U. S. S. R.

RTH POLE

ALASKA

BERING STRAIT

ARCTIC OCEAN

EAST
SIBERIAN SEA

BERING SEA

LAPTEV SEA

KOLYMA

SIBERIA

KAMCHATKA

OLENEK

LENA

Magadan

Petropavlovsk

Okhotsk

Yakutsk

SEA OF OKHOTSK

SOCIALIST REPUBLICS
FEDERATED
REPUBLIC

Aldan

ALDAN

Nikolayevsk

SAKHALIN I.

KURILE IS.

LENA

Soretskaya Gavan

ANGARA

Kirensk

AMUR

Blagoveshchensk

Khabarovsk

Bratsk

Kansk

L.BAIKAL

SHILKA

AMUR

Birobidjan

AMUR

rasnoyarsk

Nerchinsk

Cheremkhovo

Chita

USSURI

Angarsk

Irkutsk

Ulan Ude

Nakhodka

Vladivostok

JAPAN

Ulan Bator

SEA OF
JAPAN

Tokyo

MONGOLIA

N. KOREA

Peking

S. KOREA

PACIFIC
Ocean

CHINA

YELLOW SEA

Miles

0   500   1000   palacios

RUSSIA ON OUR MINDS

Reflections on Another World

By Delia and Ferdinand Kuhn

BORDERLANDS

THE PHILIPPINES YESTERDAY AND TODAY

DELIA AND FERDINAND KUHN

RUSSIA
ON OUR MINDS

Reflections on Another World

1970

DOUBLEDAY & COMPANY, INC., GARDEN CITY, NEW YORK

Library of Congress Catalog Card Number 71–103764
Copyright © 1970 by Delia and Ferdinand Kuhn
All Rights Reserved
Printed in the United States of America
First Edition

To Xenia

CONTENTS

RUSSIA ON OUR MINDS

Reflections on Another World

I

PROLOGUE

(With a Note on Being a Tourist in the Soviet Union)

> Russia had nothing in common
> with any ancient or modern
> world that history knew.
>
> —Henry Adams (1907)

This book is an attempt to set down some thoughts about the Soviet Union, and to do it in an undogmatic way. They are the thoughts of reporters rather than of scholars. Russian studies have not been our lifework, nor have we just stumbled upon them. Anyone who has spent most of a lifetime writing about foreign affairs, reporting and traveling in Europe and Asia as we have done, is bound to think and learn about Russia and want to see it for himself. In the fall of 1967 we crossed the Soviet Union from the Baltic to the Pacific, by way of Central Asia and the Trans-Siberian Railroad. The seven-week journey sharpened our thinking and gave us a frame for the chapters that follow.

While we respect hard facts and figures, as reporters should, our book is not heavily burdened with them. There are hundreds of volumes that make data on the Soviet Union available—as available as facts can be when the subject is a closed society and when all too many official figures conceal as much as they tell. What we have done is to report and reflect on the nature of the Soviet system, the condition of the people, the strength of their national heritage. What we hope to do, also, is perhaps to bring fresh ideas to a well-worn theme.

Inevitably we came up against basic questions in Russia and they have been on our minds, as this book will show. One question that engaged us particularly was this: is the Soviet Union holding fast to its Marxist-Leninist course, in

action as well as rhetoric? Or are there signs of a change
in course? We explored subsidiary questions too. For
example, is there a New Soviet Man in the making, as the
Russians would have us believe? Are the Soviet and American systems likely to converge, as some American and
European scholars believe? Could the Soviet Union hold
together as an open society, giving its people access to a
diversity of ideas? Is the Soviet Union indeed "another
world," as our subtitle suggests? All these questions became,
in a sense, companions on our journey both in the crossing
of the Soviet Union and in the writing of these pages.

One more personal note: two minds have worked on this
book, and occasionally the authors have been of two minds.
The book represents a meeting of minds, but we shall not
disclose how the meeting was arranged.

Although we have said that our subject is the Soviet
Union, it would be nearer the truth to say that our primary
concern is Russia. For Russians built the empire; Russians
made the revolution; Russians imposed Marxist dogma and
centralized control upon a hundred minority peoples; Russians rule them today. So it is Russia and the Russians that
we are really reflecting about, although we shall have plenty
to say about the non-Russian Soviet citizens as well.

It is not a subject that one can pick up and put down.
Touch it once and it gets under your skin. This was less
true before the Bolshevist Revolution. For most Americans,
nineteenth-century Russia was just another European
power, bigger than the others, more backward and perhaps
more wicked than most. Americans knew it was wicked
because it oppressed, jailed, and sometimes killed its minority peoples, especially the Georgians, the Poles, and the
Jews. But Russia was a "faraway country" and Americans
were glad to keep it that way. What brought it closer to
American consciousness was the flood of immigrants from
Russia to the cities and farms of the United States. They

were indeed the "huddled masses," the "wretched refuse" of the Emma Lazarus poem which is inscribed inside the Statue of Liberty as a monument to American smugness as well as bigness of heart. What kind of a country was it, Americans asked, that harbored such misery and then exported it?

Then Lenin and his comrades seized power. Since 1917 there has never been a year when Russia has not been on American minds for one reason or another. This partly explains our title. Is there an American alive today whose outlook on Russia and on his own country has not been conditioned by the Russian Revolution? As individuals and as a people, Americans have let Russia fascinate, baffle, anger, or repel them for one quarter of the entire life of the Republic. Neither the England of George III nor the Germany of the Kaiser and Hitler preoccupied the United States so continuously or so long.

There was something toxic about the effect of the Russian Revolution. Lenin had dropped poison into the well of American life and thought. Where Russia was concerned, it became hard to see clearly, to think rationally, to act responsibly. The Soviet system found apologists and defenders among teachers, workers, writers, and youth. One of the first of the youthful admirers was John Reed, the Harvard graduate who is now buried in the Kremlin wall. Lincoln Steffens, the muckraking writer and civic reformer, came home from a visit to Moscow announcing, "I have been over into the future, and it works." Paul Robeson, the singer, said of Stalin's purge-torn Russia that it was the only country where he felt completely at ease.

On the other side, everybody who was anybody in the two major political parties saw that the new Russia was attacking the very system on which America had been built. The Bolshevists were, in the words of former President Taft, "this gang of robbers and cutthroats." Old-line progressives like Robert M. La Follette could not forgive the Revolution for its mass killings and terror.

As early as 1920, at a cabinet meeting, the partly paralyzed President Wilson turned to A. Mitchell Palmer, his Attorney General, and said, "Palmer, do not let this nation see red." Palmer had just rounded up thousands of alleged anarchists and Bolshevist agents, and was about to deport more than two hundred of them to Russia.

But the nation did see red again and again. It saw red in the American Communist Party, a feeble thing bolstered by front organizations of pacifists and youth. The Party never elected anyone important but it had no trouble attracting articulate left-wing writers and enlisting agents around the country and in Washington. Americans saw red in the courtroom trials of alleged communists, and in the investigations by congressional committees of alleged subversives. Some of the public hearings were no more rational than the hunting of the Salem witches. They played into communist hands, for they spread fear, distrust, and bitterness far and wide through American society. The poison in the well was still at work.

Russian communism left two other scars on American minds. One was its hatred of religion, the other its contempt for America's most cherished values. Not since the French Revolution had the leaders of a Christian people rejected God. And never before had anyone said such Terrible Things about American democracy. Suddenly, foreigners were calling America vicious, greedy, and oppressive, and they have never stopped. "For the first time in American experience," wrote Walter Lippmann in 1960, "we are confronted with a rival power which denies the theory and practice of our society, and has forced upon us a competition for the leadership of the world."

Competition, in the American lexicon, is a healthy word. It is a cardinal principle of the American way of life, and there are laws to protect it. But there is nothing healthy about the race in arms, power, and influence that has kept the Soviet Union on American minds since the defeat of Hitler. Everyone knows the long history of Russian expansion in the aftermath of wars. This time the Russians used not only their army but also communism to entrench themselves in the heart of Europe. Where the Red Army and communism took control, no opposition, no competition, could show its head. Not until the middle nineteen-fifties, in areas far beyond the reach of Russian or American occupation troops, did Soviet-American rivalry take the form of true competition. This was a rivalry for friends and allies among the new and developing nations of Asia and Africa. It was the product of a momentous change in Soviet political strategy and tactics. And we, as reporters on foreign assignments, happened to have front-row seats to watch the Russians in a brand-new role.

Although Russia's symbol has always been a bear, the image of a mollusk sometimes suits her better. Even as she has expanded her territory, Russia has secreted a shell around herself. Alternately the shell has opened, permitting a trickle of traffic of people, ideas, and goods, and then has shut again, sealing the country and its people from the outside world.

One can only marvel at the effectiveness of the shell. How can a people without natural frontiers defeat geography? Only, it would seem, by equipping themselves with an absolute ruler, a tight police system, a large standing army, and by assuming that foreigners are carriers of contagious disease.

Our own generation has witnessed both the closing and opening of the shell. The great mollusk was never more tighly sealed than in the last eight years of Stalin's life. But hardly had his body joined Lenin's inside the mausoleum on Red Square when the shell of the mollusk began to crack. Stalin's successor, as head of both Party and government, to almost everyone's astonishment, was a shell-opener. He not only opened the shell but he himself came out of it. Between 1954 and 1964, when he was dismissed from office, Nikita Khrushchev toured Asia, Europe, and the United States. Risking exposure as no communist, to our knowledge, had ever done outside his own territory, he stood on the backs of open cars, waved to millions, shook hundreds of hands, and survived more confetti than any athlete or astronaut.

We saw Khrushchev's performance for the first time in India. It was in three parts: Act I, politics; Act II, economics; and Act III, pure propaganda. On assignment in India for an American magazine, we flew into Calcutta's Dum Dum Airport. Usually the road into town is blocked by taxis, ox-carts, and reclining sacred cows. That day the road was clear, but lined with school children waving small flags and shouting "Hindi-Russi bhai-bhai"—Indians and Russians, Brothers, our taxi driver explained. He said two Russians were expected that afternoon and this spontaneous demon-stration was for them. In the city, the crowd of brown-skinned Bengalis in white cotton dhotis stood body to body along Old Courthouse Road. To join such a dense crowd was to abandon all hope of leaving it at will, and we hoped that its gay mood would not turn to anger or fear.

Nikita Khrushchev rode into Calcutta in an open car perched on the rolled-back canvas hood. He had brought with him Nikolai Bulganin, a benign father figure, just the foil for the exuberant Party chairman. Together they were touring Asia on what came to be called the B. and K. Road Show. About halfway along the eight-mile route into town the crowd had pushed through police lines, overrun the Russians' car, and broken it down in pure enthusiasm. The police had rescued their guests and put them into a paddy wagon for the rest of the triumphal journey. That was how we saw the rulers of Russia pass by. Next day, the Calcutta *Statesman* reported accurately that the whole thing was "unprecedented and unique." The Russians, it said, were "overwhelmed with happiness." At a giant mass meeting Khrushchev talked about the evils of colonialism and "countries which sucked other countries as leeches sucked human blood." He proclaimed brotherly love between the Soviet Union and newly independent peoples. He did not mention the word communism, although Calcutta was the stronghold of Indian communism and the scene of the 1948 Cominform meeting, which had decreed insurrections in Burma, the Philippines, Indonesia, and Malaya.

From Calcutta the road show moved on to Burma. Then, as ever since, two competing bands of communist guerrillas were terrorizing the Burmese countryside. Khrushchev ignored them. He spoke, instead, of his fraternal love for a people which had suffered so grievously from its colonial masters. At the Shwe Dagon Pagoda in Rangoon he congratulated the cheering Burmese on having won their freedom. The English, he reminded them, had sat on their necks, robbed them, and called them "savages."

To qualify for Soviet love, one did not have to be a card-carrying communist, just a card-carrying anticolonialist. What we were watching was the beginning of a new orientation in Soviet foreign relations: Russia's embrace of what came to be called the third, or uncommitted, world. The unchallenged ruler of the world's largest remaining empire, the Soviet Union, was taking advantage of a moment in the painful history of the people of Asia, a moment when they were as unsteady on their national feet as newborn colts and needed powerful friends. He was able to persuade them that the Soviet Union was not only their friend but their practical helper. It was a virtuoso performance.

And so the curtain went up on Act II, the offer of Soviet help in addition to Soviet friendship. For the first time in their history, Russians were sent outside their empire on errands of teaching and giving rather than learning and getting. Khrushchev had the supreme and, as it turned out, justifiable confidence to let other Russians see and rub shoulders with the world as he had done. They were, of course, carefully picked men and women sent out to do various chores. One chore was to show that Soviet socialism held the secret to quick economic development.

We ran into these new Soviet men all over Asia. In Afghanistan we found them paving the streets of Kabul, boring a tunnel through the Hindu Kush, building bakeries, oil tanks, roads, and airports. In Nepal we found them cutting a road through the jungle. In Burma a Russian hotel was going up in the outskirts of Rangoon, a hospital outside Taunggyi. In Pnompenh another Russian hospital, in Djakarta a giant sports arena, and in India steel mills.

These new Soviet men, we discovered, were having some of the same cross-cultural difficulties as their American competitors, the technicians who had come on similar errands. In central India, for example, a team of Russian engineers had come to build a steel mill. Being lonely men (few Russians were allowed to bring their families on these temporary assignments) they spent their evenings drinking warm beer in the local government rest house. There they met an American water engineer, a bachelor from Wisconsin who had worked in that part of India for almost three years. The Russians confided to him that they were suffering from heat, thirst, and frustration. How did one deal with these Indians, anyway? How did one make them do the things they had agreed to do? The American gave them what help he could out of his own experience.

The only other place where we found Russians and Americans consulting on technical or cultural problems was in Kabul. As economic advisers they found themselves sitting around the same table with Afghan officials, and agreeing that the Afghan development plan was too ambitious. These, however, were not stock situations. Usually Russians and Americans competing in Asia went their separate ways.

This new kind of Soviet man came to do a specific job, and, having done it, went home. His mission, so far as we could tell, was not to propagandize but to let his contribution speak for itself. More often than not, it was a status symbol in Asian terms: a sports arena, a dam, a steel mill. Khrushchev's gamble was relatively inexpensive in rubles, for Russian aid was on a loan or credit basis. The intangible return to the Soviet Union seemed to us large. Asians saw a new kind of Russian, one who had probably come up from illiteracy in one or two generations. He was a spokesman for economic planning, for a system—namely Marxian socialism—which claimed to know the secret of quick development. The new breed of Russian in Asia wore the halo of Soviet achievement in the short space of forty years. He did not have to propagandize.

We discovered, finally, that both Russians and Americans working in the new countries of Asia wore halos. But they were of different materials. The American halo was, and still is, made of gold. Even a homespun county agent from Mississippi could not escape the patina of affluence. He could not convince an Iranian or a Pakistani or an Indian that he himself was not a rich man or that there was such a thing as poverty in the United States. The Russian, on the other hand, would deny, as all Russians must, that poverty exists in his homeland. But he would not be believed. He wore a different halo—made of something that educated Asians call "social justice."

In almost twenty years of intermittent reporting from Asia, we heard these words applied to the Soviet Union over and over again: social justice. We heard them from a Burmese professor in Mandalay, from an Indian Cabinet minister in New Delhi, and from other educated men. "They may not be as rich as you Americans, but, by God, they have social justice." Or, "I envy your wealth, but I respect the Russians' social system. They've done away with privilege. In their country every man is as good as every other.

You see, they haven't been corrupted. They were never a colonial power."

To us this was the final achievement, Khrushchev's Act III. The risk he had taken in opening the shell of the mollusk had paid off, in Asia at least. Somehow his political embrace and his economic helping hand had not only made friends for the Soviet Union. They had convinced educated Asians, the few who matter, that Russia was a paradise of social justice, a truly egalitarian society. Furthermore, Russia, the world's largest empire, had escaped the taint of imperialism. We ourselves never stopped wondering how this giant deception was achieved. The Russians had offered their friendship at a propitious moment, just as Asian intellectuals needed a champion that was both socialist and anti-imperialist. So perhaps we should not have been too surprised.

How the great coming-out affected the Russians who were allowed to participate in it is quite another matter. A meeting with a Russian circus troupe in Ceylon gave us a small and hardly representative sample. They had just toured Europe and the Middle East. The leader of the troupe, a juggler, told us that of all the European countries England was his favorite. Why? "It was very orderly. I had a sense of security. The people were well behaved—as I said, orderly." And in the Middle East, which country did he like best? This time the juggler's judgment was instantaneous. "Kuwait—yes, certainly Kuwait." Why? He grinned and rolled his eyes to heaven: "All—that—money!"

After years of watching Russians outside their country, the time for us to go inside the Soviet Union was long overdue. We went not as correspondents, but as ordinary tourists, equipped to read the Cyrillic alphabet and speak tourist-Russian. There was no deception; our applications for visas described us as writers. To go without credentials or assignments made it possible for us to travel light, free of protocol and official briefings. The official line is avail-

able anyway, at all times and everywhere. We got it everywhere. As ordinary tourists, we submitted an itinerary
which would take us from the Baltic to the Pacific on a
roundabout course. Moscow considered our plan for three
months, and then gave its answer: approved.

Our journey itself is not the subject of this book. But as
in a child's kaleidoscope, the pieces of Russia that we had
collected in so many years fell into place, making a kind
of pattern when we looked at them from the inside. The
picture still has many missing pieces and perhaps distor-
tions too. It is at least something we can try to put into
words, and this we have done.

A Note on Being a Tourist in the Soviet Union

Only about four hundred Americans, usually diplomats
and journalists, live and work in the Soviet Union. Some
thirty thousand other Americans go there each year as
tourists. Travel, like drink, can be a sedative, or it can
sharpen the senses and the mind. Our reflections on tourism
in the Soviet Union are meant primarily for the traveler in
search of a stimulant. Anyone who feels the need to be
unwound or soothed would do better to invest his time
and money somewhere else. For our taste, travel in the
Soviet Union turned out to be worth the cost in effort
and money, if only for the discovery of its art treasures.
They include masterpieces and wonders: Scythian gold,
Russian icons, Byzantine churches, and the ceramics of the
Tamerlane tombs. Having digested these, the tourist may be
full, but he has come only as far as the fifteenth century.
There are five other centuries to explore, including the performing arts of today: ballets, concerts, operas, dramas, and
the circus.

If a traveler wants not only to be stimulated but also to
be stretched, then the Soviet Union can offer him something

that has no counterpart anywhere. This is the chance to learn what it means and how it feels to be a ward of the Soviet state. For that is what he and all other foreigners, including tourists, in fact become when they set foot on Soviet soil. He will learn right away that the state tells foreigners where in its vast domain they may go. It tells them by what means they may travel and where they must stay when they arrive.

The foreigner who lives and works in the Soviet Union is constantly asking for permission of one kind or another. Like the citizen, he must apply to the state for living space, and he is usually obliged to take what is assigned to him. The state puts foreigners in apartment houses with other foreigners. These are known as foreign ghettos, and the state stations guards at the gates to report who goes in and out. A foreigner cannot employ a citizen in his home or his office without express approval of the state. He can be sure that the approved employee reports on him. If he or his family want to take Russian lessons, they must ask the state for a teacher.

All this suggests that the state frowns on random contacts between foreigners and Soviet citizens, which is the case and always has been. It tries to organize and structure every contact between a Russian and a foreigner, whether he is a resident or a tourist. Every unscheduled encounter the state regards with suspicion, as it always has. Are the stranger and the Russian engaged in smuggling letters, manuscripts, or secret data out of the country? Are they black-marketing rubles? Are they selling valuables for illegal export? Is a Russian planning to defect or to become an agent of a foreign power? Or is the state itself setting a trap for a foreigner it means to expel? This is not Ian Fleming speaking. Every foreigner and every Russian knows about such contingencies, or ought to know.

In a police state, it helps to learn the rationale and it is essential to learn the ropes. A good part of the Soviet rationale is pre-Soviet, going back to the czarist state, when

Russia lacked natural frontiers, as it still does. The absolute rulers compensated by building a fortress society, herding its people inside, and closing the gates. So it remains. But now communism, and the supposed hostility of all the noncommunist peoples outside, fortify the rationale. Another part of it derives from the state's distrust of the scores of minority peoples which it rules, many of whom dislike their Russian masters.

What is all this to the tourist? Whether or not he knows it, he, like everyone else, is under the suspicious and watchful eye of the state. Even though he is a bird of passage he is subject to unwritten rules that limit his movements and his contacts with Soviet citizens. But when you compare him with most other foreigners—diplomats, journalists, businessmen, and members of visiting delegations—you make a useful discovery. It is the tourist who enjoys more mobility, more freedom.

The tourist has not earned his advantages over the foreigners who must live and work in the Soviet Union. He does not deserve them, and if he understands the reasons for them, he should feel guilty about having them, as we did. We know only too well, having been resident correspondents in Europe, how the in-and-outer—the man on special assignment—can breeze through a country and come out an expert. Meanwhile the man who is stationed there has painfully acquired the language of the country. He has plugged away at the daily business of knowing the people and their culture. In the Soviet Union the resident is at a disadvantage precisely because he knows so much. The state can afford to let the tourist run around, because he is apt to be deeply ignorant.

For both the resident and the traveler, the rules of mobility are hard to catalogue. They disappear and reappear without notice or explanation. For example, journalists find that the green light to cross the continent by rail or to visit Alma Ata may be on today, off tomorrow. We accomplished both as tourists but met no newsmen along the way. After the clash with China on the Ussuri River, the whole of Siberia from Novosibirsk east to the Pacific temporarily went off limits to all foreigners, tourists and residents alike.

A resident foreign diplomat or journalist must get Foreign Office approval for each journey, however short; he may wait for months, then receive an unexplained *nyet*. For the tourist, the state publishes a list of places, mostly in the western third of the empire, which are predictably open to him, though subject to change. The list invites him to stay in more than a hundred cities and towns and to visit many others. He can join a group or be on his own. He has at least six kinds of transport at his disposal. He can enter and leave the country at twenty-eight points, which include eight airports, six seaports, nine railroad and five motor road crossings, all of course subject to prior approval of the state. To repeat: he is free to leave the country, as most Soviet citizens are not.

When the tourist enters this test tube of communism at one of the twenty-eight points, he is an alien particle not germane to the experiment. If he has no interest in the experiment, he should not travel alone, and perhaps he should not come at all. But if he wants to learn something about it, then tourism becomes something of an art. It is the art of using his freedoms to the farthest limits of the law and custom of the land. We have known tourists who have set out to overstep the boundaries of law and custom. They would stray from their approved itinerary; they would hand out forbidden books; they would teach those Russians about freedom. This is an idle sport. It can put the tourist out of the country or in jail. In any event, he is the loser; while teaching he is too busy to learn; while talking, too busy to listen.

Like a giant squid, the Soviet state has many arms. One of them exists only to embrace, guide, and cushion the tourist throughout his stay. This arm, known as Intourist, is

more than an official travel agency concerned with itinerar-
ies and reservations. As an agent of the state, it owns and
operates hotels, buses, and cars. Wherever tourists stay or
visit, it maintains service bureaus to handle their needs. It
employs and trains guides who speak foreign languages; it
publishes a considerable volume of travel literature.

Whoever doubts that the state does want to open its
doors to tourists should scan this literature. It spreads a
veritable banquet before the touring public of the world.
In 1969, for example, for Americans alone, it offered fifty-six
standard group tours lasting from two to six weeks, with a
choice of many departure dates; also sixty-seven excursions
from twenty-seven cities, by car or bus or train. These were
just the meat-and-potato dishes for conventional tourists.
To the specialist, Intourist suggested art tours, music, opera
and ballet tours, Soviet education tours, language seminar
tours, wine-tasting tours, camping, hunting, and fishing
tours, river cruises, skiing and winter festival tours, and
more. For the ailing there were medical tours. No fewer
than nine Soviet health resorts provide sea or mountain air,
bad-tasting waters, and a chance to be relieved of a terrify-
ing list of intestinal complications. Or the chronic victim of
too much food and drink could simply do penance in pleasant company with other sinners.

How much of this travel banquet Intourist can deliver we
do not know. But its size and variety suggests the scope of
the Intourist catering business. Compared with the growing thousands of European and Soviet tourists who take
advantage of it, Americans are only a handful. In the path
of the rising tide of tourists, the Soviet Union is visibly short
of everything that tourism needs, including a tradition. Intourist is just one of the arms of the state that compete for
slices of the available money, materials, and trained people.
That the state supports and even encourages tourism reflects primarily the Kremlin's need for foreign exchange,
and secondarily its constant need for prestige. What else

would induce the rulers of this fortress state to lower the
drawbridge to so many sophisticated strangers?

In spite of its handicaps, Intourist does grow and func-
tion. We saw hotels going up in Tbilisi, Samarkand, and
Alma Ata. We sampled old and new: the relics of czarist
elegance in Leningrad and Tbilisi, the hotel of the future
in Moscow. This will be the world's largest hotel, the
Rossiya, with six thousand rooms and no room service. The
hotels we saw going up around the country are decently
functional and clean.

Like the hotels, Intourist services vary in style and
quality. The independent traveler depends on them utterly
and is conscious of them daily, as the group tourist may not
be. We were met at each airport or railroad station with
"Mr. and Mrs. Kuhn, American? I am from Intourist. Give
me your baggage checks. Please come to the Intourist
lounge with me. A car will take you to your hotel." To us,
this was a new experience. As members of a group tour we
might have taken such services for granted. Perhaps Intourist has all the more reason for seeing that lone foreigners do
not go astray. At each hotel, the Intourist service bureau
provided our guide, transportation, and tickets we wanted
for opera, concert, theater, ballet, or circus. In addition to
all these, we loaded our individual needs and interests onto
them. May we visit a day nursery? Certainly. A language
school? Perhaps, but it is difficult. A Russian church service,
a synagogue? Of course. Our guide will take you there but
will not go inside. Babi Yar? Why not? An excursion to Gori,
Stalin's birthplace? We think you would prefer the drive
to the mountains; it is more beautiful. The inside of a new
apartment house? A collective farm? We'll try. With patience and persistence we achieved them all. All except the
collective farm, probably because of special conditions on
the edge of China. After a while we came to feel that the
hard-pressed staffs of the service bureaus, as well as the
men and women who guided us, really wanted to meet our

wishes. As much as any loyal agent of the Soviet state can be on the side of any foreigner, they were on our side. In return we tried to understand them.

Judging by what we heard, Intourist does not have many satisfied customers. The agency has probably sent more blood pressures up than its medical tours have been able to bring down. The kindest opinion we heard came from a French diplomat. "Its services are not yet à point, but they improve," he said. For the anxieties and frustrations that tourists feel as wards of the Soviet state, Intourist is naturally the wailing wall.

Consider, for example, the problem of a dear white-haired woman whom we shall call Mrs. Shapiro. She had come all the way from Brooklyn to visit her ancestral home in Russia. She had been led to believe that she could go to the small town where her grandfather was buried. Now, in Leningrad, Intourist told her she could not go there. No wonder Mrs. Shapiro was angry.

Her husband turned to us. "I can't control my wife. She is determined. She will not go home until she has put flowers on those graves. I tell her maybe they are not even there any more. I tell her to be reasonable. I tell her to forget it and enjoy this beautiful city. It's no use." What Mrs. Shapiro could not know was that Intourist had tried to help her and had failed. The ancestral town was outside the Intourist circuit. Intourist had asked the security police for permission to send her there and had been turned down. If Mrs. Shapiro had had influence, the security police might have been persuaded to assign one of its own agents to take her to the town. But concessions of this kind are rare. You have to be somebody or know somebody. In matters that concern the security police, Intourist is helpless—and so is everyone else.

Tourists who feel the embrace of the security arm of the state may be badly shaken. The experience is not to be compared with ordinary culture shock. For example, the cultural impact of a rude Frenchman or of a half-starved Indian or an Arab beggar has been explained to the tourist and he is ready to cope. The impact of the Soviet state is of another order. How does one explain the nature of this giant squid? It is largely invisible and usually unpredictable. To find himself a ward of this thing can frighten a foreigner and sometimes enrage him. Mrs. Shapiro was not the only one we found to be suffering from this kind of shock.

There was a young Mr. Bryant, a New Zealand scientist who had been invited to the Soviet Union, or thought he had, to meet with colleagues of his profession. The visit had gone wrong, or at least not as he had expected. He felt neglect, intrigue, even deliberate insult all around him. If he had his way, he told us, no New Zealander would ever set foot on Soviet soil again. He would see to that. He would get the promise from his prime minister. Nor would a Soviet citizen ever again enter his country. He would see to that too.

Another was Monsieur Gaillard, a young Frenchman who joined us in Samarkand. He could not cope with the Russian language and had not been able to order a decent meal. Would we object to his eating with us? Moreover, he had a sense of being followed. Although he had lived and worked for two years just across the border in Afghanistan, and had not been free of surveillance there, still he felt differently about it here.

Our own experience of surveillance is probably routine. The telephone rings in our hotel room. "Don't bother to answer it unless you're expecting a call," a friend had advised us. "It just gives a click and turns on the wire-tapping machine." But one does answer the telephone out of curiosity. It does click, then silence. Probably a wrong number. Would they tap every room in this vast hotel? If not, why not? We shall never know.

On an afternoon stroll, a young man attaches himself to us. This is no longer a novelty; it happens to many foreigners. Somehow Russians have an unerring eye for who and what is foreign, and an urge to make contact with the outer world. We welcome it though we make a point of not inviting it. The youth who joins us on our walk seems to want more than just a fleeting whiff of "outside." Is there a chance we might become friends? he seems to be asking. The face is wide open and charming. What can one think? Could he be an agent of the security police? Are we being shadowed? There is not the slightest sign that we have been, no reason why we should be. Still . . . we shall never know.

If our rooms were searched anywhere, we had no evidence of it. Yet we had to assume that they were, and to take a few simple precautions. These included keeping our notebooks always on our persons and never discussing people we knew unless we were fairly certain that our conversation could not be overheard or taped. For most Europeans or Americans this is a new discipline, and not an agreeable one. It affects all travelers alike, whether they come alone or in a group. From other kinds of annoyance or shock, the group tour is designed to be a shield. The group tourist can move about enveloped by people of his own kind, who speak his language. He does not have to meet a single Russian, except his guide. This is the way the vast majority of visitors tour the country. They reap a harvest of beauty and the right to say, "I was there."

Organized tours swirled around us in western Russia and Central Asia. The season had ended but still they came: Finns, Swedes, Americans, and Germans of both East and West, as well as British swimmers, Polish soccer players, North Koreans, Balkan comrades, and Soviet minorities from all over the empire. All seemed to be on rigorous schedules, but the most industrious and the most punctual at meals were the Germans. As if responding to a bugle call, they trooped in on the dot of one o'clock. Their tables, like those of other groups, were reserved and already laden with hors d'oeuvres, bread, and bottles of beer or yogurt. Never in a lifetime of travel have we seen a better-behaved tourist brigade. Not excepting our own countrymen, to whom we were especially sensitive.

Almost a hundred Americans in a single group surprised us one morning in Moscow. We had come down to breakfast in the snack bar and were helping ourselves to caviar and hard boiled eggs, when a familiar sound stopped us. From the adjoining dining room came a volume of talk and laughter that could only mean Americans on the move in the mass. We found them at three long tables, eating fried eggs, as well-dressed, well-groomed, and well-mannered a country-club set as one could meet at Grosse Pointe or Shaker Heights. From the ease of banter one might guess they had been bridge-playing companions on the same world cruise, which was exactly the case. Their ship had anchored at Odessa. They had flown to Moscow on a twenty-four-hour package tour as visitors from another planet might swoop down in their spaceship, look around, and lift off toward home.

If we seem critical of the group method of travel, it is because we ourselves prefer the independent way. The choice is, in the last analysis, a personal one. The lone traveler will define freedom in his own terms. For him, it consists precisely in not being surrounded by his own countrymen, in not hearing his own language spoken. A tight schedule of excursions and mealtimes will confine him. He may miss many sights, but he would rather move at his own pace, pursue his own interests, let the sights and sounds of the country roll over him. On a specific day, he may want to use his Intourist guide for the full six hours, or three hours, or not at all. It is up to him. So long as he observes the Intourist rules, he can take its services or leave them. Such freedoms have their price, in terms of possible irritation, discomforts, or shock. But with practice and care, the independent traveler will discover within himself the resources to keep on an even keel.

We tried to analyze why some of our fellow tourists seemed able to navigate serenely, while others floundered and sank. Neither in age, nationality, or sex did we find the clues. But among those who sailed with conspicuous balance and verve, three happened to be lone women: an American, an Australian, and an Englishwoman. They never knew one another, but each confided to us that she considered the Soviet Union an excellent place for a single woman to wander.

They had something else in common. All seemed to us to be traveling light. By this we mean that they seemed unencumbered by prejudices and stereotypes. It is hard not to bring some of these in one's baggage. They can be a burden, like a fur coat in Calcutta. This is not to suggest that anyone should come empty-headed even if that were possible. Nor do we recommend a mind so open that the brains fall out. What the independent traveler can use most conveniently is a store of experience and curiosity. From a medical tourist in Moscow, for example, we were able to get an expert opinion on the composition of Lenin's corpse in Red Square. A retired New Zealand farmer gave us informed crop data in eastern Siberia. Our own experience in Afghan Turkistan helped us to evaluate the effects of Soviet rule on the peoples of Central Asia whose cousins we had known across the border.

One problem is likely to defeat the independent traveler, and there is little he can do about it in advance. This is the daily pursuit of food and drink.

A study has been made of the logistics of achieving three meals a day when traveling as independent tourists in the Soviet Union. We made the study.

We had been warned, "You'll probably spend as much as six or seven hours a day in restaurants and cafés just struggling to get fed." This proved to be an exaggeration. But it is true that the process takes time, patience, and special skills. These add up to a package which we call food-manship.

The road to foodmanship is apt to be marred by emotional scenes. We shall not forget the American woman standing among the half-empty tables of Moscow's finest restaurant and shouting, to no one in particular, "I've been all over the world, and this is the first place where nobody wants me to eat!" With her in mind we decided to approach each meal as a sporting event.

Our research was done entirely in the field. Instead of seeking out Soviet officials in the various ministries, we collected our data in dining rooms, on the playing fields themselves. Nowhere in this study will the reader find statistics of agricultural production or the norms, in square meters, allocated by the state for eating space per tourist. We did observe the state's system of privileged groups and persons.

For example, a lone tourist enters one of the several dining rooms of Moscow's Rossiya Hotel. (We liked it, and so confess to what the communists call an "objective" attitude.) The tourist has remembered to bring his book of Intourist meal coupons, which he hopes to use up and never will. That morning he has been plodding through the museums and churches of the Kremlin. He is sated with icons and ready for his *ikra* (caviar). His stomach signals for attention. The dining room has just opened its doors for midday dinner, which is the main Russian meal. There are long empty tables for twelve and round empty tables for four. Some of the tables have flags on them, others have placards that seem to say "reserved." The tourist finds a small unmarked table and drops into a seat. A big blond waitress brushes past him with a *nyet* and is gone.

Now the tourist, like Goldilocks, begins to canvass the tables. The long ones are reserved either for group tours or for a *delegatsia,* meaning an official delegation from a

friendly country. If the tourist were not so weak, he might be
interested in the exotic flags on the delegation tables. One
flies the big gold star of North Vietnam on a red field.
Another has the red, white, and black stripes of the United
Arab Republic. That table has just been taken by two of
the most dejected Arabs he has ever seen. He has an impulse to join them and ask, "Did things go hard at the
Ministry of Defense this morning?" But across the room he
sees a table already loaded with plates of dark bread and
bottles of yogurt. It bears the red-blue-red flag of Mongolia.
No matter—the Mongolians will understand, if they should
come. He sits down and reaches for a piece of bread. A
waitress swoops on him with *"nyet—delegatsia!"* This time
he is firm. He finishes the piece of bread before taking once
more to the trail.

At last he gets an idea. He sits down at a "reserved" table
and repulses each attack with a loud *"Ya delegat"*—I am a
delegate. The first obstacle is happily behind. He approaches
the second: a menu. As he entered the restaurant he thought
he had seen one on a table by the door, but now the door is
defended by a clutch of waitresses. They are deep in gossip
and in no mood to help him. If he wanders over there, he
may lose his seat, but it's worth a gamble. He plants his book
on his table and achieves the menu. The waitresses do not
even notice the maneuver.

Our study now attacks its first piece of printed data. The
master menu is an all-Soviet document of some twelve pages
printed and bound between plastic covers. It lists more than
a hundred items, classified into various categories of food
and drink. To master this document is not a simple matter.
Reading and translating is only a first step. Out comes the
word book. Under the first heading, *Zakouski*, we scan the
fifteen or twenty items of Soviet hors d'oeuvres. Go no
further; *ikra*—yes, caviar—leads all the rest, served with
white bread and fresh butter, even when you don't order
them. In Moscow and other big cities of European Russia,

caviar is not only on the menu but usually available. But in Central Asia or Siberia you will have to beg for it, often in vain. Well, you are in Moscow, and here is caviar on the menu. Turn to page twelve and among the liquors find vodka. Now you are in business, if you can get a waitress. Reserve the rest of the hors d'oeuvres items until the evening meal, for they are most of what Russians eat for supper. The list is cheering: salads of tomato, cucumber, egg, or crab; a jellied sturgeon that has no equal anywhere and is worth waiting for till evening.

Next the soups and fishes. Except for borsch and *solianka*, the soups are strange, the fishes likewise. The meats, fried or boiled, are easy to recognize but hard to chew. Potatoes are the only vegetable except in soup or salad. Desserts are fruit (in season) or ice cream. Now, altogether, we have scanned some eighty items. The game is to find out which are available, for this is an all-season, all-Soviet master list, compiled somewhere in the inner recesses of a ministry. Any relation to supply is purely coincidental. The document probably was headed "Tentative Plan for Projected Soviet Meals in the Years 1969–70. One clue turns out to be misleading. Some items have prices opposite them in the right-hand column; most do not. Perhaps the priced items are on hand. So the tourist chooses from among these. If he does, he goes up a blind alley. Borsch (forty kopeks) will not be served until four o'clock, and by the time he arrives for his supper it will have gone. But here is a pilaff, unpriced—and it is on. Because, one later discovers, today is Tuesday.

By now the tourist has been on the playing field for thirty-five minutes and he has surmounted two obstacles of the course: reaching a seat and a menu. At the next small table sits a man who is obviously a Russian. He came in only fifteen minutes ago and his stew is already before him, in a brown earthenware crock. The waitress hovers over him, only six feet away. Clearly the Russian has her. Can the tourist entice her away? The answer is no. To get attention, he is ready to pick up all the silver on the table and drop it in one crash on the floor, or shout like the American woman. At this point a trim, dark waitress wanders over to him from across the room, whips out her pad, and takes his order. She tells him she is a Pole, married to a Russian, and home-sick for Warsaw. Ten minutes later he has his caviar and vodka, 150 grams of it in a small carafe.

The game is virtually won; suddenly the obstacles seem small and he sails over them. Only the check and coupon clipping remain to be negotiated. Now the tourist is joined by a tall, red-faced Englishman. He has tried many tables in vain. Shyly he says, "I hope you don't mind if I join you. You seem to have made it." The American is suitably modest. He knows that the game has only begun and he is still a rookie. There will be other rounds, with many fumbles, tonight and tomorrow and tomorrow.

The moment the lone traveler breaks out of the main tourist circuit, which is Moscow, Leningrad, and Kiev, he will find the game more varied. The farther from Moscow, the less the pressure of group tours on the feeding grounds. He can often get seated, and sometimes he will get service that is almost ungrudging. He has a pleasant sensation of being spoiled and is in danger of losing his hard-won food-manship. In Tashkent there are even tables reserved es-pecially for independent travelers. If he should happen to leave the Soviet Union aboard a Soviet ship, as we did, the game is over the moment he sets foot on the gangplank. With excellent food and a helpful crew, his only problem is how to use up his surplus coupons. If only the ship's bar would accept them—but it does not.

The scattered provinces of the Soviet Union deserve food studies of their own. But we shall report only a few of our discoveries. We were struck first by the diversity of peoples and their food habits. The all-Soviet master menu still con-fronts the tourist at every meal, whether he is in Kiev or

Khabarovsk, but he will learn to make end runs around the
printed pages. For instance, Tashkent hides a fine local
pilaff (pronounced "ploff"), Tbilisi an eggplant salad, and
Alma Ata a lamb-noodle stew.

Moving southward, we were struck also by the splendor
of the free markets. Under the Soviet system, most markets
and everything in them are owned by the state. The traveler
discovers two exceptions to this rule—and there may be
others. One is the licensed commission shops, where secondhand clothing and household goods are bought and sold, at
state-fixed prices; the other, the free markets where home-
grown produce is on sale. The Soviet citizen who has a backyard or a private plot (on state land) may grow things for
himself or as a cash crop to be sold in the free market. Foods
in the free markets compete with those in the state markets,
and they compete successfully. It is said that 60 per cent of
the fresh vegetables and fruits sold in the Soviet Union come
from the free markets.

Comparative shopping expeditions in ten Soviet cities
convinced us that the free markets have consistently better
quality, variety, and service, and that they are consistently
more expensive. For example, the state market stocks small
green apples at forty kopeks (about forty-five cents) a kilo
(a little over two pounds). They are displayed inside a
glass counter so you cannot examine them. You ask for a
kilo. The saleswoman disappears backstage and returns with
apples which she dumps into your string bag. Those inside
the counter look sound, but some of those you get turn out
to be wormy.

The free market is usually a covered shed where scores
of farmers and their families spread out their produce on
long counters. In the autumn, big red apples are on display for eighty or ninety kopeks a kilo. They are piled high
on the open counters, and you can inspect them and make
your own selection.

The free markets of the Soviet South are the socialist

Gardens of Eden, botanically if not politically. Bushel baskets of crimson tomatoes, mounds of fresh figs, counters heaped with pomegranates and peaches, cherries and grapes, radishes and peppers, cauliflower and eggplant: this is the kind of profusion that would cause a stampede in Moscow or Leningrad. In Tbilisi, the capital of Georgia, it is a routine display and the season is long. For the best in melons, which rival those of Afghanistan, one must go to Samarkand; for apples and roses to Alma Ata. A supply of fresh fruit and flowers in the hotel room does strange things for a traveler's morale. If he can also find a peeling knife and some paper napkins (most unlikely) in the local shops, he is in clover. He can almost forget about tables, stony-faced service, and coupons.

A traveler can become addicted to free markets not only for food gathering, but also for face gathering. The mosaic of faces to be found in these free markets is one of the rewards of Soviet travel. As far north as Moscow, the free market introduces you to swarthy Georgian farmers among the paler broad-faced Slavs. The Georgians seem at first to look like gypsies and act like Neapolitans, but they are highly individual, as we were to learn. In their capital, Tbilisi, Armenians are also active in the free market, both as buyers and sellers. In Bukhara, one finds an absorbing and puzzling mosaic of Uzbek, Kirghiz, and Turkmen, all of Turkic stock, as well as Tadjiks, who are Persian.

To become fascinated with Soviet minority peoples is to run the risk of inflating their political importance. Indeed, the well-intentioned tourist in the Soviet Union can take home even more mistaken ideas than those he brings. There is no easy way out of this dilemma except to attack the vast literature on the subject and then, if possible, to go there again. As long as the Soviet state wants the tourist's dollar and underestimates his capacity to look and listen, he can continue to learn. Perhaps he will even begin to understand this other world.

II

Leningrad:

PETER, LENIN, AND THE GREAT DECEPTION

The more I looked at everything in the house, the more I was struck with its quasi-European character. . . . And yet everything was slightly different. . . . It was not at all like going to China or Japan, where everything one sees is strange.

—Samuel Butler
Erewhon (1872)

Long before Sigmund Freud invented psychoanalysis, they put Mother Russia on the couch. They were, first of all, her own sons, the intellectuals of Russia. They drew from her a stream of consciousness to which the literature of Russia owes its genius. After the Revolution, this kind of probing was officially frowned upon as unsocialist and it became dangerous business. But interested Russian émigrés, Europeans, and Americans carried on the analysis. They have not been able to leave their subject alone. She is too intriguing and too baffling.

Concerning, for example, her heredity: which strain predominates, the Slav, the Norse, or the Tatar? Concerning her environment: how has she adapted to a home without walls, to cold and to loneliness? Regarding her behavior: why should so stalwart and gifted a subject be so prone to suffering, to misrule, and to acceptance of both? Finally, in the matter of her identity: is Russia basically European? Does she belong to Asia? Is she a part of both? Or of neither?

The Russia-is-Asian argument says: "Consider her religion; she learned it from Byzantium. Look at her propensity for autocratic rule; she learned it from the Mongols. How can you explain her capacity to suffer and endure except in Asian terms? Even communism acquired an oriental character under Stalin's rule. Stop expecting Russians to behave like Westerners and you will not be disappointed or misled."

The Russia-is-European argument has a different tone,

perhaps because so many of its protagonists are themselves European by birth or heritage. It says: "Russia is indeed a member of the Western family, a wayward member who has strayed from the highway of European history and culture. She belongs to us and she will come back." The argument passes lightly over the eight hundred years when the Russian state was small, landlocked and remote in the eastern plains, being overrun by Asian barbarians and ruled by them for two of those centuries. The case rests primarily on the two recent centuries, those Romanoff years during which Russia became a wholesale borrower of European ideas.

Today Leningrad is the prime exhibit of the two centuries of borrowing, during which it was still St. Petersburg. And to approach the Soviet Union by way of Leningrad, as we did, is to walk right into the argument about Russia's European character. Two of the borrowers overshadow all the rest, and they dominate the argument as well as the city. One of them conceived the city, and for two hundred and twenty years it bore his name. The other tore the city bodily from its past. Quite logically, they renamed it for him.

About Leningrad itself there is no argument. For Westerners and Russians alike, the city is a pool of aesthetic satisfaction and joy. What Russians created here is a facsimile of Europe that is in many ways grander in concept, purer in design than anything we have found in Europe itself. The Russians borrowed from Athens, Rome, and Versailles, among other places. Because it is a city of islands, canals, and more than six hundred bridges, Leningrad is often called a northern Venice in the literature of great cities. This easy judgment we respectfully deny. Leningrad is blessed by far more restraint and understatement than most great cities, including Venice. It belongs under a northern sky; it has to be washed by cold gray waters. The Adriatic or the Mediterranean would not do. Here one gives thanks for the sun, one does not expect it. Yet this is a place where Westerners, European and North American alike, can feast on beauty and digest almost every bit.

Peter, the "only good czar," started the city and what historians call the Petrine period, which lasted for two hundred and fourteen years. He had overriding reasons for coming here. At the age of eleven, the story goes, this Moscow child of a river country met the sea for the first time. He saw it at Archangel in the Arctic, Russia's only access to the sea at that time. What he saw was probably encrusted with ice, but never mind. It filled him with a longing from which he never recovered. At twenty-two, he took another look at the sea and decided that Russia must be made a maritime power. How he apprenticed himself to European workshops and shipyards, how he brought engineers and artisans back to Russia, created Russia's first professional army, defeated Charles XII of Sweden, took a wedge of seacoast for Russia, all this is in the schoolbooks or should be, and it is true.

This "good czar," they say, was a great brute of a genius, addicted to violence and terror as well as to technological change. Lenin, who ended the Petrine period, is remembered as small, chunky, bald, and agile, gentle in his personal relationships but otherwise addicted to similar means and ends. Between them, Peter and Lenin engineered two revolutions that changed the course of history for Russians and for the rest of the world.

Peter accomplished most of what he set out to do. (Whether Lenin did is still a matter of controversy.) Having gotten a bit of marshy land on the Gulf of Finland, facing westward toward Europe, he sent out the order to "assemble a few thousand thieves for next summer . . ." On reclaimed land and islands, the city of St. Petersburg began to rise with the help of European architects and domestic convicts, like so many of Russia's monuments, old and modern.

On one island he built a fort, a modest four-room house for himself, and a church from which, in 1711, he proclaimed himself emperor of all the Russias. Two years later he moved his capital from the Kremlin to St. Petersburg. The imperial virus seems to have cost him his personal simplicity. Soon a miniature Russian Versailles appeared on a hilltop overlooking the Gulf of Finland, complete with waterfalls, statues, and fountains. One fleet of ships took shape in the harbor of St. Petersburg, another in the lower reaches of the Dnieper River to be sailed southward to the Black Sea. To man these ships, Peter again sent for convicts. Their sentences read "condemned to the galleys." Since then the Russian word for "galley," which is *katorga*, has become the general term for forced labor.

After Peter died, his Romanoff kin spent two centuries, minus eight years, trying to make Russia into a European power. This was something the old Moscow czars had never seriously attempted. For the Romanoff czars of St. Petersburg, Europe was not just a battleground; it had been that in past centuries. They made it also a playground for the game of power politics. They took German, British, and Danish spouses, thus acquiring royal cousins in Europe, as well as invitations to royal weddings, funerals, and hunting parties. They competed in the arms race, ending up with the largest standing army in Europe, if not the best equipped or the most belligerent. They intervened in European wars, thus earning alliances, seats at conferences, and the right to carve up the spoils. They helped to put down European independence movements and liberal revolutions that threatened their fellow monarchs. They mucked about in Balkan politics, backed their fellow Slavs in Serbia, and fueled World War I from a nasty threat into a tragic certainty. That they caught the European fever for empire building is not strange. South and east of their own borders potential colonies were waiting to be conquered, vast, empty, and unclaimed. The Romanoffs overran as much adjacent land, an-

nexed as much colonial acreage, as Spain or Britain. Most
of this empire the Soviets rule today.

Arms, power politics, empire: these demanded an industrial base. The Romanoffs did what they could to provide
one. Mainly in their last half-century, the state dug minerals,
built steel and cotton mills, laid railroads and ran them.
Investment capital came from England, France, and Bel-
guim. In the end Europe could not but accept Russia as a
great power, to be feared, disliked, and distrusted, as great
powers are. And the rulers of Turkey, Persia, Afghanistan,
and China could only curse the fate that had put Russians
on their borders.

The Romanoffs gave Peter's city a splendid window dress-
ing in the European style. Cathedrals modeled on St. Peter's
of Rome and St. Paul's of London; baroque palaces rem-
iniscent of Versailles and Schönbrunn; a neoclassical stock
exchange, an Admiralty with a golden spire; acres of parade
grounds and parks; statues, regiments of statues. Peter himself on a fiery horse, marble lions, stone sphinxes, memorials
to glorious military victories. Of defeats, only one remembrance can be found today. It is a bas-relief of Russian
sailors scuttling their ship in 1904 to prevent its capture by
the Japanese. Finally, the museums, overcrowded with
icons, tapestries, sculptures, and paintings.

As the city grew in splendor, so did the Romanoff court.
Power radiated from the czars and czarinas, from the czar's
church, his ministers, his nobles, his military elite, his police,
and his bureaucracy. As might have been expected, a crust
of human barnacles attached itself to this ship of state. The
decisions handed down by the court were in the main
rigidly conservative, designed to fortify the structure. To
all liberal movements in Europe the Romanoff answer was
firmness. The Russian masses, traditionally humble and
docile, with few exceptions worshiped their czars. If ideas
should seep through cracks in their window on Europe, the
police could take care of them.

In December of 1825, ideas did seep in and were quickly expunged. About a hundred upper-class army officers demanded a constitutional monarchy. They went so far as to suggest that the incoming czar should step aside for his brother to head the state. For this nonviolent but treasonous request, five rebels were hanged, the rest exiled to Siberia.

The rebellion was ended. But the Decembrists had shattered the myth of czarist immunity. After that, European ideas of political and social change drifted into St. Petersburg and a new life began for the city on the Neva. It was a revolutionary life, and for the next ninety-two years, Romanoff St. Petersburg had to live unhappily with it. These were fascinating years.

Every great metropolis lives separate lives within itself. But what other tyranny tolerated rebellion under its very ramparts for so many years? Every great city has its crime problem. But what other city bred generation upon generation of such gifted political criminals? They were the children of nobles and tycoons, of generals and peasants, of schoolteachers and priests. Of necessity they led roving lives in and out of jail and exile, in and out of Russia itself. For revolutionists it was the best of times, it was the worst of times.

The times inspired creative writers, such as Pushkin and Lermontov, Dostoevsky and Chekhov. They searched Russia's soul and documented her sufferings. The times encouraged radical theorists of change, such as Alexander Herzen, the socialist philosopher; Georgi Plekhanov, the Marxist teacher; and finally Lenin, the practitioner of revolution. The times incited brave terrorists, some of whom were also idealists, to plot and murder under the very beards of the secret police. The times produced, in short, such a firmament of personalities, so much brilliant disputation— and fragmentation—that revolutionaries as diverse as Jeffer-

son and Paine, Milton and Voltaire, Sun Yat-sen and Gandhi
would have had no trouble finding kindred spirits in St.
Petersburg during those ninety-two years.

What the times did not produce, it seemed, was a revolution or even a basic reform of the czarist system. It can be
said that Russia was not ready for revolution, but how many
revolutions have waited "till ready"? It can be said, too,
that the rebels began by setting their sights too low. With
the exception of the anarchists, they sought to wrest reforms
out of the czars rather than to bring the czars down. Then,
in 1887, something happened that was to inject a new element, like oxygen, into the atmosphere. A chemistry student
at the University of St. Petersburg was hanged for plotting
to kill the czar.

His death, like that of many other brave and foolhardy
young people, had been a waste of idealism and a price of
amateur plotting. This particular young man had come from
a provincial middle-class family of educated and thoroughly
respectable people. His father had been a school inspector,
his grandfather a doctor. When he was hanged at twenty-
one, his brother of eighteen was made to suffer guilt by as-
sociation. The brother courted guilt too. At the provincial
university of Kazan he quickly got himself expelled for joining in a demand for student rights. After that he devoted
himself to the study of law and the works of Karl Marx.

The education of young Vladimir in the Marxist creed
has become schoolbook and bedtime reading for every Russian child. There is another side to his education, it seems
to us, that deserves more attention today. It was young
Vladimir Ulyanov who, as Lenin, was to raise professional
revolution to the level of a science. When first he was seized
of the subject, the science was primitive. He gave it intensive thought and creative understanding, so that in about
twenty-three years he had developed, institutionalized, and
perfected it and had become its acknowledged master.
Moreover he left the fruits of his experience behind in a

bible which has never been superseded, although it has been enlarged.

Today no student of professional revolution can afford to ignore Lenin's teachings, any more than a physicist can ignore Newton, a political scientist Plato, a physician Pasteur.

Lenin had no lack of time to think his problems through: two years in prison and three in Siberian exile before he was thirty. He pursued three themes to their logical conclusions, among many others. First, revolution was no job for amateurs or moonlighters. (He remembered his brother Alexander.) The best full-time professionals, he thought, would come from the working class, not from the intelligentsia, "who in the majority of cases are somewhat careless and sluggish in their habits, so characteristic of Russians." Even with total dedication "it takes years," he said, "to train professional revolutionaries" and they must be "no less professionally trained than the police."

Second, nothing can be done without an organization. The place to begin is organizing. And for the model of an organization, "take the modern army." Organize from the top down; do not be misled by the false "democracy" of "building the Party from the bottom upward."

Third, perfect your weapons. Begin by publishing an "all-Russian" newspaper with a national circulation. Organize a secret smuggling and mailing system for its distribution. "A paper is not merely a collective propagandist and a collective agitator; it is also a collective organizer," like the scaffolding around a building under construction. Create certain weapons, but use any at hand. If you are given a ballot, use it against your enemies. Tomorrow you may be given a rifle—"take this weapon of death and destruction, do not listen to the sentimental whiners who are afraid of war." As for other weapons, terror by itself and used at random is nothing more than "single combat," a primitive and wasteful instrument. The same holds for partisan warfare. It, too, must be integrated into the whole arsenal and "be in harmony with the most important methods of combat."

Like other bodies of scientific literature, Lenin's contains inconsistencies. He changed his mind about such things as when and how the Marxian revolution would come to Russia. But in the main, his dictates on organization, strategy, and tactics are consistent. He did begin with an "all-Russian newspaper," first published from Geneva in 1900. He did organize a party from the top down. And because of him, St. Petersburg became a successful laboratory for the teaching and practice of professional revolution, as Vienna became the recognized center for the development and practice of modern medicine.

Today Lenin's laboratory is a source of pride to Leningraders. They show it off with no less pleasure than when they point to the relics of the Romanoffs. Both are lovingly preserved. In fact, there is nothing a visitor can do that pleases a Leningrader more than to say, "Let's do a Romanoff tour today and take a revolutionary walk tomorrow." In practice, the two cannot be done separately. For example, you will stand on the west front of the Admiralty, one of Peter's first and best monuments, and you will find yourself standing also in Decembrist Square, where the first rebels assembled in 1825. Walk a quarter of the way around the Admiralty and you are in the Workers' Garden, which is no less hallowed as revolutionary soil. Here, in 1905, and in the adjoining square of the Great Winter Palace, a procession of humble petitioners to the czar was mowed down by his soldiers. The fort that Peter built to defend his new city is also the prison where most of the best-remembered revolutionaries languished, including young Alexander Ulyanov, Dostoevsky, and Gorky. The corridor wall outside the cells is a photograph gallery of its inmates. It reminds one of Russian cemeteries where a photograph of the dead hangs over each grave. For many of these wretched revolutionaries the cell was the waiting room for the cemetery.

Lenin's St. Petersburg, later renamed Petrograd, is different. It begins in the mean working-class district where he lodged and plotted as a young man, and thence to the Finland Station. Standing under his statue in the station square, one would give much to have been there on that night in April 1917 when his train pulled in. Under the floodlights, Lenin called on his welcoming friends to follow him to insurrection. They shrank from the mere thought of insurrection, and melted away from him.

The next six months, which Lenin spent partly in hiding and partly in Finland, can be rated his most remarkable as a professional revolutionary. He achieved the insurrection he wanted, and he came back to Petrograd, to take power over the Russian empire. The place where he and Leon Trotsky lived and worked and had their Party headquarters was a sedate little palace which had been a seminary for daughters of the rich. It was called The Smolny, meaning "pitch," because it had been built on the site where Peter first stored pitch for the building of his navy.

The fact that Leningrad was the breeding ground of revolution and the home of rebel heroes is important to the people of this city. Equally important is the actual event of October 1917, which reversed the course of history for them. If it had happened in Moscow or anywhere else, Leningraders would feel cheated, as Bostonians would feel cheated if the tea party had occurred off Sandy Hook. Leningrad is the home of revolution, and that is part of its pride.

It is a part also of its sorrow. For the city has a special history of suffering. To say that Leningraders are the most long-suffering of all Russians is to make a very big claim. But they are inclined to make it, and with justice.

There is a memorial to more than a million of them who are believed to have died of hunger and cold in World War II, a cemetery dominated by a heroic statue of Mother Russia. Standing under this figure you will probably be told by your guide that nobody, Russian or foreign, can understand what the people of Leningrad went through, and you will agree. Leningraders tend to assume also that no foreigner has more than a vague idea of their trials in the revolutions, purges, and wars of this century. This is not necessarily true. They may be taken aback if they learn that a visitor is not wholly ignorant of their past. "Really, so you have heard. Then of course you won't want to hear any more about it." To which you hasten to reply, "Of course I want to hear. Please go on."

Leningrad churches are crowded on Sunday mornings because so few of them are open for services. St. Isaac's Cathedral, the Romanoff version of St. Paul's in London, is now a museum. So is the Kazan Cathedral, which houses an exhibit to promote atheism. The oldest church, in the Peter and Paul fortress, is on view as the burial place of the czars. Where services are still held, they follow the traditional Orthodox ritual. The choirs chant with resonance, and bearded priests intone in Old Slavonic, one of the most musical of all church languages. Elderly men and women and young children make up the vast majority of the congregations. The women's faces, framed in head scarves, seem worn and tired.

There are no pews in a Russian Orthodox church, so everyone stands or kneels, or wanders about. Among the kneeling there is some prostration of forehead to floor, and among all there is more crossing of oneself than in a Roman Catholic service. Also, there is weeping. Never have we watched so much weeping in a church, even during a funeral service. It is a silent weeping, with an occasional dabbing of eyes and nose, but mostly just the coursing of tears down unselfconscious faces.

Are these people moved by the music or the words of prayers in a dead language? Is weeping a conventional expression of piety in this church? Our intuition, perhaps wrong, told us that these were not the reasons. We had a strong feeling that this closely packed throng was thinking its individual thoughts, weeping for its private sorrows. Can there be a family in Leningrad that has not lost a brother or a son in war, a mother or father in the purges? How many of the worshipers around us could have escaped tragedy of some kind in the siege? And where else but in church can a Leningrader give way and have a good lonely cry? The home is too small and too crowded for private emotion. Life is too demanding for reverie over the past. Church is at least one place where nobody notices, nobody cares, and one can indulge in the luxury of personal grief.

Leningrad knows how it feels to be stripped of its power and left with its glory. This is what happened when Lenin moved the capital to Moscow. Like the descendants of a feudal family, Leningraders inherited a great estate in shocking disrepair and a family business that was on the rocks. Shifts of power have presented other capital cities with the same predicament. We think of Kyoto, Isfahan, and even Boston. All of them have responded in somewhat the same manner, rallying to preserve their legacies of art and culture that nobody could take away from them; rallying also to cherish whatever pride had set them apart from the less cultured hinterland.

Today tourist Leningrad, the monuments of the Romanoffs and the Revolution, has been retrieved from ruins and converted into as shining a museum city as any we have seen. Such is the public legacy.

The private glory is something that many Leningraders seem to carry around with them in their threadbare daily lives. This statement is hard to document. But we think we detected something in Leningrad that for want of a better word we would call civility. It is the sort of quality that Henry James would have recognized and valued.

Leningraders, we have found, make a point of deferring to one another. Deference in a city of almost four million is not something to be taken for granted. In the crowded buses riders will insist that foreigners, male or female, accept their seats. They will push you onto a bus, but only to make sure that you get on. When the fare box is out of your reach, willing hands will pass the five kopeks to the box and return the ticket to you. (The fare box is the only evidence of an honor system, the only example of public confidence in private honesty that we found anywhere in the Soviet state's dealings with the people.)

Behind its elegant European facade, Leningrad tries to put the best face on its shabbiness, which is another clue to its pride. Like the Poles, its people have a flair for the added touch of style and color in their dress. They still cover the windows of dilapidated mansions with grandmother's lace curtains. Inside a mansion, six families may share one cracked bathtub and one antiquated kitchen. But the look of old Europe remains on the weather-beaten outside.

The pride they inherited encourages Leningraders to pursue certain kinds of excellence. Their symphony orchestra is still by all odds the finest in the nation, superior to Moscow's. Their university may not rival Moscow's in size or pretentious buildings, but it commands higher respect in some fields of learning. Finally, Leningrad has a reputation for the excellence of its language schools.

As befits the Russian city that had the closest affiliations with Europe, the schools equip children to be bilingual in English, German, and other European languages. We spent a morning with a group of privileged youngsters whose second language was English. They had passed language aptitude tests to get into the school, and they had begun the study of English in the third grade with three hours a week. Before they finish in the tenth grade, English and the subjects taught in English will occupy twelve hours of the six-day school week.

The school principal, who neither spoke nor understood

English, suggested that we spend an hour with fourth
graders. We found them wrestling with the irregular verb.
A pretty young teacher with a silvery voice and a drill
sergeant's manner was asking, "Did you go away for your
vacation, Olga?" A pigtailed ten-year-old leaped to her feet.
"Yes, I did go away."

"And where did you go, Olga?"

"I went to the Caucasus with my grandmother."

"And did you go away for your vacation, Yuri?" A small
boy jumped up and stuttered, "Yes, I—I—" The teacher in-
terrupted, "All right, Yuri—and now Sasha." She knew the
answer and passed the question on to Irena. So it went
around the class of twelve. After that, it was "Did you see?"
and "Yes, I saw." We could see that most of the children
had learned to take high-tension drill in their stride. Yuri
and two or three others clearly needed special help, which
the teacher was not about to give them in class or while
visitors were watching.

After class the principal invited us to meet with products
of the system. He summoned four of the seniors to his office,
two boys and two girls. We asked them about their future
careers and they asked us about Washington. Their plans
included three years of language institute, then teaching
or guiding of English-speaking visitors for three more years.

One of the boys caught up with us as we were leaving.
Did we think his English would be understood in Washington? We assured him that it would.

These are the lucky children of Leningrad. What about
the others? Can a museum city nursing its past glories offer
a hopeful future to the generation that is coming along? It
can in Soviet terms. For they are growing up in a working-
class city, and if Russia should ever become a paradise, it
will have to be a workers' paradise.

St. Petersburg is the place where Russian industry began
a hundred years ago. Today, Leningrad is a great industrial

complex, second only to Moscow, which has more than twice its population. Ships and shoes, textiles and turbines—you name it, Leningrad probably makes it. Behind the glamorous European facade that gratified the Romanoffs, this city of Soviet workers has not an ounce of glamor, but it is alive and real. Gone is the icing on the cake. The rich and the royal, the merchants and the middle-class environment, the flunkeys and the footmen, melted away in the first revolutionary years.

The mansions of the rich now serve as flats, clubs, and clinics for the workers. A splendid ducal palace on the Neva is the place where young couples come to be married in style by the state. Except that the ritual is not held in church, it preserves all the symbols of bourgeois marriage custom: the bride in a white veil and holding flowers; the bridegroom in a dark suit, white shirt, and tie. Attendants and family gather around them in a white and gold reception room on the ground floor. When they are called, they form a procession up a broad, red-carpeted staircase. An amplified recording plays Mendelssohn's Wedding March. They file into a ballroom, where the registrar stands beside a bust of Lenin. Under Lenin's gaze and a crystal chandelier, the ceremony takes place. A rather formidable woman official performs it. She talks to the young couple earnestly and kindly. When it is over, the family and friends embrace the bride and bridegroom and they all go into an adjoining hall for a champagne party. Or they may go home to celebrate. The marriage palace maintains a flower shop and a gift shop where silver, china, and glassware can be bought for the trousseau. It looks as though the state were trying to make up to its young workers and their parents for the loss of their colorful old religion and for the general drabness of their lives.

In time the state will have moved its workers into new apartments that already ring the outskirts of the old city. The ones we saw lacked beauty, and charm and variety.

But young Leningraders can hardly wait to move into them to enjoy their privacy and freedom from parents. We know a newly married pair that had just bought a co-operative apartment. They had to put down a thousand-dollar cash deposit on a one-room efficiency apartment. The rest they would pay in monthly installments, like rent, over ten years, and the cost worked out at about sixteen dollars a month, including utilities.

We cannot judge the quality of working-class life. But it seems to us that the factory workers of Leningrad have come a long way since the day in 1905 when they walked in humble procession to the Winter Palace to petition their czar, the Little Father, for relief from desperate poverty and hunger. The city was not a decent place for workers then. It is not a bed of roses now, but the worker is no longer on the outside trying to petition his way in. He stands at the center of his society.

Nor does he appear in the least humble. He walks instead with the head-up air of the cockney in another northern city we know. It would not have surprised us to meet Eliza Doolittle or her father selling blue plums on a Leningrad sidewalk.

To be able to look down on someone is surely a sign of progress in the world of labor. Leningraders undoubtedly look down on Moscow somewhat as proper Bostonians sniff at New York. Perhaps they would resent Moscow less if they were not in its power.

There is no better place to sense Moscow's power than in the spacious bookshop on the main street of Leningrad. It is called "Book World" and it reflects just one world, the one the Kremlin permits its people to see. Everything behind the broad counter or in glass cases is out of the customer's reach. There is no honor system here, no way to browse. The shop belongs, of course, to the state, and all the books on its shelves have been approved somewhere in the recesses of the bureaucracy. The stock, and it is large, leans chiefly on the classics and on technical subjects. There is never a time when Book World seems anything but crowded with people trying to shoulder their way to the counters. Buying a book in Leningrad is like buying a loaf of bread. You know what you need and you get it. Except among technical books the element of surprise is almost sure to be missing. Could anything be less European? The Western European mind thrives on the unexpected. There is no quarantine of ideas. They move freely across borders. The winds blow across Europe carrying the seeds that nourish the intellectual soil. No one can predict the crop, and though it may be full of weeds, it never lacks excitement.

If the spirit of this Soviet city was ever European, and there is at least reasonable doubt, it is European no longer. Whoever looks only at the glorious facade is the victim of a great deception.

III

Moscow:

COMMAND POST OF THE EMPIRE

It was the autocratic power, with the centralized administration as its necessary complement, that first created Russia, then saved her from dismemberment and political annihilation, and ultimately secured for her a place among European nations by introducing Western civilization.

—Sir Donald Mackenzie Wallace (1877)

Our window just below Red Square looks out on the Soviet Valhalla. At dawn the crenelated walls of the fortress turn rosy. The tiny golden domes far inside begin to sparkle. At noon, with most of the color drained, we notice the red of the flag that ripples over the fort. It is a mystery, this flag, because it never stops rippling. Could a wind machine be hidden at the flagstaff base?

Under a full moon Valhalla projects its silhouette into the sky. It would not surprise us to meet the god-kings, Wotan and Lenin, striding arm in arm through the Saviour's Gate on Red Square.

One could easily pursue the Valhalla-Kremlin analogy to an illogical conclusion. We know that Richard Wagner was a revolutionary in politics as well as in music; that he spent twelve years in political exile, and that he was a premature, if mixed-up, Marxist. We know, too, that his pagan gods had it in mind, as do the high priests in the Kremlin, to breed a new race of heroes. But Valhalla went up in flames some time ago; the Kremlin stands before our eyes today as a massive concentration of power, and—for Russians—a symbol of glory as well.

No nation is nearly as large as the Soviet Union and only one exceeds it in power. In this largest of nations, this empire of more than a hundred different peoples, power resides in one place: the Kremlin. So when you raise your eyes to the Russian Valhalla you know that its ancient walls

surround and conceal more power than is concentrated anywhere else. You might say, well, a nuclear warhead has
quite a bit of power, but you would have to add that the
Kremlin has the power to loose a thousand of them—a
power restrained only by the certainty of retaliation.

Trying to reduce this thing to scale, we should look at
power centers in other great nations. In Britain we would
have to list at least two: Whitehall and Westminster, perhaps adding Downing Street, depending on its occupant.
The United States has power stored in many places: the
White House, Capitol Hill, and the Supreme Court, not to
mention New York, the leading state capitals, and the vot-
ing booth. Here in the Soviet Union there is just one syno-
nym for power and it is the Kremlin.

The reason is simply that the Communist Party heads up
in the Kremlin, and, as everyone knows, the Party rules the
empire. The Soviet state also heads up in the fortress. In
theory it governs, but in fact it takes its orders from the
Party, which sits at its elbow making all important decisions
and seeing that they are carried out.

The Kremlin began, in the fourteenth century, to shelter
both the Russian church and the state, which is what it does
today. For communism is Russia's new religion, the Party
bosses are its high priests, the Kremlin its Vatican.[1] Only for
two centuries, when St. Petersburg was the capital, did the
temporal power reside outside the Kremlin. And even during those years the czars would return to the Kremlin for
their marriages and for God's blessing on their military adventures. So when Lenin in 1918 brought the government

[1] Naturally, Marxist-Leninists deny that their creed has anything in common with religion. But we are convinced that Russian communism can be
understood only as a religion in competition with other religions. This is the
position of Nicholas Berdyaev (1874–1948), the Russian philosopher with a
deep insight into both communism and the Orthodox Church. See his essay,
"The Religion of Communism," in *The Russian Revolution* (London:
Sheed & Ward, 1931).

back to the Kremlin for reasons of security, the return was not only symbolic but traditional.

Oliver Wendell Holmes the elder once called the Boston State House "the hub of the solar system." Today the Kremlin has a stronger claim. Atatürk was to follow Lenin's example in taking his revolutionary capital out of his window on Europe and into the Turkish heartland. But he went further and renounced all claims to empire, all desires to rule over alien peoples. This the anti-imperialist Marxists were not about to do. They made it clear they had not come to power to preside over the liquidation of the czar's empire. They even added to it, in time, territories in Central Europe and Central Asia which the czars had never ruled.

Lenin, the future god-king, took over the Kremlin quietly one morning in March 1918, by the Trinity Gate. Looking around for a place to live, he bypassed the elegant czarist apartments and settled in a four-room attic flat with his wife Krupskaya, his sister Maria, and a maidservant. An armed guard of Lenin's favorite Lettish regiment patrolled the hallway outside his rooms. The flat was in the arsenal building, a heavy neoclassical block designed for Peter the Great. For the czars it had been a barracks and a military storehouse. One can imagine the dirt and disarray into which the barracks had fallen after four years of war and almost sixteen months of revolution. The place, we are told, smelled permanently of carbolic acid and cats. Lenin had lived there for three years when Trotsky moved in just across the hall with his wife and two daughters. The two families shared a dining room and a bathroom. They ate their communal meals, often meager, off the czar's priceless china and silver. The two wives held demanding jobs in the new Ministry of Education, helping to overhaul it from top to toe.

After a series of strokes, Lenin was taken to his country place near Gorky, to deteriorate and then to die in January

1924. Trotsky stayed on, or rather held on, until 1927. Then he took refuge in a friend's apartment, from which the secret police dragged him, and put him on a train bound for exile in Alma Ata. Trotsky was not to see the Kremlin again.

Stalin, the next god-king, was to take over the Kremlin for thirty years. In his last days there his apartment included windowless and bulletproof rooms. One of the few Westerners whom Stalin ever welcomed to his private quarters in the Kremlin happened to be a raconteur named Winston Churchill.

Churchill flew to Moscow in August 1942 to break the news to Stalin that there could be no second front that year. The Prime Minister found some conversations during that visit "most unpleasant" and he was "offended" by much that had been said. At the final meeting, Stalin suddenly became cordial and said, "You are leaving at daybreak. Why should we not go to my home and have some drinks?"

The answer is authentic Churchill: "I said I was in principle always in favor of such a policy." The Prime Minister continues: "So he led the way through many passages and rooms till we came out into a still roadway within the Kremlin, and in a couple of hundred yards gained the apartment where he lived." (Stalin's daughter reported that he used these quarters rarely and spent most nights in his suburban villa.) That night, Churchill saw "a very aged housekeeper," and "a handsome red-haired girl who kissed her father dutifully" and laid the table. A dinner of "many choice dishes" with "excellent wines" lasted for six hours. At 1 A.M. a "considerable sucking-pig was brought to the table." When no one would join him, Stalin "fell upon the victim single-handed." Churchill was a man who chose words with care. Did he perceive behind Stalin and the sucking-pig the ghosts of the millions of victims upon whom his new ally had fallen? Among political leaders no one was harder to fool than the Prime Minister. He knew with whom he was spending a jolly evening and why. A year earlier he had said, "If Hitler invaded Hell, I would make at least a favorable reference to the Devil in the House of Commons."

Of all the secret and sacred places, none that we can think of has been more secret and sacred than the Kremlin during Stalin's reign, not even Mecca or Lhasa, or the palace of the emperor in Tokyo. His people saw little of his public life, knew nothing of his private life. Yet they worshiped him. Once a year he appeared on the reviewing stand above Lenin's tomb. Twice, in utmost secrecy and security, he ventured outside the Soviet Union, to summit meetings in Tehran and Potsdam.

Hardly had Stalin's mummified form joined Lenin's inside the mausoleum in Red Square when the shell of secrecy that had encased the Kremlin began to crack. Nikita Khrushchev was not the kind of man to spend his life inside a windowless shell. He not only came out of the Kremlin; he opened it and fumigated it as people used to fumigate their homes after the children had recovered from scarlet fever. Not since Peter quit the Kremlin had its halls vibrated to so unconventional a person.

Surely the people of Moscow thought they were dreaming when Khrushchev opened the gates of the Kremlin to them in 1958. It was an act of confidence that must have changed the very climate of the city. Today tourists and Muscovites wander in and out at will, and it is taken for granted. A considerable area is open to them. It includes the Byzantine cathedrals, the treasures of the czars, and the new Congress Hall. Khrushchev commissioned this modernist building of marble and glass for Party conclaves. But when the Party is not meeting, it makes an ideal hall for concerts, operas, and ballets with its oversized stage, its good acoustics, and its six thousand comfortable seats. So of an evening you will see streams of people converging on

the Saviour's Gate and, after the performance, hurrying out
of the Trinity Gate to catch a late subway train home. For
a foreigner who last saw Moscow in the Stalin years, this is
an almost incredible sight, one he admits he could never
have dared to predict.

"You really were here in 1947? You must see tremendous
changes, then."

Responses of this kind came from Muscovites when they
learned that one of us had worked as a reporter in their city
for a couple of months soon after World War II. To some
young Russians, 1947 seems as long ago as 1812; they assume that a returning visitor can hardly recognize Moscow
today. The city has indeed experienced a face lifting as
well as some drastic surgery in the past twenty-odd years.
But this is nothing new or out of keeping with the past.
Unlike old Leningrad, Moscow is anything but a museum.
Its life since the Revolution has been one of restless clear-
ing, widening, tunneling, rebuilding, and redesigning—and
the process still goes on. Europeans like to conserve old
buildings and make traffic squeeze through old streets,
whether in Rome or Bonn or London. Moscow, on the other
hand, is un-European; it shows a passion to tear down and
widen and build again, not for profit, not primarily for the
comfort of its people, but chiefly, one suspects, for the
greater glory of the Soviet state. In spite of its new streets,
new skyscrapers, and the biggest new hotel in the world,
Moscow has kept its physical character basically un-
changed.

Several intangible changes make a deeper impression
than the physical on a Westerner coming back after twenty
years. One we have already mentioned: the opening of
much of the Kremlin to the public. Another change, related
to the first, is a partial easing of security. In 1947, for example one could not buy a street map of Moscow. Even to ask
for one was to invite suspicion. Today Intourist distributes

street maps, guidebooks, and that essential companion of
Moscow living or touring: a map of the subway system.

Moscow citizens must still do without a directory of personal telephone numbers. The authorities still do not want
names, addresses, and numbers scattered around the city.
In 1968 the authorities did issue a new directory of organizations, institutions, and enterprises. But to find a personal
number, the Muscovite can only go to a public information
kiosk, where a woman attendant will try to locate it for him.
Talking from a public phone booth is less likely to be
monitored now than it was in the late nineteen-forties,
when it led Volodin, in Solzhenitsyn's novel *The First Circle*,
to his doom.

Still another change, harder to measure, is that people
think there is less eavesdropping than before. Twenty years
ago it was universal. Big Brother listened to everyone and
everything. The bugging of hotel rooms was obvious and a
source of fun—if you were a foreigner, not subject to a
secret trial and a sentence to Siberia. When Trygve Lie,
Secretary General of the United Nations, came to Moscow,
his official Soviet car failed again and again to show up
when he needed it. Finally he strode to a wall of his hotel
room and said in a loud voice: "I have waited fifteen minutes. If my car is not downstairs at the entrance within five
minutes, I'm leaving Moscow and this mission will be over."
The car arrived.

Today—who knows? No one can be sure that eavesdropping is not going on. Younger Russians are confident that
one form of snooping has disappeared. This was the Stalinist practice of having informers in every apartment building, like the block watchers in Nazi Germany, to eavesdrop
and spy on the other tenants. "I'm sure this kind of thing
has stopped," one youth told us, "but my parents don't believe it." The parents remember too much, and are still
afraid.

One change is concrete and visible. It affects the physical

well-being of tens of thousands of Muscovite families, and also their attitude toward the state. This change is the mass production of housing. It has moved so fast in the last few years that if you ride the subway to the city's outskirts, especially in the southwest, you will find an urban revolution under way.

It was long past time for this Russian revolution. Housing in Moscow and other Soviet cities had become more wretched year by year. Who in the West has not read about the millions of Russian families crowded into one-room flats, sharing kitchens and cold-water bathrooms, if any? Foreign correspondents used to write endlessly about apartment buildings where walls cracked and leaked, and where nothing worked as it should. For forty years, housing remained one of the best-publicized failures of the Soviet regime.

In the late Stalin years, a look at the inside of a one-room one-family apartment was enough to prove two truths. The first was that the Soviet system had failed to meet the most basic needs of its people. (So had the capitalist system in tolerating the old tenements of New York, Glasgow, or Rome.) The second truth was that the human spirit could surmount discomfort for years and decades—especially the Russian spirit. In one of the better old-style Moscow buildings, one of those high-ceilinged brownstone apartment houses built just before 1914, a seven-room apartment had been split into seven units. One room about sixteen feet by twelve housed a government translator, her mother, and her eleven-year-old daughter. An old upright piano served as a partition that gave the schoolgirl a sense of having a cubbyhole of her own. The kitchen, bath, and toilet had to be shared with six other families.

Today a large proportion—no outsider knows exactly how many—still live in such one-room crowding, many in smaller rooms and shabbier buildings. Even in some of the newest buildings, three families have to share—temporarily at least

—the space intended for one. What rankles is not the crowding, not the leaks and cracks, not the lack of cleaning and maintenance, but the lack of privacy. A Russian peasant may not need privacy in his one or two-room wooden house. He finds privacy and loneliness at work in the fields. But a Russian city man or woman spends most hours in crowds of people: at the factory, on subways and buses, in the communal lunchroom. Home ought to offer a refuge, and too often does not.

This has been the city dweller's complaint for decades. But now the tide appears to have turned. The Soviet Government has become the world's biggest builder of genuinely low-cost, low-rent mass-produced housing. As the nineteen-seventies begin, the Soviet Union claims it is putting up close to three million dwelling units a year, and says it will reach its goal of thirty million, for about a hundred million individuals, before the decade ends. Westerners who have made fun of Soviet jerry-building for many years, and with reason, will have to respect the quantity if not the quality.

How has the breakthrough occurred? The answer is a combination of elements, most of them not available in Western countries that also suffer shortages of low-cost housing. The Soviet Government, for one thing, does not have to buy the land; it already owns it. It has no union rules to obey, no speculators' profits to allow for, no threats of strikes or slowdowns to consider, no building codes but its own to obey, no competition to watch, since it is a totalitarian state with all the powers of coercion in its hands. Moreover, the Soviet Government has set a universal limit as well as a goal of nine square meters of living space, or about ninety-seven square feet, for each person. That is, each member of a family is entitled to not quite ten feet by ten, not including space in a hallway, kitchen, and bath.

No doubt there are favored ones like ballerinas, high in the system, who get more than the nine square meters.

62   RUSSIA ON OUR MINDS

Thousands still living in old buildings have not, on the other hand, yet attained what the Kremlin calls the "norm." One hears from Russians that there is much bribery of housing inspectors to get into one of the fancier new buildings. Yet the defects should not blind a capitalist observer to the achievement. The fact remains that the Soviet Government knows how to house more people in more new buildings, more cheaply and quickly, than in any country we have known.

One reason for the breakthrough is a sudden new mastery of the secret of quantity production. According to a 1967 report to the United States Department of Housing and Urban Development, a report commissioned by the agency, the most successful of the Soviet methods is the panel system of building. To quote from the report:

> In this approach each wall, floor, and ceiling of a room is designed to be factory-produced as a single prefabricated unit, a "panel." Openings such as doors and windows are easily provided by inserts in the panel castings. An entire apartment building containing hundreds of family units of from two to six rooms each may comprise only four or five basic panel types. The building will require no framework or skeleton even though it may be up to sixteen (or more) stories in height. Speed of erection is astounding.[2]

The cost? For a two-bedroom apartment with private kitchen, bath, toilet, and hallway, with a total space of 560 square feet, the same report carefully estimates a cost of $3,560, a figure unattainable in the Western world. It includes the cost of materials, transportation, structural labor, finishing labor, and overhead. If this estimate is correct, the

[2] Two years later, an American construction expert, visiting the Soviet Union, found the Russians "far ahead of the United States in producing mass housing." He was W. Burr Bennett, Jr., executive secretary of the Prestressed Concrete Institute.

Russians have put their Western rivals in the shade for years, perhaps decades to come. And the cost to the tenant, for rent and utilities, is a pittance by Western standards.

Of course the bed-sitting rooms, as the British would call them, are not exactly ballrooms in size. The Soviet apartment dweller must know how to squeeze himself and his few possessions into what is little more than a vestibule. Space is such a treasure that in the newer apartments families use their outdoor balconies as storerooms, thus advertising the overcrowding and the discomfort inside.

All mass production has its flaws, and in Russia they are not just structural flaws. One is the lack of finish, especially in the boxlike new buildings that are not prefabricated. Like many Western observers in Moscow and other cities, we have noticed the bricks that lack pointing, the balconies that sag at one end, the doors and windows that need patching to make them fit. But in Soviet priorities, perfection takes second place to speed. So long as the new apartment stands up and gives a few hundred people their long-denied privacy, it serves its purpose. A second flaw in Russia is ugliness. In outer Moscow, for example, some of the buildings rise from the mud or sand of flat fields, without a shrub or tree to soften the slablike or boxlike look.

A third defect is the distance of many new apartment buildings from shops and buses. One of Khrushchev's errors was his refusal to let the ground floor of new apartment buildings be used for shops. He did not want to divert a single square meter from precious living space. One result is that the downtown shops are constantly overcrowded. Lacking refrigerators, Russian women must buy food every day. Lacking private cars, they must tote their purchases home by subway, bus, and on foot. The distance of shops from homes is an error of Soviet housing and Soviet planning, and it is only now being corrected in the newest buildings.

The Moscow woman can share complaints of this kind

with countless other women around the world. But to compare women in the Soviet Union with women anywhere
else would be misleading. No other women are like them
in background, history, or achievement.

The Soviet woman suffers from two handicaps, neither of
which she is likely to overcome soon. On the one hand, she
is a stubborn old stereotype, the kind that most foreigners
bring with them to the Soviet Union and take back home as
well. The trouble is that the stereotype still dots the Russian
landscape, since this country, like many others, is living
simultaneously in at least five generations. On the other
hand, the Soviet woman has been converted into a new
statistic. This is an injustice, for statistics can be boring and
the Soviet woman is one of the least boring of human beings. To us she is a wonder of this modern world, a possible
overstatement we shall try to support.

Let us start with the stereotype. She was one of those
outworn symbols of czarist Russia that we had decided not
to bring with us to the Soviet Union. And so, along with the
bearded old Russian revolutionist carrying a bomb, she was
left behind. It was of no use. There she was—on our very
first morning in Leningrad.

Our window looked out onto a small park, and beyond
it to the majestic dome of St. Isaac's Cathedral. At seven in
the morning the park looked empty. But no, something was
moving along the low rail that separated the patch of lawn
from the encircling pavement. What moved was a tiny
black bundle topped with a white scarf. The bundle worked
its way around the rail wielding what looked like a twig
broom. When the broom had pushed together a few leaves,
the bundle swept them into a pail. After several such sweep-
ings, the pail was about half full. The bundle moved slowly
halfway around the park to empty the contents of the pail
into a metal trash container.

The sweeping and emptying process went on—we timed

it—for thirty-seven minutes. When the park looked spic-and-span, which it had looked to us from the start, the bundle moved to a small hut at one corner, fished out a key from some inner pocket, opened the door of the hut, and put the broom and pail inside it. Having relocked the door and carefully rehidden the key, the bundle hobbled off, turned a corner and disappeared. But not from our lives. She was there every morning, rain or shine, while we were in Leningrad. We accepted her as we came to accept the women we saw digging ditches and spreading tar in advance of paving rollers. Russian women wield brooms. Russian women dig ditches. Why not? Have not women been the traditional cleaners and earth-movers, and are they not moving the earth still, in all but the most affluent societies?

Day after day we watched this ritual in the square. We watched it not because we were making a sociological study with the bundle and twig broom as primary source material. Her age, her wages, her working hours did not matter to us. What mattered was that this little old woman, however deceptive a stereotype, however outworn a symbol, was part of the living past. Without her to tell and show us, we could not know and appreciate how far and how fast the Soviet woman has come in a little more than fifty years.

The bundle is prologue. The subject of the story is her granddaughter, or perhaps her great-granddaughter. This youngish Soviet woman we have come to know. She is the new statistic. She is a teacher in the local language institute (six out of ten teachers are said to be women). Or she is an engineer working in the Ministry of Defense (among Soviet engineers, 30 per cent are women). She is a practicing pediatrician (eight out of ten doctors are women). There is a chance that her mother went to college (52 per cent of the college-educated public are women). Women crowd the physical sciences with chemists and physicists and even with an astronaut. Women pervade the social sciences not only as teachers but also as lawyers, judges, and bureaucrats.

Nobody pretends that the new professional woman has equal opportunity—nobody except the official propagandists. A girl's best hope of getting higher education now, as always, is to have educated parents. Her best chance of entering a university or a polytechnic is to have parents who are members of the Party elite, as well as native ability of her own. Nevertheless, the granddaughter of the little bundle in the square is making the grade today.

The Soviet professional woman is her country's best propaganda tool. A measure of her value is the comparative ease with which she wins the most coveted prize: a chance to go abroad as a delegate to a conference, as a student, and even as a tourist. Carefully selected and briefed, she is effective propaganda because she is true. Just by being herself she demonstrates that the professions are hospitable to women in her society.

Not just the professions, but the crafts and industries and service trades as well. Women work in the building trades, and after a while the visitor accepts it as natural. Pick your way through the mud of almost any new housing project, and you may collide with women, large country types, pushing wheelbarrows full of cement or bricks. Stop under old buildings being renovated and peer upward. High in the scaffoldings you will see young women in dungarees with scarves wound tightly around their heads. They are slapping plaster on the cracked walls and paint on the cornices.

When you ride the subways one woman may drive the train, another may guard the platform and manage the signals. They are smartly uniformed with peaked caps. Women monopolize the enormous cloakroom service trade. In the Soviet Union you cannot go into a museum, a theater, a public building, or a restaurant without checking your coat, umbrella, boots, and bundles. The cloakroom of the Kremlin's new Congress Hall, which seats six thousand people, extends the whole width of the building's basement and keeps at least fifty women checkers busy.

Women are museum guards and guides; they are post office clerks, train conductors, and signal tower operators along the railroad tracks. Women operate all kinds of machines, including cranes in factories (six out of ten industrial workers are women). Women are barbers as well as hairdressers, musicians as well as ballerinas. To get ahead of our story: we have actually seen a woman concertmaster in a provincial symphony orchestra, and a woman director of a midget circus.

To say that women have been offered opportunity in almost every field of work, and have taken advantage of it, does not seem an overstatement. We should say in every field but one: the Communist Party, which rules the country. This is a curious and conspicuous exception. In the Party membership the proportion of women is said to be one in four. In the hierarchy women are consigned to the least responsible positions. Only one woman, Ekaterina Furtseva, has reached the Party Presidium since the beginning of Stalinist rule. She was soon demoted to the largely honorary post of Minister of Culture. Our experience with Party women has been sparse, but when we did have to deal with them, we found them formidable. Their zeal and officiousness suggested to us that they were new at their jobs and a little tipsy with unaccustomed power and importance. We hoped they would simmer down.

There is one last statistic which overshadows all the others and, in part, explains them. It is this: there are about twenty million more women than men in the Soviet Union. The reasons for the imbalance, which did not exist fifty years ago, are not far to seek. They are primarily the purges of the Stalin years and the casualties of the Second World War.

Many women died in all these catastrophes, but their casualties were small compared to those of the men. In the labor camps, for example, women accounted for about one in ten of the prisoners. We are told that the women in these hells on earth were more adept at survival than the men, even though they were harnessed to the same killing labor. Because these are now the tragedies of bygone years, the large preponderance of women today is mainly in the population of fifty-five and over. In this age group women outnumber men by almost two to one. Looking at the very young, aged twenty-five and under, we find that the disparity has virtually disappeared.

To reach where they are today, women have trodden a lonely path as their men vanished by the millions into work camps, army battalions, and mass graves. Most of them came from the land. (More than half of the women in the Soviet Union are still farm wives and farm workers. Nobody mentions this; it is taken for granted.) But during those terrible decades (1933 to 1953) there was a great trek of women to towns and cities to find work or friends or relatives and thus to survive. They had almost nothing to offer in the way of education or skills, but they moved massively into the work vacuum left by the vanishing men.

Lenin came to power in 1917 proclaiming that women would be educated, freed of household cares, and put to useful work. He had no illusions. He knew that his proletariat had to be created out of a 90 per cent peasant majority sunk in such poverty and ignorance as Europe and America could not even imagine. That the czars had never bothered to put Russian children to school, except for a small urban elite, was strange. Being autocrats, they might have reasoned, as did the Japanese rulers of the Meiji era, that literacy, if kept at a low level, would facilitate their rule and enhance their power. But they reasoned otherwise or did not reason at all.

Mass education was high on the Bolshevik list of priorities, but more desperate problems intervened, including the problem of staying in power. As a result, elementary schooling was made compulsory for the first time in Russian history only in 1930. Even then, the law required only four years of primary schooling, so that millions of children had to leave school at ten to go back to illiterate parents and to homes without paper, pencils, or books.

When you remember the upheavals on the farms, the purges, and the wars, it is a miracle that schools did get built, teachers did get trained, books did get printed, and children did get packed into schoolrooms. By 1949, for the first time, the socialist ideal of universal education for girls as well as boys was close to becoming a reality. Having lagged so far behind the West and Japan, the Russians were to catch up and to outstrip Japan, Western Europe, and the United States in one important respect. Soviet women are ahead of all others in putting their education to skilled and productive uses.

Like almost all great cities, Moscow suffers from over-crowding and tension. The distances between home and work and shopping facilities are wicked. The pace of life seems to keep people always on the run when they are not waiting patiently in queues. In most of the great cities, New York and Paris for example, it is men who do most of the straphanging, commuting, and worrying about the conflicting demands of job and family. In Moscow these burdens fall equally on women. They outnumber the men to begin with; eight out of ten of them hold full-time jobs. Moreover, most of them are mothers and housewives as well.

Why do they work? Nobody forces them to, but they are under pressures, and in the Soviet system it is not easy to distinguish between incentives and pressures. When asked why they do it, they give two kinds of answers, depending on the questioner. Privately they say, "I have to work; we need the money. Our family has to have at least two wage earners to get along." For the record, to official questionnaires, for example, they reply: "I want to do socially productive work. Besides, I feel that my work gives me economic independence and social status." There is truth in both kinds of reasons, we would guess.

The state encourages women to work. It has an economic plan to push through. The work force is a key element in the plan; women are a key element in the work force. The Party smiles on working women. It says "There is only one standard for measuring the contribution made to social life by a citizen, and that standard is his [read also 'her'] labor." Labor is for the Party, the state, and Russia all rolled into one. Work is the moral duty of every Soviet woman no less than every Soviet man.

To ease a working woman's life the state does a number of things. It fails to do other things which women want to see done. A working mother gets two months of paid leave before her baby is born, and another two months after. She has no medical expenses, of course. After the child is born she can take a year's leave without pay and get her job back at the end. When she goes back to work the state provides a day nursery and kindergarten to care for the child until it reaches school age at seven. The new housing developments have nurseries nearby, and factories that employ women provide them as well. The hours of child care are flexible. A mother can leave the baby on her way to work and pick it up on her way home. Or she can board it during the work week and take it home over weekends. Parents pay a small part of the cost, the state the rest.

We spent a morning with children of working mothers in one of Moscow's newest day nurseries. It was a complex of small buildings near a four-year-old housing development, with playgrounds around it. The nursery was staffed by smiling women in white hospital gowns. The babies seemed to be getting plenty of loving care. One and all looked over-fed and spoiled. (A favorite propaganda line is that Russians do indeed have a privileged class. "It's our children, you know," Russians will tell you.)

This particular nursery was under-used to say the least. At least half of the cribs stood empty, which seemed to bear out what we had heard: that working mothers prefer

to keep their babies at home if they can possibly find someone to look after them. Often it is a relative, usually a grandmother, as anyone who frequents a Park of Culture and
Rest on a sunny day will discover. The state frowns on the
use of grandmothers for child care, but can do nothing about
it. Communal state-run nurseries can start the making of
good socialists, while grandmothers can do all sorts of harm.
They are apt to be superficial socialists or not socialists at
all. They probably cherish all kinds of superstitions; they
may even believe in God. The grandmothers we talked
with seemed to enjoy corrupting the young, whether with
bourgeois fairy tales or stories of the Christ child, we could
not tell.[3]

When we moved from the nursery into the adjoining
kindergarten, we sensed a different atmosphere. Now the
air of permissiveness had vanished. The spoiling had ceased.
Doubtless they were showing us company manners, but
never have we seen so orderly, so disciplined a bunch of
five- and six-year-olds. They sat very straight at their small
desks; they went through a question-and-answer drill. A
child cleanup squad went into action. When the room was
tidy, out they went for supervised play in the yard. The way
the children had performed reminded us of the old-fashioned
word "deportment," on which teachers used to grade us,
and to which our parents gave special attention when we
brought our report cards home. Next year many of these
children would go into first grade, and they seemed more
than ready to make the leap.

The state has a special interest in helping working
mothers—namely, their children. It has less interest and concern about working daughters and working wives. Moscow
women contend with overcrowded apartments, to begin
with. When they have to shelter indigent parents the tension

[3] For a gay but serious discussion of the grandmother's role in Russia today, we recommend Chapter 5 of *Return from Red Square* by Stephen and
Barbara Rosenfeld (Washington, D.C.: Robert B. Luce, Inc., 1967).

at home may drive them out to church on Sunday morning. We had this plight described to us by a cheerful girl who finally turned her face from us and wiped her nose. She told us she had been born in the Caucasus Mountains, where her mother still lived alone in an old farmhouse. "We bring Mama to Moscow for the winter," she said. "It's not good for her to stay there alone in all that cold and snow. So we make room as best we can. It means putting a curtain across my son's room so she can share it with him. Yuri, that's my son, is fourteen and he is doing very badly at school. He just doesn't want to work. He looks at television when he should be doing his homework. Did you have this trouble with your boys? Well, when Mama is there she just sits and looks at television all day, and when Yuri comes home from school he sits and watches with her. I ask her to send him away but she doesn't understand. She never went to school herself. Television is her one pleasure. Of course I am never home so there's nothing I can do."

The idea of a working husband sharing the domestic duties with his working wife is highly controversial in the Soviet Union. We suspect it is disapproved in principle by working husbands—and tacitly done in practice. We observed the number of late women shoppers, and the crowding of the better-paid women into the beauty parlors between six and seven in the evening, and wondered how many husbands and children were waiting for their suppers at home. Of one thing we are reasonably sure: the Moscow working woman is stretching herself to the limit of her energies—and liking it.

The word "government" is not in common use in Russia. Occasionally someone refers to what we would call the government as the "state." When, for example, we asked about the range of hotel prices we were told, "The state sets the prices of hotel rooms." That seemed to wrap up the subject.

Russians do talk about their government; sometimes they even joke about it. But they have a special word for it: "They." As everyone knows, "They" means authority, the all-powerful, all-pervasive state. Until 1917 They was the interlocking directorate of the czarist regime and the Ortho- dox Church. They is now, of course, the interlocking directorate of the state and the Communist Party. Under both systems the army and the police have loomed large in the lives of the people. The Revolution brought basic changes with one exception: They still hangs over the life of every Russian.

Thus for the Russian an understanding of They and his relation to it has been and remains the beginning of wisdom. He carries a heritage of this wisdom in his bones. He goes on accumulating it for generations to come.

Understanding They means accepting it as a fact of life. Like the weather, They may be capricious but there is noth- ing you can do about it. You simply protect yourself as best you can. Occasionally we meet a Russian who frightens us because he or she seems too lightly clad. Our impulse is to warn, "Wrap up, your skepticism is showing." But most Rus- sians we know wear plenty of protective cover and seem to take it for granted, like the clothes they put on each day for privacy and warmth. One has to respect this privacy. For They creates a climate in which only fools or heroes expose themselves.

We have hesitated to describe They as an octopus, an animal with such a sinister reputation. But the octopus, ac- cording to Webster, can also be defined as "an organism with many branches through which it maintains a hold on the interest of others, as of the public in general." This is a fair description of They. Translated into Russian terms, it means that the arms of the octopus reach and encircle every citizen, claiming usually to be helpful and always to be just and wise. There is the arm, for example, that embraces the Russian baby—even before his mother's—when he is born.

The kindly midwife or nurse or doctor who brings the baby is an agent of They. It is They who makes and prescribes drugs and medicines.

When a mother goes back to work, They offers to take care of her baby. At the age of seven a child enters first grade and from then on continues under the supervision of They all the way through his education. They shapes the curriculum and runs all the youth activities such as clubs, athletics, and summer camps.

Coming out of school or university into the working world, a Russian has only one possible employer: They. Wages, working conditions, holidays, promotions, all come from the decisions made on high by They. From these decisions there is no real recourse. The Soviet system has no place for independent labor unions or strikes. Changing jobs requires permission from They. Moving to another city depends on whether They will make a new job and living space available there. Thus They guards the gates of Moscow like St. Peter, admitting only the favored few.

A young couple just married by They looks to They for a home. For They is everybody's landlord. The state, of course, is the sole owner of land; it builds or renovates most flats and most houses. And of course They allocates all living space. They designs furniture and styles clothing to the last plastic boot and cotton slipper. Excepting home garden produce, They decides what food shall be grown and how it shall be packaged down to the last pound of gray salt.

When it comes to feeding his mind, a Russian is almost totally at the mercy of They. For the state is the sole publisher of newspapers, magazines, and books; the sole producer and importer of films, plays, operas, concerts, and ballets, circuses, and sporting events; the sole programmer of radio and television broadcasts. Rare exceptions to this monopoly can be found in the Voice of America and the BBC broadcasts. But these are subject to jamming, as They sees fit.

Every single thing that comes into the Soviet Union and everything that leaves it is subject to state control. The same, of course, applies to persons. This is an exercise of arbitrary power which many educated Russians find frustrating. It makes them feel like prisoners in the world's largest nation.

At the other extreme are the arms of the octopus that protect a Russian and feed his pride. He is strongly aware of the formidable military establishment which guards him from outside enemies. If he lives in Moscow, he has seen samples of monster new weapons rumbling across Red Square in the May Day parades. If not, he may find pictures of them in the newspapers and magazines. They has, after all, earned the credit for sputnik and other achievements of Russians in space. One hears grumblings about the cost, but no real complaints on this particular score.

Almost everyone complains about They more as a habit than as a serious questioning of its power and permanence. One might as well question the wind on the steppes and the permafrost that grips Siberia's soil. If anyone can rule the winds and melt the permafrost, it is They. And it would be ordered from the Kremlin. As we have said, the Soviet system has only one powerhouse, and it is in Moscow. Symbolically, all the planes and trains that operate throughout the eleven time zones across Russia's two continents run on Moscow time. This is just one example of how far the arms of the octopus can reach. There is no reach and no power quite like it in the other world outside the Soviet Union.

"Dear Father Lenin is with us every day," chant the treble voices of Russian children in their classrooms. Lenin is with us too. We live with bigger-than-life statues of Lenin in stone, marble, iron, and clay in public parks; busts of Lenin in all sizes in shops, schools, ministries, and museums; Lenin in oils and camera portraits on the walls of public buildings and over the prosceniums of theaters; Lenin's head in flowers—begonias and sedum—in the Parks of Culture and Rest, an old man weeding his goatee, another trimming his nose.

And finally, today, Lenin in the flesh.

On this sunny morning Red Square is alive with hurrying people. The only people not moving are in two queues bound for the red granite mausoleum under the Kremlin wall. We join the shorter of the queues, the one reserved for foreign visitors, children, and other privileged people. Just ahead of us about a hundred eight-year-old schoolchildren are lined up under the eyes of their teachers. They wait patiently, as we do, to see their god in the flesh.

About thirty minutes later we step out of the sunlight into the mausoleum. A dark stairway leads us down into the holy of holies. It is a chamber surprisingly small and dim. A single light floods the glass case in the center. Inside the case lies the body. Only the head and the hands are bare. A small man he was, with a large head; "squat and solid," Gorky called him, "with all-seeing eyes of a great deceiver." Here the eyes are shut. The familiar face seems etched in parchment, the hands as if carved in wax.

Sharpen your mind and your senses, for you cannot linger. Soldiers keep the line moving and in a moment you are back in the sunshine of the square, blinded and bemused.

This thing raises questions, some of them morbid. First, the children just ahead of us: what do they make of their dear Father Lenin in a glass case? Childhood has a way of accepting what seems to adults incongruous.

We are just getting used to Russian children. They have a wholesome quality straight out of Johanna Spyri or Selma Lagerlöf, so healthy, so well-behaved, almost sedate. As the English nannies say, "so old-fashioned." We had not expected to see Lenin's corpse framed in Russian children.

Was it truly Lenin in the flesh? Since our visit to the mausoleum we have talked with a renowned American doctor and asked him this question. His answer was cryptic:

"Probably half Cairo, half London." Seeing our puzzlement, he explained, "I suspect the head is a mummy, the hands Madame Tussaud's waxworks." It was one of those things one unaccountably wants to know, even though it doesn't matter. For practical purposes, we have stood over the body of Lenin.

Where in the world except here in Moscow can one stand over the body of a god-king? Among sacred relics, this one is surely the ultimate. Compare it, for example, with the Buddha's tooth. We remember Kandy on the island of Ceylon. An ancient temple shelters the tooth in its innermost shrine. Once a year thousands of pilgrims gather reverently in the great hall. They prostrate themselves and wait. After a while, the high priest emerges and holds the tooth aloft for one dramatic moment.

The advantage of a tooth is that, once extracted, it is eternal. This one, at any rate, is believed to have survived almost twenty-five hundred years since the death of the Lord Buddha. The artificial teeth of another venerated man are on view near where we live in Washington. The dental school of the Johns Hopkins University displays the ivory denture of George Washington. The Founding Father owned two such dentures, which was a good thing in those days because he had to send them to New York to get them repaired. The denture that survives in Baltimore has more clinical than sacred value. Still, it did belong to a revolutionary leader, a man who had a state named after him, as well as a hundred and twenty-one towns, numerous mountain peaks, lakes, rivers, and highways, a man whose face on canvas, coins, postage stamps, and paper money is so common that Americans no longer see it.

To find anything that remotely rivals the object of worship which the communists offer their faithful, we must go far afield. The search takes us all the way to West Irian on the island of New Guinea. Tucked away in the highlands, a tribe of brown-skinned Papuans came to light only about

78 RUSSIA ON OUR MINDS

thirty years ago. The Kapauku have become the darlings of anthropologists because they are stone-agers who defy the word "primitive" in some of their institutions and ways. For their most respected leaders, or headmen, they build a house on stilts. According to a Czech-American scholar who has made them his specialty, they place the corpse in it, with the face at the window. They pierce the body with arrows so that fluids drain away and it is mummified. There it remains for years. Although the Kapauku are a markedly secular, nonreligious people, they do believe the spirit of their leader will protect them.

Short of the highlands of New Guinea, and short of the Kapauku, there seems to be no other place or culture that delivers a whole god in the flesh to its faithful, three times a week at no charge.

For about eight years, the communist hierarchy was able to do even better. It offered its believers two gods.

The thirty-year reign of Joseph Stalin ended on March 5, 1953. His remains joined Lenin's in the mausoleum in Red Square. Lenin's body had to be moved to one side to make room for the body of the colleague he had distrusted and tried from his deathbed to demote. Stalin's name went up next to Lenin's over the entrance to the tomb. The duo-theism looked eternal. Who could have foretold that after three short years it would collapse?

When the Communist Party elite assembled for its twentieth congress in February 1956, their leader, Nikita Khrushchev, came armed with a seven-hour speech. On the next to the last day of the congress, he delivered it. When he had finished, the Stalin cult lay in ruins. Although secret, the news leaked and by June the ruins had been laid bare to the world. The last people to get the news were, of course, the most concerned: the Russians themselves.

Doubtless many had read the political weather from small clues. One clue was the new Khrushchev slogan, "Back to

Leninism." Another, the names of a few of Stalin's victims began to reappear, after having been unmentionable for eighteen years or more. Little by little the faithful understood that one of their gods had ceased to exist. He had been transmuted not just to an un-god, but to an un-person.

There are, of course, precedents in the legion of heroes of the revolution who have evaporated from the scrolls of history, beginning with Trotsky and ending with Khrushchev himself. In Stalin's case, there was a ghoulish difference. The body of the un-god continued to lie under glass and spotlight in the mausoleum on Red Square. It lay there until October 30, 1961. Then, by order of the twenty-second congress, it quietly disappeared. A few months later Lenin's corpse retook the center of the case. Stalin's remains reappeared in a conventional grave under the Kremlin wall. It is there today, the only one without a headstone, in a row of heroes' graves.

So the Russians, those who are no longer "believers," and those who never were, make do with a single god to worship and love. This would be tolerable if they had not for thirty years been conditioned to the cult of Stalin, if they had not learned to love him as a father, worship him as the savior of their country, and trust him as a god. In these words the cult was explained to us by young Russians who were brought up in it. And these words can only begin to measure their disillusion. For if Stalin was "evil," they reason, who is "good"? Lenin, the Party tells them, only Lenin.

What would the lone god say to all this? It is impossible to pass through the shrine in Red Square without wondering what Lenin would make of it. The thought arises: suppose the spirit that once inhabited the corpse could return to it. Suppose Lenin could open his eyes and discover where and what he is today.

Lenin appears to have belonged to that rare breed of political animals, a modest man. The adulation that poured over him in his later life drove him to boredom and fury,

which he did not bother to hide. We read this again and
again in the writings of people who lived and worked with
him. To an old friend and right-hand man he grumbled,
"I consider this completely un-Marxist emphasis on an individual extremely harmful. It is bad, entirely inadmissible
and unnecessary. And these portraits! Everywhere! What is
the purpose of all this?"

On the wild April night in 1917, the night a train bearing
Lenin steamed into Petrograd's Finland Station, the returning hero was caught in a deluge of welcoming words. He
behaved, Trotsky tells us, "like an impatient pedestrian in a
doorway waiting for the rain to stop." Whenever possible,
he ducked ceremonies in his honor, as on the Party's celebration of his fiftieth birthday. After the oratory was all
over, Lenin looked in to say, "Comrades, I must thank you
for two things: for today's greetings and even more for excusing me from listening to the anniversary speeches."

Lenin's personal habits tend to bear out the picture of a
modest man. He never had enough money to live well, and
never worried about it. If his simplicity was a pose, he fooled
everyone. No one seems to have doubted it, not even those
who detested his political creed.

We can then imagine Lenin opening his eyes, breaking
out of his tomb, and berating the Party faithful who put him
there. This would bear out one side of Lenin. But there was
another side, and we can well imagine the reanimated
Lenin in his glass case shutting his eyes again to take stock
of the situation.

For this was a man who spent his life at the wheel of a
bulldozer called Revolution. This was a man who said often
and in many ways that "Everything is moral which is necessary for the annihilation of the old exploiting social order
and for uniting the proletariat." The Revolution was all, he
insisted; the means did not matter. When Lenin died, in
1924, the Bolsheviks had only begun to strip the Russian
people of their ancient Orthodox faith, and to discredit the

clergy, although most churches had been closed and some demolished. The need for "uniting the proletariat" around another faith was perhaps not as obvious then as it became in the Stalinist years. We have not heard any Russian deny that the cult of the dead Lenin and the living Stalin did sustain the people through their trials of World War II. Knowing his people, knowing their dependence on authority, both religious and secular, would not Lenin perhaps close his eyes again, stifle his disgust, and resign himself to continuing as the means to a necessary end?

IV

Kiev:

A QUESTION OF IDENTITY

To fly from Moscow to Kiev, the handsome capital of the Ukraine, is to come back unexpectedly into Europe. One is not out of the Soviet Union, of course, but one is out of Russia. The difference is subtle and important to understand, for Russia feels unsure of the Ukraine, and many Ukrainians feel unsure of their future. Which helps to explain why we felt, ourselves, a vague unease around us (and within ourselves) during our days in Kiev.

Between Russia, still known as Great Russia, and the Ukraine, which used to be called Little Russia, the distinction is not one of ideology. Party members in Kiev can say with truth that they are just as good communists as those in Moscow. So dependable, so firm, has been the control of the Ukrainian Communist Party that the Kremlin has not needed to send Russian agents to head its police apparatus. Why bother? The Ukrainians have plenty of trustworthy men of their own. Leonid Brezhnev himself is Ukrainian-born. If there is an independence movement seeking to break away from the Soviet Union, it survives mainly in the hearts and dreams of the irreconcilably anticommunist Ukrainians abroad.

Not ideology, but identity: there's the rub. Culturally the Ukrainians consider themselves as distinctive as the Poles, Slovaks, Magyars, and Romanians, whose communist-ruled countries lie just across their borders. The Ukraine wants to keep more significant symbols of its identity than, for example, its national ballet, which Moscow has always promoted, or its seat in the United Nations, which Moscow has always used for Soviet and Russian rather than Ukrainian purposes. One all-important symbol to the Ukrainians is their native tongue, a modified version of Russian; they want it taught in the schools, not smothered by the all-enveloping Russian language. They also want their children to learn about Ukrainian poets and heroes. Devoted as some of them are to Marx and Lenin, Ukrainians feel no more Russian than the Viennese feel Prussian. And many of them have a nagging fear that Russia is trying to take their language, their heroes, their identity, away.

Largely because of this fear, there remains within the Ukraine today an instinctive, inherited resistance to Russianization, and the Russians know it. Stalin knew it in his later years. So did Khrushchev, who was Stalin's viceroy in the Ukraine. In Khrushchev's secret speech to the twentieth Party congress, the speech that exposed the dead dictator's crimes, he talked of Stalin's "monstrous" deportations of entire communities during World War II. Among them were the Crimean Tatars, sent to the Tashkent region, and still in 1970 forbidden to return; the Volga Germans, who had lived in Russia for almost two hundred years, sent to Kazakhstan; and two small mountain peoples of the Caucasus, likewise uprooted for no good reason except that Stalin did not trust them.

"The Ukrainians," said Khrushchev, "avoided meeting this fate only because there were too many of them and there was no place to which to deport them. Otherwise he would have deported them also." There are forty-five million people in the Ukraine today, a Slavic but largely non-Russian population too big to move or to push around. Not just their numbers but their industries and farms make the Ukraine second only to Russia itself in economic production among the fifteen republics of the Soviet Union.

To the men in the Kremlin the Ukraine is an absolute necessity. They must have a quiet, reliable Ukraine, free of capitalist and bourgeois poisons. It would be only natural in these circumstances for the Kremlin and its agents to be protective, and overprotective, in guarding the Ukraine against infection. We cannot document the Kremlin's state of mind, but we do know that Kiev gave us an impression of edginess and tension. (It is a traveling reporter's business, among other things, to sense the climate of a place; we have had some practice, in forty-odd countries, in this kind of unscientific reading of the barometer, even when we have been tourists on holiday.) In Kiev, we felt, the security apparatus was on its toes, as if wary about something or someone.

"While in Kiev," said an Intourist folder, bright with color pictures, "you will certainly get to know its people. They are always glad to welcome guests." Taking this assurance literally, we tried to find two young people who had been exchange students in the United States. A friend had asked us to look them up. But to make contact with Soviet citizens, we discovered, was no simple enterprise, especially in Kiev. In other cities Intourist would go through the motions of helping, even to the extent of asking the police for an address. In Kiev, on the other hand, the answer was no from the start. "You will never find them," was the response to our request—and it was said with a finality that made further efforts a waste of time. Thus Kiev achieved a distinction, a negative one, in our minds among the cities on our route to the Pacific.

Another distinction: Kiev was the only place where we sensed that people were either inconsiderate or afraid to be friendly. Elsewhere (except in restaurants), Soviet people usually went out of their way to show goodwill and good manners toward two strangers in their midst. Passengers on buses helped to make change, pedestrians on street corners pointed the way, and all did it with gestures and smiles that broke linguistic barriers.

But in Kiev, on a crowded excursion boat on the Dnieper River, no one smiled, no one helped. No one offered to make room at the deck railing. The looks we got from the other passengers were blank if not hostile. They brought to mind the expressionless stares from Muscovites in the late nineteen-forties, when contacts with foreigners were enough to send innocent Soviet citizens to Siberian prisons. Again we had the sense, maybe only imagined, of a city and a people inwardly disturbed, outwardly on edge.

We shall report another incident that we thought betrayed official nervousness. In Kiev, for the first and only time, we were told to leave a public café because we were with local citizens.

One sunny afternoon two university students had come up to us during a stroll and asked if they might walk and talk with us. They gave the usual explanation: they wanted to practice their English. At first we wondered if this could be a plant by the secret police, but it was not. After an hour or so in one of Kiev's lovely parks, high above the Dnieper River, our acquaintances asked if we would like to come to a student café. What tourist could refuse?

The young men showed an interest in our Russian-English phrase book. As the four of us sipped hot tea from glasses, Russian fashion, they amused themselves repeating English phrases. One, to help a foreigner approach a Russian girl, "You are so beautiful!" delighted them and they repeated the English, over and over. Another, "I've been robbed!" made them frown. They assured us that such things could never happen in the Soviet Union. Next they sampled the questions to be used (so the book said) in a Soviet restaurant. "What do you recommend?" (to a waiter) produced loud laughter from both young men. And "What wine do you recommend?" brought down the house. Russian waiters have not been known to "recommend" anything helpful, or to care what a customer eats and drinks, since the Revolution. What they are apt to recommend to foreign tourists is to find another table.

The laughs brought looks from other tables, as if to ask "What's the joke?" They also brought looks of a different kind from two young men in business suits, shirts, and ties (most of the student customers were tieless) standing near the cashier's desk. One of them walked over to our table and courteously asked one of our hosts to follow him. They talked quietly out of our hearing. No voices were raised, no iron fist shown. The student came back. He said he was sorry, but the café was closing and we would have to leave. The other patrons stayed at their tables, but we paid and left.

There was no mystery about the two men near the entrance. They were not police, and wore no badges that we could see. They were, our companions told us, members of the volunteer militia of the Komsomol, the communist youth organization. One of their duties is to watch foreigners and Soviet citizens as well, and report to the police any un-Soviet or suspicious behavior.

If these experiences of ours can be interpreted as evidence of an edginess in Kiev, what is it, precisely, that the ruling party is afraid of? Why should the militia fidget about the foreigners? One reason, among others, could well be that the Ukraine is comparatively open to foreign influences. It borders on four countries of the Soviet bloc: Poland, Czechoslovakia, Hungary, and Romania. Foreigners fly directly to Kiev from Vienna, Prague, or Sofia without having to go to Moscow first. Respectable motor roads cross the frontier and lead to Kiev, dating from the days before 1939 when much of the present-day western Ukraine was Polish or Czechoslovak or Romanian.

Because Kiev is so accessible to Europe, and because the Ukrainians are non-Russian, the Ukraine was a particular worry to the Kremlin before and during the Soviet invasion of Czechoslovakia in 1968. The liberal reforms of the Dubček government in Prague had set up vibrations in the Ukraine more pronounced than those elsewhere in the Soviet Union. One cannot prove it, but it has been suggested that the Party leaders of the Ukraine asked Moscow to take stern action against the Czech reformers, and in a hurry; for if the Dubček heresy should prevail, it would surely jump the frontier and infect the Ukraine as well. More than one consideration must have induced the Soviet leaders to push the button for military invasion; but one of the reasons, it seems clear now, was concern about the Ukraine.

When we were in Kiev it was the Poles who seemed to be the neighbors with strong influence and close ties. Poles in Kiev behave with the assurance of old friends. We happened to be there while the city was playing host to the European Games, a kind of rehearsal for the Olympics. The planes from Vienna and Eastern Europe had brought scores of sports writers, commentators, and photographers from bloc countries, including Poland.

The Poles seemed to be the biggest contingent and they virtually took possession of our hotel. Judging from the number of vodka, brandy, and champagne bottles on their restaurant tables, Poland was under the thumb of the Women's Christian Temperance Union, from which those reporters had just escaped. They carried on with the hotel waitresses as they would not have dared to do in puritanical Moscow. They switched the table flags of the various countries represented at the games. In communist countries it is the custom to put the appropriate flags on tables reserved for foreign delegations or even, as we found in Cracow some years ago, for unofficial reporters like ourselves. The miniature flags have at least three uses. They are supposed to insure seats for visitors who might otherwise complain; they signal people of some nationalities to keep away from others, and thus avoid political contamination; and they make surveillance easier for secret police, if any.

In Kiev one mischievous Pole took possession of a table with an American flag (we never discovered for whom it was intended). Then he called his friends over to laugh at him. These Poles felt at home in Kiev. They reminded us of visitors from the United States in Canada, or Danes in Norway.

Geography, ethnology, and history can create barriers as well as links. After all, the Poles ruled the Ukraine from the fifteenth to the seventeenth century, and the present Ukraine includes the Polish city of Lvov as well as a large slice of what used to be eastern Poland. But recent events seem to have pulled these former enemies together. Poles and Ukrainians now sense an affinity as fellow Slavs; they feel themselves different from those other Slavs, the Great Russians, who dominate them. They also share a fear of the Germans, who destroyed their cities in World War II, ravaged their farmlands, herded their men and often their women off to Germany for slave labor. And they share memories of unspeakable crimes committed on their soil: the Poles at Auschwitz, the Ukrainians at Babi Yar.

"Could we see Babi Yar today?"

"Why not?" the Intourist manager answered. The reply was not as casual as it sounded, nor was our question. Babi Yar (literally, women's ravine) was the scene of one of the indelible crimes of World War II. On three successive days in 1941 the Germans rounded up the Jews remaining in Kiev—those who had not fled eastward with the retreating Russians—stood them on the edge of the ravine, and machine-gunned them. The bodies fell into the trench and lay there unburied. The number of victims of those few days is usually put at 50,000; those killed during the German occupation at 200,000. The returning army of General Vatutin found the traces at Babi Yar and learned the story when it retook the city in 1943. But for some reason still unexplained, the Soviet Government put no marker on the site, as if it were trying to blot out the whole episode—until Yevtushenko denounced the silence in a memorable poem.

We had imagined Babi Yar to be deep in the countryside. Actually it took less than fifteen minutes by car to get there from the center of the city. Kiev has spread so fast that the ravine is within present city limits—which somehow deepens the stain. For if the crime was so close to them, wouldn't hundreds of Kievans have known what was going on? How many of them hid prospective victims? How many delivered them up to the Germans?

The place itself looks evil. We drove at first through old and shaded streets, then through new ones lined with apartment buildings. Where the buildings ended we came to the site of the massacre. On the right of the road was the site of an old quarry, with a pool of stagnant water. On the left, a piece of level ground dropped off into a ravine. It was just an ugly ravine. Of course there was nothing to see.

In spite of Yevtushenko, nobody was interested in the place, not even morbid sightseers. We did notice, on the side of the road near the quarry, a boulder with an inscription: "On this site a monument will be built to the memory of those who perished in the occupation of Kiev, 1941–1943." Not the Jews who perished; to give them special mention would not do, least of all in the Ukraine. A car drew up and two well-dressed women got out. One of them laid a bunch of white chrysanthemums on the stone, stood almost furtively for a moment, then drove away. We drove off too, wondering, among other things, what it would be like to live in an apartment with a view of this place from the window.

Nobody has yet explained the twenty-five-year Soviet effort to hide Babi Yar. In neighboring Poland, the policy of the communist government is to make sure that German crimes and victims are remembered. Polish schoolchildren over fourteen are taken in groups to visit the extermination

camp at Oswiecim, or Auschwitz. A few years ago we saw
them there solemn-faced, staring at the piles of hair and of
children's shoes in glass cases, or at the gallows where the
commandant of the camp was strung up after the war. Flags
of twenty-eight countries, including the United States,
showed that their citizens died in the gas chambers. The
whole place seemed to say, "Let us remember them." It
stirred subsidiary emotions, such as pity and terror, and
shame for the human race, but remembrance came first.
Why the victims of Babi Yar cannot be remembered, why
their fate must be wrapped in an official silence, passes
understanding.

Kiev does not show off Babi Yar. It offers other sights for
tourist snapshots and diaries. As the city from which
Byzantine art and Christianity first radiated through Old
Russia, it has its own relics of olden times. The ninth-
century church of St. Sophia, a small-scale masterpiece of
design, has not been used for worship since the Revolution;
it is a museum. But somehow a mosaic of the Praying Virgin,
under the golden semi-dome, imparts reverence to the older
Soviet tourists among those who crowd the aisles. Even as
museums, the old churches of Kiev keep religion and history alive. It is odd that the two celebrated St. Sophias, one
in Kiev and the other in Istanbul, are now museums in
states that have disestablished organized religion.

In the summertime Kiev is crowded with foreign tourists
from all over, but especially from East Germany. We encountered troops of Germans in St. Sophia and still more in
the many-towered Pechersky Monastery above the Dnieper
River, three miles from the center of the city. Here a heap
of stones and a single small tower are all that remain of
the Church of the Assumption, built in the late eleven-
hundreds. The Nazis carted off its gold and silver and blew
up the building. A fence now surrounds these ruins, as if

they were a bear pit at a zoo. The German tourists stand at
the fence and gaze at the ruins, with thoughts unspoken
and unknown.

Why should Germans choose to come to Kiev? In the
Soviet Union one sometimes feels that World War II is not
yet over. The Kremlin keeps memories of the war alive,
fanning the flames of national hate and pride. The cinemas
have never stopped showing films of World War II. One
that is reissued again and again is the story of Zoya, a young
girl who fought with the guerrillas behind the German lines,
was captured and tortured, and then, still refusing to give
information, was hanged. Soviet television seemed to us to
alternate sports events, ballets, and films of German cruelty.

While we were there, the official Soviet radio proclaimed
a "Friendship With Germany Week"—with East Germany,
that is. There was no interruption in the official attacks on
West German "revanchists" and plotters of a new war.

In spite of all the violence it has known, Kiev keeps the
air of a queen among Soviet cities. It cares about its looks,
and it obviously likes to be admired. If guidebooks rated
cities as they do restaurants, Kiev would surely get four
stars for its apparent wholesomeness and charm. Among
the secrets of its looks are its site and its attachment to a
woody plant, known as a tree, that is going out of fashion
in other parts of the world.

Kiev sits at the back of forested heights that overlook
the Dnieper River, as the Palisades overlook the Hudson.
From the heights, and from places in the city itself, a view
sweeps eastward for miles across the Ukrainian plains, and
south toward the Black Sea. What a private real estate developer could have done with this site! He could, for example, have planted multistory apartment buildings high
above the river. This would have given the city a brand-new
skyline and a brand-new source of tax revenue. Next, the

developer could have improved the opposite shore by putting up factory buildings at the river's edge.

The city fathers of Kiev, of course, did nothing of the kind. Being able under the Soviet system to do what they liked with land, they built mass housing far off on the flatlands. They connected these apartment communities to the city by a subway line that crossed the Dnieper on a bridge and tunneled under the riverside cliffs. The cliffs themselves they preserved as parks.

There are fifteen miles of parks along the Dnieper, most of them green and leafy refuges from the city streets. An official statistic says that Kiev has 194 square feet of parkland for every man, woman, and child among its million and a half people. The river itself remains a playground as well as a busy industrial highway. How the people of Kiev have kept their river relatively unpolluted for bathing and boating is an enigma that dwellers on the Rhine or Hudson might like to solve. On summer days and until the end of September, thousands of sunbathers crowd the beaches on the sandy islands in midstream. Individually most Ukrainians would not win beauty contests in their swim trunks and bikinis, but collectively they make a gay sight. They are an example of city people making the best of their environment.

The city itself preserves its environment, and thus preserves a human scale. Its main street, the famous Kreshchatik, or Crossroads, was past preserving in its old form; the buildings on both sides were blown up by the retreating Russians in 1941, as part of a scorched-earth policy. Under Stalin it was rebuilt with some of the most pompous structures of the postwar period. But its rebuilders also gave it trees, so many trees that now it is one of the greenest as well as widest avenues in the world. Its sidewalks are fifty feet wide for walking or idling. Some of the side streets, climbing steep hills, are canopied with trees. The air sparkles on sunny days, partly because of the parklands, partly because factories have been kept well outside the town, and partly because the streets are blessedly free of traffic.

The lack of cars and the banishment of industry to the suburbs have forced the city to provide mass transportation. Most people have to take buses or trolley cars or subway trains from their cramped homes to the city center and to the factories. We rode the Kiev underground line to the end, ten stations and about six miles from its start, wishing that our own city of almost a million might have a line as useful, as clean, as well maintained as this one.

But decentralizing a big city also imposes burdens on those who live and work there. Kiev's subway, like Moscow's and most of London's, is of deep tube construction. It adds at least five minutes to each journey to ride the long escalator to or from the trains. The stations are far apart, so that in Kiev as in Moscow the shoppers must do a lot of walking in every kind of weather. Now the government is moving back toward a more centralized plan. A flat stretch at the river level, known as Podol, an ancient part of the city that corresponds to Quebec's lower town, will soon be rebuilt with tall apartments. The process of moving outward seems, in Kiev, to have reached its limits.

It has been the fashion for years in the West to disparage Soviet cities and city planning. A communist bureaucracy, we used to be told, could not possibly plan cities for human beings. Some of this theory was justified, as we saw in the inconveniences of new housing in Moscow. But in Kiev we felt that state control of land had paid dividends to the urban population. Freed from speculation in land values, the municipality has been able since World War II to design and build a livable, workable city. Who knows? The time may soon come, if it is not already here, when city planners and municipal officials from the industrialized

West will take a professional look at Kiev, and perhaps learn from its example.

"They know we're socialists—why don't they leave us alone?"

The question came not from a Czech in Prague, but from a Russian on a park bench in Kiev.[1] It was a morning for soaking up the September sunshine and looking up at the cloudless sky. In this position you did not have to look at the beds of public flowers, the inevitable red salvias and red canna lilies in geometric designs. But your ears could not avoid the inevitable loudspeaker that afflicts almost every Soviet Park of Culture and Rest. The public voice on this particular morning was leading setting-up exercises to appropriate band music. Nobody in the park, so far as we could see, was doing setting-up exercises. A few middle-aged grandmothers and one young father were pushing go-carts or sunning themselves on nearby benches. A young woman who shared our bench had seemed absorbed in a book. But the loudspeaker finally caused her to put it down and look around. After surveying the two strangers, she said shyly, "May I speak English with you?"

The conversation began cautiously. No, we were not English. We sensed a shade of disappointment. "American then?" The encounter survived. The young woman was a chemistry student.

"The English language is necessary when you study chemistry," she said. "I try to learn it by myself, but it is hard." We agreed.

No, I do not come from Kiev. My home is a small village in the Crimea. My father is dead. My mother works in a collective. My parents did not have education but my sisters and I have all finished eight years of school. I came to Kiev

[1] In the following discussion we have, for obvious reasons, masked the identities of the people who talked with us and the settings in which we talked, but we have reported faithfully what they said.

to attend the university. I was lucky. Everybody wants to
go into science and there are not enough places. I think five
people qualify for each place. But I got good marks in my
examinations.

The setting-up exercises ended. Across the park came a
procession of schoolchildren with their teachers. A bunch
of healthy eight- or nine-year-olds, they wore dark pinafores
and red scarves around their necks.

"Octobrists," said the young woman. "It is a socialist
youth group, the first one. After the Octobrists come the
Pioneers from ten to fifteen, and then the Komsomols."

"Were you an Octobrist and a Pioneer?"

"Yes, of course."

"And a Komsomol?"

"*Nyet*, I mean no. I did not belong to the Komsomol."

"Why not?"

"Well, I did join when I was fifteen. My friends persuaded
me. But I did not stay very long." There was a pause, then:
"It took too much time away from things I wanted to do. I
am not really a person who likes to belong to things."

There was another pause. The young woman stood up
and looked around. Then she said, "They know we're
socialists—why don't they leave us alone?" She pulled a leaf
off a bush and chewed it. "Shall we take a walk?"

We strolled together down the paved path between the
public flowers. The young woman at our side was telling us
about the sights of Kiev and the boat trip down the Dnieper
that we should take. Our thoughts were on her question.
We had not heard it put so simply before.

This encounter and conversation were not the first of
their kind, nor were they to be the last along our route to
the Pacific. We had not expected to be accosted by strangers
wanting to talk. It struck us as remarkable that so many
people, most of them young, would be so eager for contacts
with foreigners that they would ignore the possible risks.

Yet it happened in every city and, with one possible exception, the motives were entirely innocent.

There was the young man in another city who bumped
into us, literally, as he came out of a food store. He
apologized in Russian, then, after a second look, in German.
The three of us stood on that spot for an hour talking about
parents and children in our country and his. The family was
breaking up in Moscow, he told us, but it was still very
strong in provincial cities and especially in Georgia. The
authority of the father had not changed. No teen-ager
would dream of defying the father except, maybe, in Moscow. Girls, of course, left home when they got married, but
not boys. They would stay under the parental roof. After all,
they owed it to the parents to help them in their old age.
How many young people in America took dope? And
wasn't it true that most of them were against Vietnam?

Suddenly the young man looked down at the package in
his hands. Something was dripping out of it, down his
trousers and onto the sidewalk. It was the pound of butter
for which his mother had sent him to the store, and it had
been wanted for lunch. We laughed, shook his buttery hand,
and said good-by.

There were the young women who sat next to us at the
opera in a provincial city. Might they translate the program
for us? And the synopsis of the plot was rather a compli-
cated episode of Russian history; perhaps they could explain it. During intermissions we talked and after the opera
they walked back to our hotel with us, not wanting to stop
talking. But they politely refused the invitation to come in
for a cup of coffee. Perhaps we could meet again and take a
walk. They wanted to know about American books, being
students of English at the language institute. Would they
like us to send them some books when we got home? Yes,
please. And what titles did they have in mind? Well,
would it be possible to send a book called *Catcher in the
Rye?*

We Americans had such wonderful highways. They had seen a movie, *It's A Mad Mad Mad Mad World,* which showed superhighways. And all Americans, they supposed, had color television sets. What! We did not have one? Why?

There was the young man who helped us buy a pocket comb in a department store. He apologized for the Moscow subway. It was so vulgar; now, the ones in Kiev and Tbilisi were in better taste. Why, he went on, did "they waste so much money on expensive and ugly decorations in the metro stations?" And why did "They" support Castro to the tune of a hundred million rubles a year? That money was needed in Russia for so many things.

There was the journalism student at a provincial university: If you want to see the world, you have to be either a journalist or a diplomat. Science and journalism are the two most popular careers here. But only the scientists work hard. In your country, I understand, everybody works hard. And so on.

On reflection we realized we had been listening to protest of a sort. What could be learned from it? To begin with, these chance acquaintances were not "average" Soviet citizens. They took the initiative in accosting foreigners. All of them spoke a second language, usually German or English. All of them were educated in the sense that they had gone beyond the compulsory eight years of schooling. Considering their isolation from the outside world, and the misinformation that is fed to them, one had to respect the scope of their knowledge, their willingness to give and take in conversation.

We learned, moreover, that these particular people were neither pro- nor anti-American. They showed discrimination, as though they had somehow absorbed both Lenin's and Stalin's admiration for American technology, along with their hatred of its capitalist creed.

Last, and perhaps most revealing, was the kind of criticism they freely expressed to us. Never did it question the basic Soviet system, but only the abuses of the system by the faceless rulers in the Kremlin. "They know we're socialists," the young woman in the park had said, and there was never any reason to doubt this in anything our chance acquaintances said to us. In that word "socialist" we sensed a pride. They seemed not to doubt that their system was the best so far devised by man, the one to which all peoples would come someday. In short, they felt about their socialism in much the same way most Americans still assume the superiority of their system. Americans, too, admit imperfections and abuses, but even those who want to bring the system down are unable to propose a better one.

Only once did we hear anyone denounce the Soviet system, and it may perhaps be a commentary on us that it shook us by its rashness. Early one morning we went shopping in a free market with a Russian acquaintance. Our string bag was full of apples and pears. Suddenly a middle-aged man stood before us. His clothes had been expensive but they were shabby. His face was deeply etched with sadness. He spoke to us in Russian in a cultivated voice: "What country are you from? Please tell me because I want to go there. This socialist system is bad. It does not work."

The Russian with us bent close to us and whispered, "Pay no attention to him. He is drunk, very drunk." There seemed only one thing to answer, "Yes, of course, he is drunk." To the stranger, too, there seemed only one thing for us to say. "Our country is the United States, and if you were able to come, we are sure you would be welcome." The courtly stranger turned away, and we thought we saw tears on his face.

V

Tbilisi:

GEORGIANS, "NOT REALLY SOCIALIST"

At least a quarter of the Soviet people live under a system that is alien and often beyond their understanding. These are the people who are not Russian, not Slav, but products of many other ethnic strains. Their problem is to stay afloat in the strange waters of Marxism-Leninism. To navigate in such an unfamiliar element, to steer a course that might lead to a relatively satisfying life, requires talent of a high order.

The people most richly endowed with this talent, it seems to us, are the Georgians. In their little Soviet republic to the east of the Black Sea, they start with natural advantages over the Russians themselves. The sun shines on them longer each year than on other parts of the Soviet Union. An ample rain keeps their valleys green and productive, except in the eastern districts toward the Caspian. More important, they possess just those skills that are needed to cope with Russian rule and the Soviet system. One of them, Joseph Stalin, coped so well that he became master of all of Russia and of the system too.

Georgians will get far no matter what kind of system may rule them. Out of every thousand of Georgia's people, thirty-eight, according to an official Soviet publication, "have received a complete higher education"—the highest percentage of any of the fifteen Soviet republics. What sets them apart from the Russians today is not primarily their thirst for learning, their sense of fun, their non-Slavic Mediterranean origin. The real difference, in our opinion, is that Georgians cling to an un-Soviet scale of values.

"Those Georgians aren't really socialists, you know," a Communist Party member had confided to us in Moscow. We had been shopping for fruit at an open market, a so-called free market, where farmers and householders sell what the state allows them to grow in their backyards and private plots. The stallholders were mostly Georgians who had brought their tomatoes, plums, and grapes by train or plane, and somehow made a profit in spite of the fare.

An outrageous price in a Moscow or Kiev free market is apt to start a customer grumbling: "Oh, he's a Georgian. What else can you expect?" The implication, of course, is that Georgians are still private traders at heart, always able to make a fast ruble, by fair means or foul. Georgians are quick to complain that their reputation is unjust. In Tbilisi, their lively capital, a Georgian acquaintance told us that such price-gougers are usually Armenians. "They give us a bad name," he said. Armenians live in the neighboring Armenian Soviet Republic, and also make up about 11 per cent of Georgia's population. Any act of boorishness, rudeness, double-dealing or crime was surely Armenian. It brought to mind the time burglars entered our apartment in Turin, in northern Italy. Within a few hours everyone in the neighborhood knew of the crime. Everyone commiserated with us and expressed outrage at such mistreatment of foreign guests. A shopkeeper assured us:

"It wouldn't have happened a few years ago, before all those people from the South came to live here. The thief must have been a Sicilian."

Hearing this kind of talk in Tbilisi made us wish we were going to Armenia—just to see who gets the blame there.

Keen traders or not, many Georgians have done well for themselves. The austerities of the Soviet system have not been enough to stop them. The cars flow along the main street of Tbilisi in traffic that is almost Western European, not Russian. They are not only the big official cars, easily identifiable, or the buses of all ages, the newest made in East Germany or Czechoslovakia, that one sees in other Soviet cities. In Tbilisi it looks as if hundreds really own private cars. The compact Volgas, the smaller Moskviches, sturdy rather than stylish, form a never ending river of traffic that sometimes made us doubt we were in the Soviet Union.

Where do Georgians find the money for this kind of luxury? Where do they get the influence? The questions puzzled us again and again, and not just because of the cars.

We imagined that we saw more cafés, restaurants, pastry shops along the half mile of Tbilisi's main boulevard than in all of central Moscow. In this city a Viennese or a Berliner, accustomed to whipped cream on every piece of cake, would not feel seriously deprived. The restaurant in our hotel was crowded at every meal; for once the headwaiters were honest when they waved us away, for our own eyes told us there was no table.

Most of the diners were Georgians and Armenians: dark-haired men, usually with small mustaches on thin faces; men without women, as in most public places in neighboring Turkey and elsewhere in the Middle East; men always talking, gesticulating, arguing in Mediterranean fashion. They talked while eating one course after another, with hors d'oeuvres, shish kebabs, and hot spiced chicken. They put away more liquor than we had ever seen consumed outside a New York bar. A table for four might have on it two bottles of Tsinandali white wine, the best in the Soviet Union, four bottles of beer, two of vodka, and two of Georgian cognac, a drink that is sugary and powerful enough to put Westerners under the table. It costs six rubles a bottle—$6.60 at the official rate of exchange—a sizable slice of a Soviet salary. Yet these Georgians emptied all the bottles and were able to walk out at eleven at night when the restaurant closed.

Again, the question asked itself: where do the Georgians get the money? Perhaps one should say "some Georgians," for it was evident that Tbilisi as a whole did not share such affluence. The conspicuous consumption we saw was mostly on one main street in one small section of the city. Apart from food and drink, consumer goods were scarce, and of a quality that Westerners wouldn't buy unless they had to. It was evident to us that a few Georgians (and Armenians) were making money out of a combination of state and private trading. The Soviet state was letting them do it, winking at trading practices in Georgia, on the periphery of the empire, that it would never permit in Russia itself.

Confirmation came in a shady park tucked away on a hillside below the main boulevard. Here an aged larch tree spreads across a junction of two park walks, and here, in almost every kind of weather, men and a few women collect like birds around a feeder. Usually they cluster around one individual, who, obviously, has some kind of business to transact. He appears to be giving information; those around him ask questions, note the answers, nod or shake their heads.

We soon discovered what was going on. It was a private, unofficial real estate exchange, a black market in furnished housing. Anyone who suddenly had an unused room in his apartment, or a few extra square yards that could be made into a semblance of a room, could rent the space here without going to the authorities. Suppose a son marries, or a daughter goes off to a university in another city, or a relative who has been sharing the apartment dies. Since housing space in the Soviet Union is allotted on a basis of nine square meters per person—ninety-seven square feet—and since housing space is the most precious of all Soviet commodities, anyone reporting unused space probably would be moved to a smaller apartment. Is it any wonder that Georgians do not always report it?

The wonder is not that they rent the space privately,

and make a little money out of it, but that the state lets
them do it. We saw the black market under that tree day
after day, and never observed a policeman nearby. Surely
the police knew about it and let it go on. If the same kind
of thing goes on in Moscow or Leningrad, we did not see
it.

One learns that private room-renting is not the only form
of private enterprise in Georgian housing. Home building
itself is private as well as public, and home ownership too.
We caught our first glimpse of this unsocialist development
from the top of Mount Mtatsminda, the 2,500-foot hill that
forms a backdrop to Tbilisi. A bourgeois funicular railway
built in 1906 pulled us slowly to the top. On the edge of the
precipice, overlooking all of Tbilisi and its winding Kura
River, the city has set up a restaurant as middle-class in
spirit as the similar mountaintop cafés that overlook Bergen
in Norway and Kobe in Japan.

A Georgian friend was showing us the aspects of socialism we were supposed to admire.

"All those buildings are new apartments for the workers,"
she said, and pointed to a white gash of new buildings
stretching, it seemed, for miles, toward the surrounding
brown hills. The new apartments always make an impression on visitors in their quantity if not their style. But something else caught our eyes in the view below, something
that did not seem to fit the Soviet scene. It was a green
hillside dotted with one- and two-family houses, and they
stood among lawns and gardens.

The next day we went to those hilly streets to view a
most unsocialist phenomenon. We learned that a Soviet
citizen who has saved enough rubles can build a house for
himself or he can join with several others. He and his
friends apply to the state for land; the state lets them have
a site that is not needed or not suited for building an apartment development. The government also allots labor. Since
there is no free labor in the Soviet Union, it makes ma-

terials available, and long-term loans as well. In due course a one-family or multi-family house is built, usually of brick, with wrought-iron grillwork covering the ground floor doors and windows for security. We did not go inside, but from the outside, the houses looked sturdy enough.

"Who gets these houses?" was an obvious question to our friend.

"Anyone who has the money," was the straight-faced answer. "Usually older people want them. They can't stand living in the big apartment buildings. They want a garden. Of course you have to heat these houses in the winter, and get rid of snow, and all that kind of thing."

Obviously, not "anyone" can get anything in the Soviet Union, even in Georgia. We knew that. We knew that there exists, as several Russians acknowledged to us, a pyramid of influence: ballerinas and athletes at the top, then army officers and Party officials, then scientists and teachers. But, making allowances for this Soviet class system, we did feel that the central government was holding Georgia on a loose rein. "Private" building now produces almost a third of all the new housing in Georgia. Without being able to prove it, we suspected that Moscow was letting Georgians make more money, enjoy more comforts and luxuries, than those comrades not on the periphery of the Soviet Union.

"My grandparents live on the Black Sea coast and they have a jeep," a graduate student told us. "Lots of the farmers down there have washing machines and cars. They grow cotton and fruits and vegetables."

Western friends who had traveled along the European frontiers reported the same story of comparative affluence in the other borderlands. A French diplomat we met in Georgia told us that he no longer needs to leave the Soviet Union for decompression after duty in Moscow. He goes to Tallinn, the capital of formerly independent Estonia, and finds good food, courteous service, civility, and ease of a kind he had not known in Russia itself. We ourselves were to see in Central Asia additional evidence of the loose rein we had noticed in Georgia.

Why? In a country where the true reasons for government decisions are seldom told, the outsider can only play the game of putting clue and clue together. Sometimes the clues mislead. One of them, for example, is the obvious distaste of Georgians for Russians. To ask a Georgian "are you a Russian?"—meaning, do you belong to the Soviet Union or are you a foreigner?—is to display ignorance as well as bad manners. "No, I'm not a Russian, I'm a Georgian, and proud of it," is the usual answer.

As one of many minor subject-peoples on the edge of the empire, the Georgians have caused Russia a disproportionate amount of trouble since their ancient kingdom lost its identity in 1801. The history of Georgia since annexation is spattered with the blood of rebellions and reprisals. What, therefore, could be more natural than a Russian policy of avoiding trouble now? Would it not make sense for Moscow to give the Georgians special privileges, and thus make sure that rebellion does not recur?

It would make sense—except that this is not the way Soviet policy works. In the face of any rebellion, incipient or actual, the Soviet response has almost always been a swift and ruthless use of force. The rulers in the Kremlin do not buy off opposition; they liquidate it. They did it in Georgia in the nineteen-twenties, when the local communist leader, Budu Mdivani, became too Georgian, too nationalistic. They purged him. They did it in Central Asia in the early nineteen-twenties, when Soviet rule was challenged. No matter how remote the border region, whether in the Middle East, like Georgia, or in the most distant Soviet territory in Asia, open discontent becomes a threat to the security of the Soviet system. The Russians do not compromise with such a threat, and would not do so if it raised its head in Georgia.

Yet Russia wants and needs what its border regions produce. Georgia supplies manganese, coal, and iron for Soviet industries; it also grows fruits and vegetables that offset the starchiness and monotony of the Russian diet. Georgian tobaccos and wines help to make the deprivations of Russian life more tolerable, and Georgian warmth and sunshine give hundreds of thousands of Russians a vacation to look forward to. Little Georgia, in other words, plays a big role in satisfying Great Russia's wants.

What the central government seems to be doing, in response, is to combine flattery with incentives. It flatters the Georgians' pride by letting them have newspapers in their own language; by training and subsidizing a Georgian national ballet; by giving Georgians positions of apparent honor, if not of power. Too much power, of course, would never do; Stalin was a Georgian, and so was Lavrenti Beria, the chief of his secret police—and two such power-wielders in one century are enough. But Georgians have learned how to adapt to the realities of Russian power. Better, they seem to be saying, to eat, drink, and be merry when you can.

Westerners stationed in Moscow have never stopped complaining about what they call the gray blight of the Soviet system. Few can define it exactly, but all know what it means. The words stand for a lack of variety and color in the shops, a skimpiness of comforts and of choice, a bureaucratic dullness spread over everyday living. In the Georgian capital of Tbilisi, on the other hand, the gray blight has vanished, if indeed it existed at all. The town knows how to laugh and be informal. "Call me Charlie," said the Intourist driver, an Armenian with an American accent, as he met us at the airport. This, we discovered, was typical of a place that lacked stuffiness, in its looks as in its manners.

Stalinist Gothic, which clothed new buildings in pretense instead of style, seems hardly to have penetrated here. In the central city only one building of any consequence, the headquarters of Georgia's Soviet Government, shows off the massive columns and sculptures that are among the hallmarks of Stalinist design. Lenin, of course, addresses nonexistent crowds from a pedestal at the foot of the main boulevard. But the street is named neither for Lenin nor Marx nor Engels. It is named, instead, for a Georgian poet, Shota Rustaveli, who wrote a national epic eight hundred years ago. If there is any outward conformity to Soviet taste in this city of many styles, one must look for it on the outskirts, in the scores of new apartment buildings. In general, Tbilisi struck us as a city of character, part Mediterranean, part Middle Eastern, and only slightly Russian in its atmosphere and flavor.

In their cultural and artistic life, too, many Georgians are "not really socialists, you know." They have too much sense of humor to follow the teachings of Nikolai Chernishevsky, the solemn Russian philosopher and teacher of the mid-Victorian age. Chernishevsky wanted all artists to enlist in the struggle for political freedom. If painting or sculpture did not have a social purpose it did not qualify as art.

This was not in the Georgian character, although Russians swallowed the doctrine and followed it. Nor do Georgians take kindly to the companion doctrine that if art is not strictly realistic it is not art at all. Lenin wanted a painting to show a tree that looked like a tree, a house that he could recognize as a house, a person with eyes, nose, mouth, and body. When he saw nonrepresentational art he exploded. Accordingly, Lenin and his successors ordered Soviet art encased in what is still called Socialist Realism. Under this doctrine, the free artistic spirit is anesthetized or kept, like the mummy of Lenin's corpse, as a kind of curio. Even the sunlight of the French Impressionists and Post-Impressionists is dimmed and deprecated.

A Soviet textbook for secondary school students has this to say about Monet, Manet, Renoir, and Van Gogh:

> Concentrating on purely visual impression, the impressionists were often guilty of lack of balance, reducing the whole diversity of life around them to the immediate personal impressions of the artist. Their works were often without deep content and rarely dealt with major socially significant themes . . .

In the Russian galleries, where foreign visitors are supposed to spend much of their time, great works of the impressionists are either confined to attic rooms, as at the Hermitage in Leningrad, or to back rooms, as at the Pushkin Museum in Moscow. Many of them still rest in storage rooms in museum basements, where the public cannot see them.

The paintings that hold pride of place and dominate all others are Russian works of a spirit that faded from Western art long ago. As we gazed at static tableaus by Repin or his imitators, of healthy, happy peasants in the fields, or of kerchiefed women harvesting potatoes, or of idealized schoolgirls running up a hill, we felt transported back to the days when Millet's "Angelus" was considered the apex of a painter's art. The Soviet realism is not realism at all; it is a sentimental romanticism of which Maxfield Parrish was a good example in the America of half a century ago. But Parrish, at least, did not preach, whereas the paintings of Socialist Realism contain a sermon in every frame.

Acres of such displays made us thirsty for art with some glow of imagination, some flash of fun. So must Marco Polo have felt as he plodded across the Gobi Desert for thirty days, all but losing his hopes of ever seeing the golden rooftops of Cathay. We, too, almost gave up hope—until, in Tbilisi, on the top floor of the Georgian Museum of Fine Arts, we came upon a treasure.

A team of film makers from Belgium had spread its wires and floodlights over a part of the gallery. The lights shone on canvases of a kind we had not found elsewhere in the Soviet Union. These were, clearly, a painter's imaginings— some of ordinary Georgians at work and play, some of deer and bears and mules, but all, obviously, as the artist dreamed them, not posed them. All were set in Georgia: so much was clear at first sight from dress and scenery. And there was not a square inch of preaching in any of them.

"He's a naïve painter—what you'd call a primitive," said one of the Belgians, adjusting his lights. He said he was making a documentary on the Soviet Union, and would include these pictures, of course. Some of them, he said, were going to Paris for an exhibition at the Orangerie.

The artist's name? In Georgian, Niko Pirosmanishvili— but since "shvili" in Georgian means "son of," Westerners can shorten the name as the Russians do, to Niko Pirosman or Pirosmani.

He was a vagrant, a bum, born in the eighteen-sixties. Nobody ever taught him to paint; he just did it, without a studio or models. Often he painted in the open streets on black oilcloth, with children looking on. Sometimes he worked as a railroad guard, sometimes as a peddler, but for long stretches he worked at nothing, and went hungry. We have seen a photograph of him taken in his fifties, looking like a man who needed even half of one square meal. Was it not natural, then, for him to paint fish and fruit and game birds, and, above all, scenes of outdoor feasting?

As in the Italian primitives, everything is happening at once in a single Pirosmani painting. A farmer stamps on grapes in a tub, a shepherd leads his flock to the field, a fisherman pulls his catch from a stream; but the focus of the painting is always a Georgian khan, a chieftain, feasting on the products of the land. The local khans in their peaked fur hats are sitting cross-legged on the ground or at tables covered with white cloths and heavily laden with food. Their faces are grave with the seriousness one ought always to bring to a memorable meal. If the pictures have any message, it is: food, glorious food! and wine, glorious wine!

Ironically, this modern Breughel died of hunger during the political convulsions that swept Georgia toward the end of World War I. In his unhappy life he had painted two thousand pictures, of which a thousand have scattered into the hands of unknown private owners. We were glad to see that *Soviet Life*, the English-language official Soviet magazine, took note of this "naïve" painter in 1969.

One can only wonder why the Soviet Government suddenly uses this most unsocialist of artists in its cultural salesmanship abroad. He seems to serve no socialist purpose. He celebrates the old peasant-landlord society without a hint of the class struggle. Like the French Impressionists, who still displease the Kremlin, this Georgian of czarist days painted only what he saw and dreamed, not what he thought would be helpful to the authorities. How could the Soviet arbiters of culture have found this free spirit "socially useful"? We can only guess that they are honoring Pirosmani, belatedly, as a gesture to Georgian pride. If he were painting today instead of sixty or seventy years ago, his works would be barred from public view, and any exhibition of them would be padlocked by the police.

A tourist in Tbilisi is not supposed to want to go to Gori. The head of the Intourist bureau thought of one reason after another why we should look at mountains or monuments or factories instead of the birthplace of Georgia's most famous son. In the end, not having firm orders to stop us, he relented. The next day we were off, in the mist of an autumn morning, to see where Iosif Vissarionovich Dzugashvili, otherwise known as Stalin, was born.

On the forty-mile drive we passed many reminders of Georgia's three thousand years. On one hilltop a crumbling fortress stood against the sky; on another, a fourth-century church with a conical steeple; and at the junction of two rivers, the ancient capital of Mtskheta, where the kings of Georgia ruled until the fifteenth century. These sights were splendid, but the relic of the past that lay ahead of us was as rare as Buddha's tooth in its temple in Ceylon.

We came upon it as we swung into the main square in Gori, a cotton mill and market city. A familiar figure stood on a pedestal, wearing the cap and greatcoat of a Soviet army marshal. Coming closer, we saw who it was. The figure had the mustached face that used to adorn every park, every building, every home in the Soviet Union.

"Why do you look so surprised?" our guide asked. She must have seen us staring at the statue, as if we had seen a live brontosaurus rearing up on the pedestal. "What's so unusual about it? Every Soviet marshal of the last war has a statue. It's put up in the place he was born."

But it was, of course, more than unusual. In all the vast empire Stalin ruled, from the Oder to the Amur, there is, to our knowledge, no other statue like this one. After 1961, when his body was taken from the mausoleum in Red Square, Stalin was virtually an un-person. Like Trotsky, he might never have existed. Only after the fiftieth anniversary of the Revolution did his successors let him be impersonated in a play and a film—and then only as a military commander. His role as politician, diplomatist, dictator, tyrant, is still hidden from those who are too young to remember him.

In Georgia, on the other hand, his memory lives. The Kremlin, wisely, has never tried to erase him from Georgian minds. One might as well forbid Corsicans to brag about Bonaparte—and he, in contrast to the Georgian-born Stalin, was defeated, captured, and humiliated after conquering Europe. Cruel as Stalin was toward all Georgians except a favorite few, contemptuous as he became toward the un-Russian culture that produced him, Georgians still keep a profound pride in what he did.

"They can't take Stalin away from us," said a Georgian as we talked with him on a street corner one quiet Sunday morning. "After all, he made a great country, didn't he? He won the war for us. Remember—our soldiers didn't fight and die for Russia. They fought for Stalin. We used to be taught to worship him."

So it is that Georgians point with respect to the grave of his mother, Ekaterina, on the mountainside overlooking Tbilisi; so, too, they like to show foreigners the statue at Gori, and much else about Stalin in his native town. His birthplace was obviously intended to be a popular shrine; the hotel across the street from his statue could only have been designed for big groups of tourists and official visitors. Today its high-ceilinged public rooms are empty caverns. When we appeared in mid-morning we were clearly the first visitors of the day, and we had to order our lunch long ahead of time. Not even Intourist, with all its government subsidies, could afford to have food in the larder for nonexistent guests.

Around and beyond the Stalin statue, an entire city block has been laid out as a formal memorial garden. One walks past the inevitable red masses of salvia and cannas to the marble steps of what looks to be a classic temple. But the temple, on closer acquaintance, turns out to be only a shell: a flat roof on columns, without walls. It shelters a one-story two-room cottage. This, we are told, is the shoemaker's home where Stalin was born in 1879. It reminded us of the temple that encases Andrew Johnson's tailor shop at Greeneville, Tennessee. The wooden bedstead and chairs, one upholstered in the plush of the eighteen-seventies, suggest a life of bleakness but not of desperate poverty. It gives you a turn, as the cockneys say, to think that the baby born here grew up to be a conspirator, a revolutionary, a dictator who changed the course of history more sharply than all the Georgian kings combined.

Of that career, an adjoining building tells the story—as it used to be told to the Soviet people, years without end. This is the Stalin Museum, built, we gathered, in the years between his death in 1953 and his indictment by Khrushchev in 1956 for "monstrous crimes." We had to push our way to the paintings, prints, and documents on display; a busload of East German tourists crowded up to the walls and glass cases and blocked everyone else's vision. What we finally saw on the walls was a scrapbook of history and a reminder of the cult of personality. The scrapbook consisted of old photographs of muddy Gori, as it looked at the time of Stalin's birth; of Stalin as a student and then as a conspirator and budding revolutionary. There were group pictures—one is tempted to call them team pictures—of the Bolshevist leaders, first in Georgia and then in St. Petersburg, posed like the crew or football team of 1889, 1890, 1891, which one sees on the walls of the university clubs in New York. Plotters and terrorists though they were, they looked in the old pictures like a cozy brotherhood of like-minded men and women.

One cannot help feeling, at the sight of these pictures and documents of revolution in the making, that the autocracy of the czars was far more permissive than the one that replaced it. The cult of personality shows its face, first, in the portrayals of Stalin as a hero, and then in the selection and distortion of material. In paintings that must have hung in some Moscow museum in Stalin's day, the crafty-eyed young plotter becomes the young hero. We see him, for example, inspiring his fellow prisoners in the far North, by the Yenisei River; we see him again as a superman escaping across the snow.

Photographs and paintings of the years since 1917 obviously leave out anything inconvenient. Where Trotsky stood with the party leadership in a famous photograph, there is now a smudge: the retouchers have been busy since

Trotsky's disgrace and exile. There is nothing in this exhibit to suggest the great purge of the nineteen-thirties. In those years Stalin is shown here only as a benign leader.

The crowning touch of the retouchers comes at the end of a series of wartime photographs. Stalin is now a world leader; he goes to the Potsdam conference at the end of World War II. He is photographed in his white tunic, sitting in a wicker armchair. The picture is a familiar one. Those who sat to his right, as one can see in any collection of Potsdam pictures in England or America, were the President of the United States and the Prime Minister of the United Kingdom. Perhaps Harry Truman and Clement Attlee are nonentities in Soviet eyes. Whether they were important figures or not, they were at Potsdam. In the Stalin Museum they were never there.

"In the end," George Orwell wrote, "the Party would announce that two and two made five, and you would have to believe it." That was supposed to happen in London in 1984. But in the Soviet Union two and two have made five, or whatever other sum the Party has decided, for more than fifty years. The most famous son of Gori was a founder of the new Soviet arithmetic, and was of course the prototype of Big Brother in the Orwell novel. It is an irony that the man who rewrote history and recast the truth for so many years is virtually an un-person now, a posthumous victim of the fraudulence he taught his followers.

We did not expect Russians to look at history as we do. An American may talk to an Englishman and a Russian about the War of 1812. The Englishman will ask him "What war of 1812?" And the Russian will not understand at all, for 1812 is to him the year of Borodino and of the tremendous events that followed. Every nation sees the past and present through glasses of its own. To look through anyone else's may bring on dizziness, which is what happened to us when we first saw the Soviet view of the world.

The experience reminded us of a talk we had had with Han Suyin, the half-Chinese, half-Flemish author of *A Many-Splendoured Thing*. Over lunch in the Raffles Hotel in Singapore she told us that she had just come back from visiting relatives in Peking.

"For the first two weeks I felt I was standing on my head," she said. "All the values around me were upside down. It made me ill at first, but I got used to it."

We never did. Day after day, in posters and pictures, newspapers and magazines, we saw our own country as a place of evil. We saw the world of Marxism-Leninism, on the other hand (except for China) bathed in the kind of glow that Renaissance artists used to paint around the heads of angels. Evidently the Kremlin still felt the need of persuading its people that they were more moral, more decent, more fortunate than anyone else. At the same time it pictured America as hungry for power, West Germany bent on revenge, and the entire capitalist world plotting to undo the Revolution. By such appeals to fear and hate it kept a latent xenophobia alive.

When a Soviet schoolboy tries to learn his country's history, or when a serious historian sets out to write it, he may find the ground shifting under his feet. "Marxism-Leninism has no need to reconcile ideas with facts," wrote Victor A. Cheprakov in *Izvestia* not long ago, looking ahead to the year 2000. "Life has run and will continue to run its course as Marx and Lenin envisaged it." Under this philosophy, historians can write only what the Party approves and requires at a particular moment. The Party can change its line, so that what was truth in June becomes heresy in July. And the historian may find his whole career in ruins because of what he wrote in May.

We could understand why they substituted revolutionary names for those of czarist days. In Leningrad, for example, Alexander's Garden, named for Alexander I, is Workers'

Garden now. Senate Square became Decembrist Square, re-named for the army rebels who failed in 1825. But how can anyone keep pace with the changes from one revolutionist's name to another? Some places have been renamed two or three times, such as the street in Leningrad that once honored N. A. Voznesensky. When he was purged and shot in 1950, his name came down and Mayarova Prospekt went up. Since Vyacheslav M. Molotov fell from grace, the city that bore his name reverted to its former name of Perm. The highest mountain in the Soviet Union, a 24,590-foot peak in the Pamirs, was changed from Garmo Peak to Mount Stalin; now it is Mount Communism. The hallowed ground of Stalingrad has become Volgograd. Examples are endless. Russians will rename anything, from a street to a mountain, at the drop of a hero.

"The idea that the truth remains the truth is admissible in a philosophical club," said the late Mikhail Kalinin, long the President, the titular head, of the Soviet state, "but in the Party the decisions of the [Party] congress are obligatory also upon those who doubt the correctness of a decision."

In a university bookstore we were lucky to find a sample of current Soviet teaching of history. It was a 1966 textbook called *Modern History*, covering the period from 1870 to 1917 in all continents. The book was in English—excellent English, by the way—because it was intended for students specializing in the English language. Thus the readers of *Modern History* might well be the diplomats, translators, Intourist guides, and teachers of the next generation.

Three main ingredients seem to have gone into this particular version of the past: economic determinism, Russian patriotism, and post-Stalinist distortion. The first of these is more than familiar. Meeting it now is like finding a former neighbor still living in the old hometown. The economic interpretation of history has influenced teaching and scholarship in the West for most of this century. To rely on it exclusively today is as out of date among Western teachers as Freud's total emphasis on sex. But in the Soviet Union economic determinism is by no means obsolete. The Marxist-Leninist canon teaches that nothing ever happens by chance. Wars are fought, treaties are written, governments are formed and overthrown in accordance with unchanging economic laws. The rich in the capitalist countries are the ruling circles, the elected officials their puppets, the masses their victims.

Conspiracies are assumed to be the capitalist way of life. Historians in the Soviet bloc like to point to episodes of American history that conform to their thesis. In the late nineteen-fifties, talking over coffee cups with a group of communist students at the University of Warsaw, we found that they knew more about the Reconstruction period in the United States than many American students. They had, for example, read C. Vann Woodward's unsurpassed study of the unwritten compromise of 1877, and of course found that this account of pressure by railroad builders fitted nicely into the Marxist-Leninist frame. But how stiff the Russians have made the frame! And how tiresome it must be for Russian students to read and write a history that is chanceless and foreordained!

The second ingredient of the Soviet history book, Russian patriotism, is as familiar as the painting of Washington Crossing the Delaware. Most school textbooks, West and East alike, teach hero worship in history and find something heroic in their country's record. Early in the Russian Revolution, Leninist teaching found nothing good in the czarist record. But Stalin soon changed that. In the nineteen-thirties he brought patriotic figures of the czarist past back into Soviet favor. The historical museum in Moscow assembled collections on Suvorov, the Russian marshal in the early French revolutionary wars, and Kutuzov, his successor. During World War II even so unsavory a figure as Ivan the Terrible, the mid-sixteenth-century autocrat, was dusted off and shined up in a Soviet book entitled *Ivan Grozny* (*Ivan the Dread*). We still have a copy of an English version, officially published in Moscow in 1947. It pictures this czar as a patriotic man whose atrocities were invented by Germans, whose severities were needed to save his country.

Patriotism also requires civilian heroes. In the world history textbook we have cited, many of the scientists, explorers, and scholars of pre-revolutionary times are held up to honor. Usually the book tries to show Russians always in the lead. The culmination is the boast to end all boasts: "The teachings of Marx and Lenin are the highest achievement of human thought."

Today, though Stalin is dead and largely discredited, national self-glorification continues as a powerful theme in all the media of state control, including the performing arts. Nothing is more patriotic, nothing more glorious than the celebration of Glorious Victories. One grows numb from repetitive stories in operas, paintings, statuary, and mosaics of Glorious Victories over Swedes, Poles, Turks, French, Germans, and of course over the foreign interventionists in the Civil War. Defeats, no matter how gallant, are not mentioned. Once, in 1931, Stalin, in an unaccustomed burst of frankness, did try to goad his people by talking about the "continual beatings" old Russia suffered.

> She was beaten by the Mongol khans. She was beaten by the Turkish beys. She was beaten by the Swedish feudal lords. She was beaten by the Polish and Lithuanian gentry. She was beaten by the Japanese barons. All beat her for her backwardness, for military backwardness, for cultural backwardness, for political backwardness, for industrial backwardness, for agricultural backwardness.

But these defeats are not commemorated, and Stalin's successors do not talk about them. If Dunkirk had been a Soviet evacuation instead of a British, it probably would be a forbidden topic now. It is only victories, Glorious Victories, that the state finds it useful to remember.

When it comes to inflating their exploits, Russians would seem to be old hands. Gibbon tells us that they were doing it in the Middle Ages. According to Gibbon, a Russian naval expedition against Constantinople late in the ninth century slipped around the defenders by the "usual expedient" of pulling the boats over an isthmus of dry land to the inner harbor, the Golden Horn. But, says Gibbon, "this simple operation is described in the [Russian] national chronicles as if the Russian fleet had sailed over dry land with a brisk and favorable gale."

During World War I every belligerent power suppressed defeats, invented victories, exaggerated skirmishes into battles, and multiplied enemy losses for the sake of home morale. The Bolsheviks found these practices ready-made for their uses. Why not continue them in peacetime? To the true believer, there is no peacetime; the class struggle is never ending war. Lenin said that "everything is moral which is necessary for the annihilation of the old exploiting social order"—including, presumably, lying.

As Stalin elbowed his way to power, he began the work of revising the past, as Lenin had not. He saw to it that historians were purged and jailed and their books banned. Under his supervision the new history made him an early and close associate of the dead Lenin, although in real life he had stood on a less exalted level.

Doctoring the historical record was one of the ways Stalin built himself up to be a popular idol and Lenin's heir. It was also an essential method of preparing, and then excusing, the great purges of the nineteen-thirties. Once Stalin had made up his mind to get rid of the Old Bolsheviks, he and his secret police had to implicate them in past crimes. And it was on the basis of manufactured history that these old warriors were arrested, jailed, and shot.

After serving Stalin's purpose in the trials and purges of the nineteen-thirties, Trotsky, too, became an un-person. The path of historical science in the Soviet Union became a Via Dolorosa for every self-respecting historian. The scholar never knew when fabrications would turn a respectable Bolshevik into a traitor.

As every historian knows, what you leave out can distort the record as much as what you put in. One small example of omission for political reasons is the account in our copy of *Modern History* of the Boxer Rebellion in China in 1900:

> The imperialist powers agreed upon joint intervention with the object of suppressing the popular rising. Britain, Japan, the U.S.A., Germany, France, and *some other countries* [italics ours] sent their troops to China. With fire and sword the punitive troops suppressed the national-liberation movement of the Chinese people. . . . In the middle of August 1900 the foreign armies seized Peking. They gave themselves over to rapine and looting, and there was no limit to the atrocities committed.

Among the "some other countries" was one that deserved to be named. Russia contributed more than 3,000 men (some estimates say 4,000) to the international army, and two Russians were the first to get inside the Peking walls. But Russian students of today, Russian diplomats of the future, are not supposed to know.

In reading *Modern History* we naturally turned with some suspense to know what this Soviet textbook would say about the United States. Its chapter on America at the end of the nineteenth and the beginning of the twentieth century tells mainly of corruption in politics, expansion of big business, repression of labor, and the start of colonial conquest. Here is a passage headed "The U.S.A. on the Eve of War" [World War I]:

In 1912 the Democratic Party candidate, Woodrow Wilson, won the presidential election. Like his predecessors, Wilson represented the American multimillionaires, and dreamt of the U.S.A. dominating the world. He wrote that a new era lay ahead, one in which the U.S.A. would evidently rule the world.

Wilson was compelled to reckon with the intensification of the class struggle in the country. . . . All Wilson's measures were undertaken with the aim of using individual reforms to check the revolutionary feeling gaining ground in the country and to create a sounder rear for the approaching imperialist war.

Pondering this, one might wonder why the Marxist-Leninist historian had been so rough on Wilson. Was it not Wilson who was "thrilled," in public, by the overthrow of the czar? Was it not Wilson who stood against the British and French and refused to permit a full-scale military attack on the Soviet regime? Then we remembered posters we had seen in Moscow and Kiev on the fiftieth anniversary of the Revolution, posters showing, among other Western misdeeds of the period, American troops in their scoutmaster hats marching through Vladivostok. The cause of the unforgiving bitterness toward Wilson became clear. Against his better judgment, Wilson had let himself be persuaded to send about 8,500 American troops to Vladivostok in 1918. Their ostensible purpose was to guard the Trans-Siberian Railroad as an escape route for the famous Czech Legion; they also kept a watchful eye on the far larger Japanese army in the area. As long as the Marxist-Leninist system endures and maybe longer, Wilson will be pictured in Russia not as reformer and idealist, but rather as the capitalist who sent troops to crush the proletarian revolution. What Sherman's march through Georgia meant to the irreconcilable South for many decades, the allied interventions still

mean to Soviet writers, teachers, and other propagators of
the faith.

Perhaps for the same reason, Russians nowadays are told
nothing about the American relief effort during the Volga
famine of 1921 and 1922. At the height of this effort, according to Merle Curti, the historian of American philanthropy
abroad, the American relief organization was feeding
10,500,000 people at 18,000 food stations. In a little less
than two years it distributed over 700,000 tons of food, plus
medical supplies and clothing. Maxim Gorky wrote to
Herbert Hoover that "in the history of practical humani-
tarianism I know of no accomplishment which in terms of
magnitude and generosity can be compared to the relief
that you have actually accomplished . . ." Yet Russians do
not know. It would conflict with the Soviet version of American intervention to recall American help in a desperate
time.

One should not imagine that tinkering with history is
just a product of Stalin's fevered mind. His successors never
swore off the habit. Nikita Khrushchev the liberalizer, who
let fresh air blow through the Kremlin, proved to be an
addict of suppression too. Although he set the record
straight with his speech on Stalin's crimes, and although he
let Russians listen to foreign broadcasts without jamming—
an enormous concession in a closed society—he, too, tortured the evidence. First he exposed Stalin; then he expunged him. He added Stalin to the ranks of the
unmentionable, including Trotsky, whom Stalin had exiled
and Bukharin, Radek, and others whom he had ordered
killed.

"What can we believe?" a young Russian girl asked us.
We were talking about Stalin in his native Georgia. "One
day he is our great leader; another day they tell us he was
a criminal. I don't know what to think."

The record of Khrushchev's successors is no less a cause
for wonder. Did we mention Khrushchev? He never existed.

In a series of television programs covering each of the fifty years since the Revolution, Khrushchev's name and picture appeared not once. A few revisions of history have been re-revised. Stalin himself has begun to come back into films and plays, but only as a respected military commander, not as a political leader. Trotsky has never come back. To this day his name is wiped out. Even Kerensky is sometimes referred to in newspaper polemics as a "corpse," but Trotsky—never. In all the historical museums we saw in the Soviet Union—and we tramped through a good many of them, admiring their chronological arrangement and their range of exhibits—his picture is still smudged out. Is there any parallel, in any other country, for a vendetta so unforgiving and so long?

The Revolution may have lost momentum but the Kremlin still finds it essential to adapt history to Party uses. The Party leaders, supposedly practical modern men, go on deciding what books Russians can and cannot read, and also what they can and cannot know about their history. The Soviet people, as Isaac Deutscher has observed, are the only ones who do not know the truth about their Revolution and what has happened since.

What does all this mean for the future? Should it be any other country's concern? The answer "yes" has been sounding in international forums for twenty-five years and more. When the United Nations Educational, Scientific, and Cultural Organization was set up in 1945, the preamble of its charter said: "Since wars begin in the minds of men, it is in the minds of men that the defenses of peace must be constructed." This seemed to call for international action against the distortion of history as well as other intellectual poisons. At the London conference that organized UNESCO in 1946, much was said, though nothing was done, about false history (or about anything else). No sovereign nation will let any other or others dictate how or what it shall teach its children—unless it is a defeated and occupied nation like Germany. Ideally, each nation ought to be willing to extract the venom from its own history books.

The Western European countries have been the first to try collectively: the six nations of the European Community conduct a four-language international school for the children of their civil servants, and have produced a community history. In this pioneering work Charlemagne, for example, is no longer a French king or a German king, as he used to be in rival histories, but a Franco-German. French children learn of the excesses and extravagance of Louis XIV and Germans of the militarism of the kaisers. Disagreeable figures of the past are not locked away, out of sight, but are brought out for understanding and appraisal. Only in Russia, as far as we know, does it remain official policy to consign historical figures to darkness.

What country is without fault in its textbooks on history and current events? American schools used to teach that the British burned Washington in 1814. How many of them added that the Americans a few months earlier had burned York, where Toronto now stands? The American public is just discovering how much was conveniently omitted from most grade-school and high-school teaching about slavery and its aftermath. Yet when all such faults have been conceded, in the Western European as well as the American record, one contrast above all others remains. In the West new historians, new researchers, can always push their way into print to set the record straight as they see it. In Russia the state would forbid them to publish, unless the state—meaning the Party—approves the content of their work. In Russia the state decides what the historical record shall be.

To look out at the world from inside the Soviet Union is a sobering experience. Is it actually the same world that Americans know? In Russia the people are taught from childhood that the world is divided irreparably into enemies and comrades, oppressors and oppressed. Their world is rigidly and fatally frozen into a Marxist mold. Their way of life is the only way, they are told, and it is sure to prevail.

Americans, too, have been conditioned to believe the worst of their communist opponents and the best about themselves. It was not many years ago that official rhetoric made America sound infallible. When John Foster Dulles was Secretary of State he talked of the wickedness of "atheistic Godless communism," of the immorality of neutralism, and of the certainty that the Soviet system would collapse if America stood firm. But no American was compelled to accept this doctrine; indeed, it was and is beyond the power of any American Government to compel anyone to believe anything. There have always been outspoken Americans, thank heaven, who stand with Jefferson against "every form of tyranny over the mind of man."

Do the Russians really believe what they are told day after day about the wickedness of the world outside? It was hard for us, not living in Russia, to know. Perhaps the Soviet people have developed blab-offs in their minds, like the one we use in our own house to switch off the sound of television commercials. One must hope that the next generation of Soviet leaders will not accept everything that the present generation has tried to teach them. If they do believe it, holding, as they will, both dictatorial and nuclear power, then surely the Russians and all the rest of us are in deeper trouble than any we have known.

VI

Bukhara—Samarkand—Tashkent:

BORDER PEOPLES UNDER RUSSIAN RULE

> Everyone can now see what great success on the road of socialist development has been achieved by the people of Kazakhstan and Central Asia, who either stood at the precapitalist stage or were only beginning to switch over to capitalism when the socialist revolution took place in our country. These people did not have to experience the painful stage of capitalist development. They succeeded in bypassing it and going over to socialism with the support and aid of more developed socialist nations, in particular the Russian socialist nation.
>
> —Nikita Khrushchev to the twenty-first Party congress (1959)

1. Lenin stands on top of an armored truck, addressing the throng, as he did at the Finland Station on the night of April 5, 1917. This is the statue of Lenin one sees all over the Soviet Union. Photo by David Gulick, St. Louis *Post-Dispatch*

2. "Where but in church can one give way and have a good lonely cry?" Photo by David Gulick, St. Louis *Post-Dispatch*

3. The marriage palace in Leningrad, formerly a ducal palace on the Neva. This is where young couples are wed in style under a bust of Lenin. Photo by David Gulick, St. Louis *Post-Dispatch*

4. Khrushchev opened the Kremlin to the public in 1958. A group of American farmers are seeing the sights.—Sovfoto

5. Russian women do all kinds of construction work. Have not women been traditional earth movers? Photo by John Launois from *Black Star*

6. A sunny morning in Red Square. Three times a week people wait in long queues to see Lenin in the flesh. Photo by John Launois from *Black Star*

7. One of the many day nurseries where working mothers can leave their children until they reach school age. Photo by John Launois from *Black Star*

8. We rode the subway in Kiev, wishing our own city might have one as useful and as well maintained as this one.—Sovfoto

9. In Gori the Stalin Museum and (lower right) the temple encasing the two-room house where Stalin was born. Photo by John Launois from *Black Star*

10. Inside the Stalin Museum, where many East Germans but few Russians now come to see his relics and ponder his life. Photo by John Launois from *Black Star*

11. Tashkent, destroyed by earthquakes, is rebuilt by volunteers from all the republics in the Soviet Union. The building at right is the gift of "Kiev to Tashkent."—Sovfoto

12. In Tashkent People's Park Uzbek men sit cross-legged, playing chess, sipping tea, and passing the time of day in Central Asian fashion. Photo by Fred Mayer from *Black Star*

13. In Tashkent's collective market the melons are among the best in the world. Photo by David Gulick, St. Louis *Post-Dispatch*

14. Bukhara used to have miles of covered bazaars. Only a few of their domed towers are still standing. Photo by David Gulick, St. Louis *Post-Dispatch*

A Soviet colonial empire? A true believer in Russian communism would say that the very notion is nonsense, like a mammal that lays eggs; it cannot be. Leon Trotsky once explained why. Defending the reconquest of Georgia by the Red Army in 1921, he wrote that the Soviet regime supported the principle of self-determination of peoples "wherever it is directed against feudal, capitalist and imperialist states." Where self-determination is used against the "proletarian revolution," on the other hand, it becomes a "fiction," like capitalist democracy itself. So if anyone suggests today that the Soviet Union runs a colonial empire in Central Asia, he is guilty of libel, and he is of course a warmonger, a revanchist, an agent of the CIA.

The Russians really do protest too much. What, anyway, is imperialism? What is an empire? The late John Strachey, a British Marxist of the nonrevolutionary kind, provided one definition. "By imperialism," he wrote, "I mean the process by which people or nations conquer, subdue, and then permanently dominate (either de jure or de facto) other peoples or nations. By empire I mean the state of things in this way established."

Applying these definitions, who can honestly deny that they fit the state of things in the Soviet border territories? Soviet Central Asia is indeed a colony, created by the imperialism of czars and preserved by that of the commissars. It is true that Russian commanders never had to cross an

ocean, as the British did, or even a sea as narrow as the
Mediterranean, as the French did, to subdue their subject
peoples. But neither did the Ottoman Turks, who once
ruled a polyglot empire from Moldavia to Mecca and from
the Atlas Mountains almost to the gates of India.

In Central Asia in the nineteenth century, non-Russian
peoples were conquered and held by force precisely like
those of other colonies. They were and are as different
from Russians as Pakistanis from Britons: different in their
Moslem religion, their Turkic or Persian languages, their
non-Slavic ethnic stock. They were not just a ragtag of
primitive tribes. Many of them belonged to settled Moslem
societies that were thriving when Moscow was only a fort
in the northern forests. Ancient and famous cities became
parts of this Russian empire: Merv, the capital of Arab
conquerors and later of Seljuk kings; Bukhara, a center of
art and learning a thousand years ago; and Samarkand, the
capital of Tamerlane's realm, the treasure chest and jewel
box of Moslem Asia.

Today, in these and other centers, Russians hold the positions of real power. They even live like colonial rulers
in separate sections of the towns. But they do not need to
be so defensive about themselves. It seems to us that in
some ways they are doing a better job than other imperial
masters we have known. They have, for example, provided
mass education; they have emancipated women, diversified
industry, raised the standard of living, and paid outward
respect to native culture. For all these gains the Central
Asians paid a cruel price, but that was long ago. Just possibly, although of course one cannot prove it, the Central
Asian peoples today would choose to stay within the Soviet
Union if the decision were up to them.

What gives special interest to the Soviet empire is the
conflict, long violent, now peaceful, between communist
innovation and Central Asian tradition. Innovation is win-

ning hands down. A visitor can see this conflict most dramatically in Bukhara, long closed to so-called progress and to foreign eyes.

If the sign at the airport did not say Bukhara—in Cyrillic letters, of course—you would not know you were in one of Central Asia's ancient centers of religion, art, and trade. You would know only that you were in an oasis in desert country. The paved two-lane road into the city passes between white-flecked fields of cotton. The republic of Uzbekistan, in which Bukhara belongs, produces three fifths of all the cotton in the Soviet Union, and the outskirts of Bukhara show it. Loading machines scoop up cotton as if it were snow on city streets. They pour it onto a mound of white already as high as a slag heap in coal country. The road passes two stone pylons, marking the little that remains of an ancient wall. Then it turns sharply and becomes an avenue that appears to have been cut very recently through a maze of alleys. Another turn into a side street, and the visitor finds himself in front of the run-down stone building that calls itself the Bukhara Hotel. (In Russian, by the way, the name is Bukhara, pronounced Boo'-ha-ra; the old name, Bokhara, with the accent on the second syllable, is used abroad.)

The evening we arrived, a few tourists, displeasure written on their faces, were making a dinner out of tinned sardines and dark bread. The cooking range in the kitchen had broken down and was being overhauled. There was no soup, no tea or coffee, not even a boiled egg. The manager, with deep and honest apologies, suggested that we walk for dinner to the Bukhara Restaurant, the best, he assured us, in the town. We took his advice, and he waved us off, showing us the general direction.

The hotel faced an open space two city blocks square, strewn with stones and weeds, as if a slum area there had recently been torn down. We crossed this space, in the gathering dark, and followed a narrow alley between the walls of mud houses.

Now, at last, we knew we were in the Middle East. We had sampled this kind of neighborhood in old cities in Pakistan, Iran, and eastern Turkey, and in the kasbahs of North Africa. Our alley was cleaner than those we remembered from other countries. The earth, hard as rock, had been swept clear of dust; there were no piles of refuse in the alley, at least, and no chickens pecking around. With our sense of direction lost, we dipped into our poor stock of Russian words. We asked a small boy, who was wearing an Uzbek skullcap and a once-white robe, "Which way is the center of town, please?" (In the old days an Uzbek boy would have known only his people's Turkic language, and perhaps a few words of Arabic if he had gone to a Koranic school.) This one understood Russian, even our Russian. He pointed down a still narrower alley than the one through which we had come. A cat slid out from a doorway and crossed our path. All of a sudden we found ourselves on a broad asphalted street that was obviously the Fifth Avenue of Soviet Bukhara.

Down the street, shaded by droopy trees, a park with paths and benches invited us. A sound of splashing water came from one end of the park—a steady sound of raindrops on a lake. In that land of heat and dust for much of the year, the sound was as cool as a martini on the rocks on a summer day. We strolled toward it, and soon had the explanation.

A dozen broad steps led down from the park to a square pool set between two majestic buildings. One was a theological school built in the seventeenth century, which makes it modern by Bukhara standards. Bits of blue and yellow tile still clung to some of the tawny brickwork, a hint of what these facades must have looked like before they began to crumble. From the sides of the pool, fountains played into the water. Their streams arched like the branches of the acacia trees above. Blue smoke and the fragrance of cooking floated up to where we stood at the top of the steps. Shish kebabs, lamb on skewers, were being grilled and served with tea at poolside tables. We did not stop, having learned in other cities that Soviet shish kebabs are too tough for joy. Near the tables were wooden platforms covered with rugs, where at other times of day men would sit cross-legged, sipping tea or playing chess or just passing the time of day.

Could this possibly be the Soviet Union? Could anything be more like the storybook East than this pond with its fountains and trees, and the reflections of blue tiles in its water? Russia and the West had disappeared—until we found the Bukhara Restaurant across the road.

The tables were crowded with men who wore the Uzbek embroidered skullcap with Western shirts and trousers. They seemed to have plenty of rubles to spend on food and wine. We found one unoccupied table in a corner, out of sight of a band that was playing from a platform. A waitress, far more prompt and friendly than those in Kiev or Moscow, took our order for lamb stew, dark bread, and a hundred grams each (four ounces) of vodka. As she hurried away the band broke into a new tune: *South of the Border, Down Mexico Way.*

In that setting, the 1939 song hit was not entirely out of tune or out of place. For Bukhara used to be south of a border between two cultures: between the Slavic peoples of Russia on the north and the assorted non-Russian, non-Christian, non-European peoples to the south. What we had seen so far suggested that the cultural border was real enough but was becoming blurred.

To conquer these Central Asian states, and thus to move the political border south, the Russians had to mount a series of hot wars and one cold war in the century before 1914. The hot wars were hot in more senses than one. Usually they involved long marches by the imperial Russian troops across burning desert country. Sometimes, though not always, the Russians had to shoot and shell their way into their enemies' walls; at other times, as at Khiva in 1873, the local ruler surrendered without a fight. Sometimes, as with Tashkent in 1865, they incorporated the conquered city directly into the Russian Empire; at other times, notably with Bokhara in 1868, the city and its surrounding territory became a protectorate, nominally free but actually a vassal state under the czar.

The rationale for all this expansion of territory was set forth in 1864 in a memorandum by Prince Gorchakov, Chancellor of the imperial Russian Government. This still stands as one of the few frank statements ever written in defense of colonial conquest. According to Prince Gorchakov:

> . . . The position of Russia in Central Asia is that of all civilized states which come into contact with half-savage, wandering tribes possessing no fixed social organization. It invariably happens in such cases that the interests of security on the frontier, and of commercial relations, compel the more civilized state to exercise a certain ascendancy over neighbors whose turbulence and nomad instincts render them difficult to live with.

In calling the Central Asians "half-savage, wandering tribes," the Prince was being less than frank. After all, these peoples knew and lived by the Koran; they worshiped one God in what even the Russians would concede to be one of the world's higher religions. They had produced men of learning and even of genius, although most of their people were as illiterate as the Russian peasants. True, they had certain unpleasant habits. Their khans or chieftains had held Russian prisoners as slaves during several hundred years, and Asian slavery was a shade worse than Russian serfdom. Their prisons were, as we were to see, less agreeable even than those of the czars. Their horsemen often made a living by raiding and pillaging caravans, and thus they annoyed Moscow merchants who had hoped to make money out of Central Asia's needs for manufactured goods. But to call them "half-savage" was less than half the truth.

Still, Gorchakov went on in a way that disarmed much criticism. What, he asked in effect, is a civilized imperial power to do? If it punishes and then pulls back, those who commit the crimes will simply repeat them. If it reduces some of the "robber" tribes to "more or less willing submission," other tribes beyond its control will create disorders and make it necessary to push the line forward again. Therefore, he said, Russia had to extend its frontiers.

The trouble with this formula was that neither Gorchakov nor his military commanders really knew where to stop. No expanding empire knows—until it hits an obstacle like an ocean or a mountain range, or a rival empire. In Central Asia it was not a natural obstacle but the British who barred their way.

The British, pushing their own empire in India north and northwestward, saw the southward-moving Russians as rivals and dangers. The Russians, in turn, were sure that the British had designs on the khanates of Central Asia. Thus began a cold war that was to last for eighty years. It started about 1838, when the British decided to launch their first disastrous Afghan War, ostensibly to protect the northwest frontier of India. Once, in 1885, the cold war heated almost to a real war over an oasis the Russians had occupied. The cold war ended in 1907, when British and Russians divided their spheres of influence because both of them feared the Kaiser's Germany.

During that cold war, which became known as the Great Game, Britons and Russians spied, intrigued, and played their tricks in the dusty bazaars and on the caravan routes of Central Asia. When the Great Game ended in a handshake and a draw, British rule in India extended as far

northwest as the Khyber Pass. Afghanistan was a buffer
state under British rather than Russian influence. The Emir
of Bokhara, sitting like a spider in his web, ruled another
buffer state, this one under Russian influence. Russia ruled
everything else, and had built an empire over alien peoples
from the Caspian Sea to China.

It was this empire and its Moslem population which the
Bolsheviks acquired when they seized power in 1917.
They found it hard to control. A rebellion against Russian
rule had just been beaten down, and there were to be
others. The process of being swallowed and digested by
the Soviet state was an especially painful one. The civil
wars lasted longer in Central Asia than anywhere else in
the Soviet Union. In the nineteen-twenties famine took an
estimated million lives in Central Asia; in the early nineteen-
thirties, when the nomad herders were forced into collective farms, millions of animals were slaughtered or left to
starve. Local leaders who protested the new policies were
often charged with treason and dealt with accordingly. In
the purges of the middle and late nineteen-thirties, Central
Asia was not exempt from the knock on the door at night,
the disappearance of father or brother, and the volleys of
firing squads in prison courtyards. The old emirs used
cruelty as a weapon, but not as lavishly as Stalin used it in
transforming a society and building a mighty state.

To justify their rule over alien peoples, the Russians now
take pains to persuade tourists of the debauchery, cruelty,
and greed of the emirs who used to rule in Bukhara. The
palace of the last emir, for example, is a showplace on every
tour. It turns out to be a seedy imitation of grandeur, like
the palace of a minor maharajah in India. The official guide
takes care to show an outdoor pool, now stagnant and
scummy, and a royal grandstand alongside it. In the grandstand, the guide explains, the last emir used to sit and watch
his harem girls, or boys, splash and play in the pool. The

effect, of course, is to remind the visitor that the old regime was rotted with vice and decay, which it indubitably was.

Other monuments of Bukharan rulers help to prove the Soviet point. Their thousand-year-old Kremlin was a citadel known as the Ark. One enters this once-dreaded place through an opening in the ancient city walls, and up a ramp, a cobblestoned version of the commuters' incline in the Grand Central Terminal in New York. Alongside this ramp were the prison cells. As the emir walked or rode or was carried in a palanquin, he could observe the miseries of those he had condemned. Today the Russians have provided a realistic wax figure of a jailer, in Bukharan uniform, on duty outside one of these cells. Visible through the bars are wax figures of the prisoners sitting with chains on their legs.

High above all this, the emir used to hold court in an outdoor pavilion on the roof of the citadel, with a view over Bukhara's walls and towers. A penthouse next to the pavilion enclosed a throne room; today it has become a museum, where the Soviets hang cartoons of the emir and the system he personified. One cartoon shows the emir on a throne at the apex of a pyramid. His subjects are writhing underneath like the figures in Doré's etchings of Dante's hell. On the wall, too, are photographs of released convicts of the World War I period, their backs still scarred from the lashes of the emir's jailers.

Not all the convicts survived the prisons. In the center of old Bukhara, outside the noblest of the ancient mosques, a brick minaret rises from a paved square, as the Campanile in Venice rises from San Marco's Piazza. The minaret is just over two hundred feet high, the equivalent of more than twenty stories in a modern office building. Built early in the eleven-hundreds, it tapers slightly like the columns of the Parthenon. Its stubby top can be seen for miles. The tower was a lighthouse for caravans on the desert, a watchtower for the capital's defenders, a place where the muezzins called Bukhara's faithful to prayer. But it was also a Tower of Death. Until the eighteen-seventies, and again during the Russian civil war, condemned wretches were thrown off the top onto the pavement below. The Russians rightly praise the tower for its workmanship and design, but they also use it as a propaganda weapon against the pre-Soviet regime.

Those who were pitched off the tower were more fortunate than some of their contemporaries. The emirs maintained a vermin pit, sometimes called the Black Well, a dungeon under the red brick walls that encircled and guarded the town. It was here that two English officers, Lieutenant Colonel Charles Stoddart and Captain Arthur Conolly, were put to rot and starve during the reign of the Emir Nasrollah in the eighteen-forties. This emir's custom was to introduce snakes, scorpions, and other disagreeable vermin into the pit where his prisoners lay. Some of the captives died there, some were dragged out to the chopping block, and few survived. Today the pit, too, has become a tourist exhibit, to show, presumably, how times have changed. The visitor looks twenty-one feet down into the pit as from the balcony of a theater. No stair, no path, leads down; a huge bucket, attached to a hawser at the top, seems to have been the elevator by which the prisoners were lowered and their bodies ultimately removed. In its effort at realism, the Soviet regime has not turned present-day vermin loose in the pit, but has provided wax effigies of two emaciated prisoners, sitting in rags on the dungeon ground. The sides of the pit slope inward to the circular opening at the top. A prisoner could not possibly escape unless he were a cockroach or an angel.

The significance of this display is not that the emirs of Bukhara applied cruel and unusual punishments. Of course some of them did—but so did other rulers of past centuries and ours. What gives meaning to the public exhibition of the vermin pit—and it is only a footnote in the record of

Soviet Central Asia—is that the Soviet state and Party have ordered it. The message from Moscow is that the old regime had to be destroyed, that times have changed. Thus the peoples of Central Asia are shown to be better off within the Soviet Union than under their former khans and emirs; better off, too, than their neighbors across the frontiers. The neighbors include the oppressed Turks, Iranians, Afghans, Pakistanis, and in the case of the Kazakhs in the easternmost regions, the Moslems living under Chinese Communist rule.

Are the Central Asians really better off today? To answer with assurance one would need to have lived in Central Asia in the old days, the days before the Revolution. Of the many revolutionary changes that have shaken Central Asia, those in the rural economy and in education are at the same time the most important and the hardest for a foreign visitor to measure.

Farmers in the irrigated valleys of southern Central Asia used to grow grain as well as cotton; thus they could feed themselves. Now, after half a century of communist rule, cotton output has increased sixfold, but the grain output is only two thirds of what it was toward the end of czarist rule. In other words, the Kremlin has outdone the czars in imposing a colonial-type one-crop economy on the region. For food, the fast-growing population must depend to a large and uncertain extent on what it can get from western Russia.

Since the early nineteen-thirties, moreover, the farmers have belonged to collectives, and are thus cogs in a state machine. Whether or not they are benefiting in health and housing, and in their general standard of living, we could not tell; we were refused permission to visit a collective farm and see for ourselves. But we did see, more than once, evidence that all is not well in the Central Asian collectives. In Samarkand, on a market day, we happened to be watching as dozens of farm workers jumped out of trucks that had brought them from the countryside.

This was "Samarkand the Golden," once the capital of Tamerlane's empire, and still the architectural gem of Central Asia after almost six hundred years. The trucks stopped at the free market, near the ruined arches of the mosque Tamerlane had built in memory of his best-loved wife. It was sad to see the mosque fallen into decay, but sadder still to look into the farmers' eyes. Their faces were hollow-cheeked. Their clothes were rags. Their general appearance was more wretched than that of any group we had encountered in the entire Soviet Union.

Was this why the authorities did not want us to go to the farms? If the farmers we saw in Samarkand were representative of others, then the collectives, not the cities, are the slums of Central Asia. (Later, on our roundabout route to the Pacific, we were to discover the same look of poverty among collective farmers in Kazakhstan on the edge of China, and in eastern Siberia.) As John Fischer once wrote, Karl Marx was a city boy.

In the cities, the regime in Central Asia can claim credit for a series of achievements. Among these, without doubt, are the spread of free, universal, secular schooling and the official emancipation of women. Related to these is the removal of the mullahs, the Moslem teachers, from the dominant position they used to enjoy. The picture of Central Asian education today is a dramatic contrast to that of the almost unrelieved illiteracy of former times. Now all children, boys and girls, are required to go to a Soviet public school for five years from the age of seven. In old-time Bukhara, some boys went to a religious school and learned some literacy—in Arabic—through learning the Koran. The girls never went to school at all.

It has been an immense achievement for the Soviets to have broken this crust of ignorance in Central Asia. As usual, however, they overstate what they have done. Although universal schooling was decreed in principle as long ago as the beginning of the Revolution, it was not until 1949 that virtually every child went to elementary school. Therefore the middle-aged as well as the elderly in Soviet Central Asia remain largely illiterate, as they do in Afghanistan and Pakistan south of the border. In their childhood they never had a chance to learn.

Moreover, the official figures usually take no account of those who drop out of elementary school after staying for the required five years, or those who fail to pass the entrance examinations for higher learning. In Bukhara we watched the men sitting in the tea shops, and those on benches in the Parks of Culture and Rest. Culture was less evident than rest. We detected nobody reading a book or a newspaper. Our guess was that literacy among the Central Asian masses does not yet run as deep as the government pretends.

One visible change under communism, and one contrast with the neighboring noncommunist countries, is the virtual disappearance of the merchant class. In the old days, of course, merchants in Bukhara and Samarkand were moneylenders, as they were across the whole of Asia from Istanbul to the China Sea. They not only committed the moneylenders' sins, but also performed services—for a price—for the poor and landless as well as for their wealthier patrons. This they did in the bazaars of Central Asia before the Russian Revolution turned their old world upside down.

We have browsed in such bazaars in half a dozen cities, the busiest of them in Istanbul, the biggest in Tehran, the darkest in Isfahan, the most colorful, because of its rug market, in Tabriz. In all of them, as every Asian traveler knows, covered alleys lead off into the shadows, lined on both sides by booths or stalls. Dealers sell shoes and boots in one alley, chinaware in another, brocades and embroideries in another. No trucks can spread their noise and

fumes in these dark mazes. Instead, donkeys pad along carrying goods to the stalls, or sometimes, as in Isfahan, instead of donkeys, a camel.

From past trips to Asia both of us remember one sound
in particular that evokes "bazaar" in our minds. This is a
tapping on metal, a tapping by a hundred tiny hammers,
without rhythm or end. The sound came from small boys,
usually from six to eleven, often thin and shrunken compared to boys in most Western societies. They were shaping
and hammering copper or silver. Their fathers and grand-
fathers had started as small boys in this respectable Middle
Eastern trade, and now they, too, were in it, although they
should have been in school.

Bukhara used to have miles of covered bazaars. Since it
was a traditional Eastern city, it exploited child labor as
other market towns did for ages past. The money that
changed hands made it one of the busiest trading centers
of Asia, especially because it was on the ancient caravan
route between Persia and China, and between Russia and
India. That Bukhara was a gigantic showcase of Asian goods
before the Revolution there can be no doubt at all.

Today the showcase has vanished. One can search the
alleys and look inside or under the remaining city walls
and not find anything like an old-time Asian bazaar. One
reason, of course, is that the Soviet regime outlawed private
profit—and profit was the bloodstream that kept the bazaars
alive. Another reason is that the Soviet authorities tore
down the covered bazaars, apparently as part of an enlightened effort to let sun and air into the inner town.

All that remains of the old galleries are a few domed
towers at street intersections. These used to be the junctions
of covered alleys, and they still contain a few stalls, bazaar
style. At one such stop we came across a bolt of brocade
of the kind that is common in India but almost unobtainable
in Soviet Asia. We asked to see it, wanting a remembrance

of Bukhara. The price, fifty-one rubles—about fifty-six dollars at the official rate—was more than we wanted to pay. Next to us stood a tall bearded man in a white turban and a robe of striped and quilted cotton. Without even bargaining—no one bargains in government shops in the Soviet Union, since all prices are fixed by the state—he said he would like that piece of silk. And he calmly took out his wallet and peeled fifty-one rubles from a thick roll that must have contained hundreds. We could only infer from this that someone in Bukhara still knew affluence in spite of the miseries of the farmers and the exactions of Soviet rule.

Today an outdoor bazaar is all that remains of Bukhara's mercantile glory. It is a place of flies and dirt and shoddy goods. In summer and well into the fall, a hot sun beats down on carcasses of lamb and mounds of melons and onions. In winter, the merchants move indoors to sheds that have as little eye appeal as bus garages. The final indignity—in Bukhara, the great market town of old—we discovered around the fringes of the open-air market. Here were the booths of craftsmen. One bearded man was repairing watches, one shoes, one jewelry; and from the last of these we heard the tap-tap of a small hammer. But an old man rather than a child was doing the hammering; the children were in school. And each booth bore a number instead of the proprietor's name. It was "Shop Number 24" or "Craftsman Number 38," just as if this were Moscow or Kiev and not a center of old-time artistry. The numbers reminded us, more sharply than the Cyrillic letters on all the signs, that we were in the Soviet Union, in the modern world. We knew Bukhara's days of art and trade had gone.

Perhaps it is a good thing for the children that they no longer have to tap with their hammers in dark alleys, as their forefathers did. In Russian Central Asia it would seem that the present younger generation has won a life of greater opportunity than the old—if opportunity is what a Central Asian wants.

What equips the young people for a new life is, of course, the new schooling for boys and girls. What gives them a choice of careers, and to some extent the specialized training for such careers, is the spread of varied industries. Neither the czars nor the commissars ever planned such a growth of factories and processing plants in what had been a cotton and livestock economy.

It was Joseph Stalin and indirectly Adolf Hitler who brought it about. For when the German armies invaded Russia in 1941, occupying and denuding the most productive parts of European Russia, Stalin ordered an unprecedented removal of industries to the East. A hundred major plants from Europe were built anew in Uzbekistan alone, and their workers were moved to the new sites before housing was ready for them. Even under the czars, some factories making cotton and silk had been set up in southern Central Asia. Under the urgencies of war, the Russians brought fertilizer plants, railroad building and repair shops, glass and machinery factories, and a wide variety of other industries—and the industries stayed.

No other colonial rulers, to the best of our knowledge, ever located so much industry among subject peoples as the Russians have done in Central Asia. Perhaps the British around Calcutta and Bombay and the Japanese around Mukden were exceptions. In general, it was a persistent fault of European (and American) colonialism to use the colony overwhelmingly for the mining or growing of raw materials to be processed in the mother country. The subject peoples usually became dependent, as Central Asia used to be, on food and consumer goods from the ruling power.

In Soviet Central Asia, in contrast, the people do not have to look to Russia for everything. Every major city shares some of the industries and the productive jobs.

Samarkand and Bukhara are no longer mere museums; each has its factories as well, and seventy miles from Bukhara a vast new source of natural gas brings added importance to the region.

The undisputed industrial center is neither of these old cities but Tashkent, now the capital of the Uzbek Republic in more than the official political sense. A little more than a century ago, when czarist troops conquered it, this place on the ancient caravan route to China was a dusty town of ten thousand. Before World War II it had become largely Russian in character, with a mixed Russian and Uzbek population of almost half a million. Today it has more than a million—or had until 1966, when calamity befell.

In Tashkent every breath of wind blew dust in the fall of 1967. Every gust stirred up a yellow cloud that seeped into our eyes and hair and pores. On windy days the safest place to be was in a room with windows shut, no matter what the heat outside.

Why? This was no normal dust of an ill-kept city, nor was it like the sandstorms that sometimes blew in on Tashkent from its surrounding deserts. This was the dust of earthquake rubble. In the eighteen months before our visit, Tashkent had felt no fewer than 868 shocks. No one of them was serious enough in loss of life to be listed among the world's most destructive tremors. But the first few, in 1966, were rumored to have cost a total of 500 lives, and all of them together had made 80,000 homeless in a city of more than a million.

The damage was worst in a mile-square area in the central city, in what used to be the old "Turkish" quarter. By the time we reached Tashkent, many of the shops lining the central streets had collapsed, and their stocks were being sold in glassed-in sidewalk stalls. One stall offered pastries; another, dark Russian bread and flat, unleavened Uzbek bread; another sold books and school supplies; another, ice cream. In the residential streets, where low houses had stood, entire square blocks had been bulldozed. Many houses on the wide streets of the Russian section had been shored up by brick or concrete buttresses. These were built at right angles to the outer walls. Sometimes they extended halfway across the sidewalks, so that one had to weave around them while walking in the dark. It was a city still in the throes of disaster.

The central city was, in a way, under a sentence of death. Of course nobody could tell when the next shocks would tumble the buildings that remained. That there would be more shocks here in the near or distant future seemed foreordained. Beneath the inner city, geologists had found a fault so serious that they warned against any rebuilding there. The ground would have to be used for parks, and the rebuilding would have to be done in the outskirts. The outer areas, at least, the experts proclaimed geologically sound.

Homeless victims had to camp in tents or double up with relatives. The textile mills and the railroad repair shops were relatively undamaged, but their workers needed homes. How could the workers attain the socialist "norms" of output if they and their families had no roofs over their heads? The authorities had to move fast. By "authorities" one means, of course, those in Moscow. Officials of the municipality or of the Uzbek Republic had neither enough money nor power to cope with such a crisis. For weeks after the first shock they did little except to bury the dead, heal the injured, put up tents for the roofless, and provide the equivalent of soup kitchens for the hungry. Then Moscow acted.

The central government sent out an "appeal" to all the fourteen other republics within the Soviet Union. Ostensibly it called for contributions of money and volunteers to rebuild Tashkent. Actually such an appeal from Moscow is a contradiction in terms. Moscow does not need to ask for money or men; it orders what it wants. Each republic is told each year what share of the national budget it can spend, and for what. Each is also told year by year how much of its own revenues it can keep for projects within its territory.

Manpower, too, is controlled by various devices, mainly by the issuance or withholding of permits for work and housing. So when an emergency like the Tashkent disaster requires 25,000 building-trade workers in a hurry, the central government does not need to appeal. It simply compels the republics, under cover of an appeal, to reshape their priorities, to do without this or that project which Moscow had promised them. It also "appeals" to the government-controlled organizations like the labor unions and the Komsomols, the Young Communist Leagues, for the needed manpower and skills.

Although there is no reservoir of rubles in private hands, the government chose to ask for "contributions" as if it were running a Community Chest drive. So convincing was its plea (a government official told us in Tashkent), so deep were the hidden springs of idealism in the character of the Soviet people, that 50,000 volunteers offered to interrupt their lives and help rebuild. The Tashkent authorities could not house or feed such an army. They told half the volunteers not to come. The rest arrived, lived in tents, and set to work.

From what we could see in the autumn of 1967, muscle and drive had been added to idealism. New apartment space for 60,000 families had risen in the earthquake-free suburbs and in two new satellite cities. In addition, 13,000 families were moved from the stricken city to new homes and jobs in other parts of the Soviet Union. Each new building around Tashkent bore a sign identifying it as "Gift from the Lithuanian S.S.R." or one of the others, or just "Kiev—Tashkent."

The buildings were varied in color and materials: some with cinder blocks showing, some with bricks, a few with prefabricated walls and windows. Yet somehow they looked alike. All had the uniform boxlike aspect that marks the buildings on the fringe of every Soviet industrial town. And all showed in their lack of finish that they were put up in a hurry. Still, with these defects, the result as a whole was a prodigy of concentrated effort. The Soviet Government had shown that it has the capacity to do well what it really wants to do. And it had shown political sense of a high order. It had demonstrated to the people of Tashkent, and to the largely Uzbek and Tadjik villages and towns around it, that the whole Soviet Union shared their sorrows, cared for their welfare, counted them members of the family.

Inevitably the new Tashkent will look even less like a Central Asian city than the old. The earthquake simply finished a transformation which industry and the movement of populations had begun. Tashkent had long been a many-layered cake of ethnic ingredients. One saw more Koreans, for example, in the streets of Tashkent than in the Soviet Far East nearer Korea—the reason being that Stalin moved something like 200,000 Koreans en masse to Central Asia because he did not trust them in a possible war with Japan. The entire community of Crimean Tatars, likewise, was moved to Central Asia; today thousands of them live reluctantly in and around Tashkent, sometimes causing riots, because the government does not let them go back to their former homes.

In the Uzbek Republic as a whole, Russians are still in a minority. But as one travels eastward from Tashkent, one finds Central Asia losing even its ethnic uniqueness. In Kazakhstan, once the home and pastureland of nomadic herdsmen, Russians and Ukrainians now outnumber all the other ethnic components combined. The Kazakhs have become a minority in the republic that bears their name.

VII

Alma Ata:

ON THE EDGE OF CHINA

The Soviet Union borders on fourteen countries, seven of which are not communist. Ironically, it is the border with a communist state that causes the most anxiety to the men in the Kremlin. This is, of course, the 4,500-mile boundary between the Soviet Union and the People's Republic of China. It is not only Russia's longest frontier; it is the longest land frontier in the world. Considering that it is sometimes vague and disputed as well as long, the border has seen surprisingly little violence in its long history. But the tensions of the nineteen-sixties between Moscow and Peking led to violence and bloodshed. Most of the trouble broke out at the two opposite ends of the line. At the Far Eastern end, pitched battles were fought where the border runs down the middle of the Ussuri River. In the west, where China's province of Sinkiang meets Soviet Central Asia, bloody skirmishes punctuated a propaganda war. Here the border defies both history and geography, for it barricades one of the great natural land bridges of the world. A few centuries ago the whole vast and empty region was called Turkistan, and it was the main highway from Asia to Europe—those two names for what is actually one Eurasian continent. Now this part of Turkistan has been cut into two pieces: the Soviet Republic of Kazakhstan on the western side of the border and the Chinese province of Sinkiang on the eastern. To plant an international barrier here is to bottle up and thus to hurt the native peoples on both sides of it.

Some frontiers, like the Himalayas, divide peoples of different races and religions. Not this one. Here Kazakhs and Uighurs, peoples of Turkic stock and language and of Moslem religion, have called the area home since long before either Russians or Chinese pushed in. The early possessors had not a drop of Russian or Chinese blood in their veins. What they do have in their blood is more than a healthy dislike of both the foreign peoples who rule them.

Until Russia and China took them and their homeland over, the Turkic peoples were nomads and shepherds. For such peoples political frontiers and border guards with strange faces and guns had no meaning. What mattered was pasture land for their flocks, for that meant life itself. But the old pastoral life is no more. Now the nomads have been more or less settled into their respective collective farms. Their rulers are flooding into the area and already dominate it on both sides.

The border is volatile for more than human reasons. China claims a large piece of territory on the Russian side, contending that the czar stole it in the eighteen-sixties. Russia would like to resume control of a section of Chinese Sinkiang that was its puppet state in the nineteen-forties, when the Chinese were occupied elsewhere. The claims surprise no one, for both territories are rich in minerals: nickel, copper, lead, silver, and oil, among others.

What undoubtedly heightens the anxiety here is a relatively recent act of border defiance. In 1962, when the Soviet-Chinese quarrel was new, about 60,000 natives crossed into Kazakhstan from the Chinese side. They streamed into the fertile valley of the Ili River north of the capital city of Alma Ata and into grasslands still further north. None of these border violators were ethnic Chinese. Most of them were Kazakhs and thus blood brothers and coreligionists of the restless natives on the Russian side. A second component of the migration was several thousands

15. A spur of the Tien Shan, or Heavenly Mountains, stood between us and China in Soviet Kazakhstan. The mountains are a stunning backdrop for Alma Ata.
—Sovfoto

16. The clinic where we sought dental services had six chairs. Two drills were attached to one wall. It was clean and basic. Photo by David Gulick, St. Louis *Post-Dispatch*

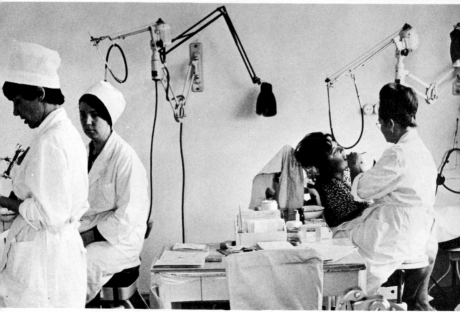

17. "The same for me . . ."—*Krokodil*

18. "Already they're making improvements . . ."—*Krokodil*

шка и лотерея.

Рисунок М. БИТНОГО

19. "The dream of an old man with a national lottery ticket . . ."
—*Krokodil*

20. We strolled among the carved wooden houses of old Irkutsk. Without central heat or running water, they are being replaced by ugly new apartments. Photo by David Gulick, St. Louis *Post-Dispatch*

21. Prefabricated panels help to speed up the building of new apartments. These were used in Khabarovsk in the Soviet Far East. Photo by David Gulick, St. Louis *Post-Dispatch*

22. Our locomotive on the Trans-Siberian, like this one, was "a monster of its kind." Photo by David Gulick, St. Louis *Post-Dispatch*

23. The old Irkutsk railroad station has a spacious, high-ceilinged waiting room that seems to dignify the traveler. Photo by David Gulick, St. Louis *Post-Dispatch*

24. On our Trans-Siberian railway car the metal letters "Moscow—Vladivostok" were kept polished, but the windows needed polishing more. Photo by David Gulick, St. Louis *Post-Dispatch*

25. On the Trans-Siberian diner the staff feeds a continuous stream of passengers from eight in the morning until eleven at night. Photo by David Gulick, St. Louis *Post-Dispatch*

26. Nakhodka, one of the newest commercial ports of the Soviet Far East, is the only one foreigners may use.—Sovfoto

of Uighurs, who are relatives primarily of the Uzbeks on the Soviet side.

Why they came over is a matter of dispute between the former communist partners. The Russians say with truth that the Peking Government had been trying to stamp out Russian influence on the Chinese side, as it has tried to do for a couple of centuries. There is little doubt that the Chinese harassed and regimented their native peoples as the Russians did theirs. The Chinese say, on the other hand, again with some truth, that the Russians had been enticing the Kazakhs and Uighurs of Sinkiang with broadcasts and other propaganda devices. One Soviet consul on the Chinese side was said to have issued thousands of visas to Soviet territory.

The Russians, always suspicious, assume that Chinese agents came over with the migrating 60,000. To what extent can these newcomers be trusted now that fighting has flared along the border? Most of the migrants were settled in collective farms far from city streets and military installations. Yet the Soviet authorities have put their secret police on constant alert along with their soldiers.

In Alma Ata, the capital of Kazakhstan, we came as close to this particular border as foreigners can. The impulse to peer into China, which we may not enter, has plagued us for years. It has driven us, like many others, to the Hong Kong-Chinese border, to be confronted by the gun barrels of Chinese frontier guards. In northern Burma we have followed the valley of the Shweli River and gazed across it at the blue hills of Yünnan. In Sikkim we have jeeped into the Himalayan foothills until our Indian army escort stopped us and said, "That hillside over there is Tibet."

Now Chinese soil began 175 miles to the south of us, beyond a spur of the Tien Shan or Heavenly Mountains. China also lay 200 miles to the east, across country that is more open, more free of natural barriers. A motor road to the north and east would have brought us to Chinese soil within a day—if we had been allowed to go. But even in 1967, before the shooting had begun, the Russians wanted no foreigners wandering around this countryside.

Evidence that this was a sensitive border came when our request to visit a collective farm was refused. Usually the Russians are eager to show off the best of their state and collective farms. Official visitors and journalists from abroad used to be plied with collectives as with food and vodka. We had been reading some of the Intourist literature which actually offered visits to farms in the Alma Ata region. The offer was several years old and apparently out of date.

Our Intourist service bureau, otherwise helpful, turned us down. We guessed that a higher authority, presumably the Ministry of Internal Security, had said *nyet*. And from this authority, as we have noted, there is no appeal.

Another example of border touchiness grew out of a chance meeting with two elderly brothers in the Kazakhstan Hotel. One of them was tall and white-haired. He wore a white shirt and tie and a well-cut jacket. The other looked more rugged and earthy. He had the leathery face of an outdoorsman; he wore a dark shirt without a tie, like most Russians.

The two were having dinner at a nearby table, talking in a language we couldn't identify. It was not Russian or Kazakh, nor was it English, French, Italian, German, or Spanish. Since we never made the first overture to a stranger in the Soviet Union, we swallowed our curiosity with each spoonful of borsch.

That evening, in the hotel lobby, the taller one waylaid us. "Excuse me," he began in English, "what country do you come from?"

"We're Americans."

"I thought so. I'm American too—from Miami."

"But what was that language you were talking in the dining room?"

"Oh, that was Greek. That was my brother with me."

He explained that he and his brother were born in Turkey of Greek parents. Then his face clouded.

"Do you know what they've done to me here? They've told me I can't stay with my brother at his house in the country. I can't even go to see it—and we haven't been together for fifty-seven years."

"Did you say seven years?"

"No—fifty-seven. We said good-by in 1910, in Turkey. We were kids then. I was only fifteen."

His family sent him west, and he ended up in Florida. His brother went east, and ended up on a farm in Kazakhstan near Alma Ata. Eventually he became the manager of a collective. Now he had retired, but still lived on the farm with his Russian wife and children. The Florida brother had lost his wife the previous year and had decided on a reunion after most of a lifetime apart.

"I wrote to my brother," he said. "He told me to come and I got my visa. But they won't let me stay with him. He can visit me here in the city, but it costs too much for both of us. The family came to the airport to meet me. They had to go back to the farm, and now I have to go back to Florida. It's a sad thing for me."

So for a week the two brothers, separated for more than half a century, talked and reminisced, either in the hotel bedroom or over glasses of beer in the dining room. It was a reunion that Soviet bureaucracy and border tension had ruined.

Russia has suffered through the ages not only from invasions but also, in consequence, from a frontier neurosis. Every neighboring people can cite instances of this neurosis in action. The Turks, for example, like to tell about the Turkish horse that strayed across the line into Soviet Armenia. The Russian border guards shot it as if it had been an agent of the CIA. The Japanese talk sadly and bitterly

about thousands of seizures of fishing boats that drifted a
few yards across their water boundary with the Soviet-held
Habomai Islands. Russians would not be Russians if they did
not worry about their borderlands, particularly since most
Soviet borderlands are inhabited by non-Russian peoples.

The Kazakh people, like all the Central Asians, do have
scores to settle with the Russians. In the first half of
the nineteenth century the fights between Russians and
Kazakhs were something like the Indian wars of the American plains. Russians would raid Kazakh villages or nomad
settlements, Kazakhs would retaliate, Russians would push
their forts farther south and east, Kazakhs would lose their
grazing grounds. Today, it seems to us, the Soviet Union
has little need to worry about the reliability of its Kazakh
people who live on or near the China border.

We say this for two main reasons. The first is that the
Kazakhs have been absorbed more successfully, from the
Russian standpoint, than the other Moslem peoples of Central Asia. They seem to have been the most willing to send
their children to Russian schools, to learn the Russian language, to make their peace with the Soviet system, and to
get ahead in it. They really had little choice, for, as we have
said, they form a minority in their own republic. Moreover,
the Moslem faith of most Kazakhs goes back only to the
eighteenth century. In contrast, the Uzbeks and other peoples along the southern frontier have been Moslem for more
than a thousand years. It is easier for the Kazakhs, therefore,
to pay lip service to Marxism-Leninism and to adapt to the
way of life which it imposes. They are not suicidally inclined.
They are not likely, therefore, to rise up against the Russians in a time of tension and trouble.

We have a second reason for not expecting a Kazakh or
Central Asian uprising now. This is that the Central Asians
can look to no outside power for encouragement and support except, of course, China. In late czarist years and in the
first years of the Soviet regime they could make trouble for

Russia, and they did. In those days Turkey was the center of a still-powerful empire, and the sultan was caliph of the Islamic world, which included Central Asia. Turkey exerted a pull on the Central Asians, with their Turkic languages and their Islamic faith and culture. Bukharans, nominally independent until 1920, used to send students to Istanbul. There some of them were drawn to the Pan-Turanian movement, which dreamed of uniting all the Turkic peoples from the Balkans to Siberia and China. As recently as 1922 Turkey's chief minister in World War I, Enver Pasha, led an anti-Soviet uprising in Central Asia and died in battle.

Today, Turkey is a compact republic; it has disestablished Islam. It has Latinized its alphabet and given up imperial ambitions. Neither in Turkey nor in Central Asia have we detected any strength in the Pan-Turanian fantasy. It is simply not relevant now. We happened to be in Samarkand the day after the Prime Minister of Turkey, Suleyman Demirel, had paid an official visit there. It was the first such visit by a Turkish leader since the Russian and Turkish revolutions. Banners in red (the Turkish as well as the Soviet color) proclaimed Soviet friendship with the Republic of Turkey. Demirel and his entourage attracted crowds so dense that the Soviet secret police were displeased. But what did it matter? From what we heard later, from Turks and Russians alike, the crowds came out of curiosity and friendliness but not out of any feeling for present-day Turkey.

Britain, too, used to be a power in Asia, a rival of imperial Russia, and a benevolent ruler of perhaps fifty million Moslem subjects in the subcontinent of India. But Britain could no longer help rebellious Central Asians even if it wanted to. Nor could Central Asians get encouragement from their direct Islamic neighbors Iran and Afghanistan, both of which are lightweights on the scale of power.

Only one country might conceivably be tempted to fan the dying embers of anti-Soviet nationalism in Central Asia.

This, of course, is China. But do the Chinese seriously think they can become the liberators of Kazakhs, Uzbeks, and others who have ancient grudges against the Russians? If they do, they may be as wrong in this as they have been in their other estimates of foreign attitudes in recent years. It would take more than propaganda to make the Soviet Kazakhs pro-Chinese. They know too much about Chinese regimentation and cruelty toward their cousins across the border.

The time for Central Asian nationalism has passed. The non-Russian Moslem peoples, it seems to us, are in no position to rise against their Russian masters. For Kazakh nationalism especially, the bell has long since tolled.

City folk in Moscow and Leningrad look down upon Alma Ata, the capital of Kazakhstan, as a kind of cow town. A Polish physicist summed up this contempt, which he had acquired from Russian colleagues. Talking of Soviet higher education, he told us: "The Russians have a right to be proud of some of their universities—but please remember that I said 'some.' The University of Leningrad is one extreme, Alma Ata is the other."

Alma Ata is a lonely city in the center of the Asian heartland, as remote from the oceans as a city can be. It is a small metropolis of half a million far from any other. Facing arid steppes to the north, mountains to the south, deserts to the west, and the endless wastes of Chinese Turkistan to the east, it would seem to be the end of the line. Yet Alma Ata has more than empty distances to set it apart from other Soviet cities. It is lovely as well as lonely. When we lived in it in early October a million roses were still blooming in its parks. Its buildings, except for a few, lack the heaviness of Muscovite design. And its setting offers one asset that most other Soviet cities lack: a jagged line of mountains against the southern sky. In an effect that we have seen in the Himalayas, the snowy peaks float above the clouds as if they were not rooted in this planet.

The city, like Leningrad, wears an air of cultivation, of good manners and good temper. With no monuments of Asian architecture or history—the place was settled as a Russian garrison town a little more than a hundred years ago—Alma Ata nevertheless gives the traveler something almost as precious as relics: a well-appointed, comfortable hotel with good food and friendly service. We felt at ease, and so, it seems, do the people of this surprising oasis, tucked away at the edge of nowhere.

Why? What explains the grace of this town? The only satisfying answer we found was the Russian exile system, not just under the czars but, most important of all to Alma Ata, in the Stalin years. For it was the exile system that brought some of the bravest and best of Russia's writers and thinkers into the heart of Central Asia and, of course, into Siberia. Wherever these political exiles had to live, they brought an intellectual life that would otherwise have been lacking. Alma Ata is one of those far-off places that owes the exiles a lasting debt.

The most famous of Alma Ata's exiles was the organizer and energizer of the Red Army, Stalin's hated rival Leon Trotsky. In late 1927, when he was hustled from Moscow on a secret train, the railroad did not reach farther than the present city of Frunze, the capital of the Kirghiz Republic. The last 125 miles from Frunze to Alma Ata was a week's journey by bus, truck, sleigh, and on foot over a snowy mountain pass. According to Trotsky's devoted biographer, the late Isaac Deutscher, Alma Ata at the end of the nineteen-twenties was still an oriental town of dirt and squalor. It was, he said, exposed to earthquakes, blizzards, floods, and heat waves, and the heat waves brought dust storms and "plagues of vermin."

True or not, this is what Trotsky wanted the world to believe. His biographer never saw Alma Ata; he had to take the word of Trotsky and his partisans. But even in Trotsky's year of exile, Alma Ata was already a place of gardens and apple orchards. The famous ex-commissar used to enjoy hunting trips and picnics in the foothills of the Tien Shan—and who would not? He had his own log cabin among the pines. The rushing streams, the straight tall trees, the sight of snowfields up against the sky—these are among the delights of the Alma Ata mountain country, as we ourselves discovered. Trotsky savored them until, a year after his arrival, he was expelled from the Soviet Union. He found refuge first in Turkey, then in Norway and Mexico, where he met a gruesome end in 1940 with an assassin's hatchet in his skull.

Trotsky's departure did not, of course, mean the end of Alma Ata's eminence as a place of exile. On the contrary, the years of forced collectivization of the farms brought streams of dispossessed kulaks into Central Asia, some into the apple growing country around Alma Ata. The town began to lose its oriental character. As early as 1936 Fitzroy Maclean, then a young member of the British embassy staff in Moscow, found that Alma Ata "must be one of the pleasantest provincial towns in the Soviet Union"—and Maclean was by no means an admirer of everything Soviet. The city's character, he remembered later, was purely Russian. Even in those days one had to visit the open-air market to be reminded that this was in Central Asia, on the edge of China.

In the hardest days of World War II, while Stalin was moving 200 factories to Central Asia, he also moved a part of the motion picture industry to Alma Ata. The cinema was important in wartime, even more than in peacetime. The Bolsheviks had relied heavily on camera propaganda from the earliest days of their Revolution. Stalin's government needed it in wartime to impress or intimidate world opinion, allied or neutral, and to rally the home front to new efforts. Thus new battalions of intellectuals became residents of Alma Ata: script writers and photographers, actors and actresses, technicians and stage setters, all exempted from military service to perform this specialized service for the state.

At the same time Stalin deported entire minority communities, among them the so-called Volga Germans, who had farmed and traded along the lower Volga since the time of Catherine the Great. Not trusting any of them in the path of the Nazi advance to the Volga, Stalin ordered them loaded into cattle cars and moved east. Some he sent into Siberia between the Yenisei and Lake Baikal, some into the Kazakh Republic.

One sees two evidences of their presence today. One is a German-language daily newspaper, *Freundschaft*, a bulletin sheet of Communist Party exhortation. The other is an abundance of German books, handsomely printed and bound in East Germany, in Alma Ata's bookshops. It would be out of character if these immigrants to Central Asia, now in their second generation, did not add their talents to the musical, theatrical, and artistic life of the city.

Like every other Soviet city, Alma Ata has its statue of Lenin. The god-king stands in this center of Asian minorities in his usual pose: his right arm aloft almost as if hailing a taxi, wearing what looks like an Edwardian frock coat of a cut Lenin rarely if ever wore in real life. But Alma Ata also has a statue of another who is honored as a national hero. The name carved into the pedestal, Abai, means nothing to most foreigners and to many Russians, but it tells much about the political and cultural tactics of the Soviet state toward its minority peoples.

The real Abai was a Kazakh teacher, translator, and poet, Ibrahim Kunanbai (1845–1904), as the Russians spell it. He was born and raised in a mountain village near where Russia, Mongolia, and China come together. In the light of his posthumous fame as a communist hero, it is worth remembering that he spent three years of his boyhood at school in

Semipalatinsk, the nearest Russian city. There he learned
the Russian language and Russian ways, there a wealthy
Russian became his patron. With his dual background as a
Moslem Kazakh and as an accepter, if not an admirer, of
Russian culture, he became a bridge-builder between the
Kazakhs and their Russian masters.

Abai never fought against the Russians, although he was
a genuine cultural nationalist. The struggle of his life was
against illiteracy, superstition, and fanaticism among his
own people. His goal was the modern education of the
Kazakhs so that they could hold their own in the modern
world. Because he was a faithful Moslem, early Soviet officials in Central Asia denounced his poetry as "semi-feudal."
But their more skillful successors saw in Abai a perfect cultural hero. It was safe for them to hold him up for admiration and emulation, since he had never been anti-Russian,
and died long before there was any issue of communism
versus capitalism in Central Asia. He was the kind of person
the Russians find it useful to commemorate in their own
art forms—namely, in plays or films or operas.

We bought tickets for an opera called *Abai*, wondering
what on earth could be done with such material on the
operatic stage. The result was a surprise. The librettist was
the son of a Kazakh nomad from Abai's tribe. The composers, we were assured, were also Kazakhs. The tenor in
the title role was one of two brothers named Abdullin,
Moslems and non-Russians as their name suggests. Both
had risen to stardom in the provincial opera and had sung
from more famous stages in Leningrad and Moscow. All
this, be it remembered, in a medium alien and unknown to
the Kazakhs of a century ago.

In the music we found the resonance and color characteristic of Russian orchestral scores. Sometimes a Kazakh folk
song gave it an Eastern flavor, but in general *Abai* sounded
to us as Russian as Moussorgsky. The Kazakh authors had
absorbed the Russian gift of stagecraft. Abai is an Asian

Hans Sachs, lamenting a world of arranged marriages, blood feuds, and violence.

Remembering that we were only 175 miles from the Chinese frontier, we noted that the chief evildoer in the plot was made up and dressed like a Chinese, while all the rest in the cast were unmistakably non-Chinese and Kazakh. At the end of the second act the villain poisons the juvenile lead, the young man whom the princess, in defiance of her family, wants to marry. The young suitor is singing a romantic aria when the pains of the poison assail him. He clutches his stomach, and sinks slowly to the floor. The rest of the cast rush to help him. The music rises to a tumult of blowing and banging as the curtain quickly falls.

When the lights went up we saw several women in the audience holding hands to their faces as if to say, "How horrible!" But in a moment the poisoned suitor bounded through the curtains with a smile and a kiss for all. Stretching his arms, he announced to anyone who might be worried, "I'm all right—I'm all right!" In forty years of opera-going we have seen harrowing deaths on many stages: Tristan's agony, Tosca's suicide, Aïda's entombment alive, and, most grisly of all, the beheading we watched in Moscow in Tchaikovsky's *Mazeppa*. But this was the first time we had ever seen a dying singer rush out to assure his audience it wasn't true.

In the Kazakh Republic, Abai is the only leader of the past whom the Soviet regime has anointed as a cultural hero of the present. True, Alma Ata does possess a statue of a genuine Kazakh nationalist warrior: he was Amangeldi Iman-uli, or Imanov, as the Russians call him. He led the fight against czarist troops in the 1916 rebellion that swept Central Asia. Imanov was the first important Kazakh to embrace Lenin's cause after the Bolsheviks seized power in 1917, and of course the communists have honored him ever since. But he is primarily a communist, not a national, hero. Of Kazakh teachers, writers, politicians of the pre-Soviet years, only Abai seems to have met Moscow's standards. And for him a mere statue is not enough, nor is a biographical novel and an opera about his life and work. The opera house itself is called the Abai Opera and Ballet Theater, and his statue stands on a wide street now named the Abai Prospekt.

In other Soviet republics, likewise, the central government seems to have fastened on just one non-Russian to honor. The neighboring Uzbek Republic, for example, was the homeland of Tamerlane. That conqueror has left his monuments of glory, and the Soviet regime has respected these almost from the moment it fought its way to power. But Tamerlane is not the officially approved hero. It is his grandson, Ulug-beg, the most celebrated Asian astronomer, for whom streets are named and for whom an opera will surely be commissioned some day. Ulug-beg fits the Soviet prescription for several reasons. First, he was grandson and successor of the greatest ruler ever to make Samarkand his capital. Thus his name rings the gong of Uzbek pride in the distant past. Moreover, the circumstances of his death can be made to fit antireligious purposes. That Ulug-beg was murdered in 1449, two years after succeeding to the throne, there is no doubt. Some historians say his killers were Uzbek adherents of a rival house, who saw Tamerlane's empire weakening and struck to win power for themselves. According to the Soviet story, however, the religious fanatics of fifteenth-century Islam hated Ulug-beg for his scientific and naturalistic knowledge, and they killed him. Finally, he was a scientist, who lived so long ago that he cannot possibly collide with Soviet theories. Now it is safe and wise to hold him up to honor.

It was an archaeologist in the czar's service who rediscovered his observatory in 1908. But the Bolsheviks make Ulug-beg almost one of their own. In a museum on the site of the observatory, a heroic painting pictures Ulug-beg's assassination. And in the churches that have been turned into museums of atheism, like the Kazan Cathedral in Leningrad and one of the buildings of the Pechersky Monastery at Kiev, Ulug-beg's bearded face appears among portraits of Galileo, Newton, and other scientists of East and West whom the Kremlin exploits in its antireligious campaigns.

The Kremlin promotes the cult of folk heroes in other republics as well. In Georgia, the hero is not a Russian communist but a Georgian of long ago. He is the poet Rustaveli, who wrote a Georgian national epic in the twelfth century. The tree-lined avenue that forms the Champs Elysées of Tbilisi is named for Rustaveli. Why not Lenin? The Russian arbiters in these matters resisted temptation and let the Georgians use one of the honored names of their independent past.

This at least fed the pride of a Soviet minority, if not its stomach. It seems to us that the Russians have shown sophistication in thus promoting non-Russian folk heroes. For once, a deft touch has replaced the heavy hand of Soviet policy. On the surface, at least, it has smoothed what would otherwise be the rough texture of Russian colonialism. The British learned this little secret of imperial rule when, for example, they knighted Rabindranath Tagore. The Americans failed to remember it when they named Manila's finest avenue Dewey Boulevard, and kept the name for almost fifty years. It was only after the Yankees went home in 1946 that the new independent republic renamed the boulevard for Manuel Roxas, its first president. The Americans should have had the wit to name it for a Filipino from the start.

Not having been allowed to sample Kazakh culture on a collective farm, we had to content ourselves with the cultural life of the city. A Leningrader or a Muscovite would scoff: Alma Ata is too far, too small, to have anything that would qualify as culture. Still, we from the provincial, parochial capital of the United States found plenty to divert us. One evening we bought tickets for the Kazakh Philharmonic Orchestra, wondering whether this European art form would show any Kazakh influence. When the orchestra appeared and finished its tuning, what took our attention was not the conductor, although his gestures were about as restrained as those of Leonard Bernstein. The center of interest to us was the concertmaster—a chunky brunette in her late thirties, who might have been Russian or German, but was certainly not Kazakh. She was the first woman we had ever seen in that particular post. She sawed away at her violin efficiently, but with a look of withering contempt for the leader whose beat she was following. The first half of the program was a performance of the Sixth Symphony by Evgeny Brussilovsky. Somehow we had missed his name in our studies of great composers. He turned out to be a contemporary and a local celebrity as well. In the early nineteen-thirties he had been sent to Alma Ata with orders to find native Kazakh themes for his music. He had stayed in Kazakhstan, in virtual exile, every since. We saw him in the audience: a thick-necked man of sixty, with a beaming face and a head as smooth as a Kazakhstan melon.

His symphony was neither Kazakh nor contemporary. It hit our eardrums as a noisy imitation of the Richard Strauss of fifty years ago. Whatever its faults, the musicians played it with Slavic passion. The woman concertmaster gave the music her all, while darting hostile glances at the conductor. Another player, who looked at least eight months pregnant, was one of two harpists, sitting with her profile to the audience. She, too, was a musical novelty for us. At the end of the performance Comrade Brussilovsky, in a black velvet jacket, took the stage to shake hands with the conductor and concertmaster, while the audience applauded loudly.

We finally caught up with Russian jazz as well as symphonic music on the edge of China. All along our route from Leningrad we had asked for tickets to a jazz concert. Always the reply had been: "Ballet and opera, yes, of course; circus, maybe, but tickets are scarce; jazz concerts, no, students play it for themselves, not for the public." Such was the official answer.

Unofficially we learned that the new jazz has a passionate public. It is the main motive of young Russians for turning on shortwave radio, chiefly the Voice of America. Listeners record the jazz that comes over the Voice, dance to it, and improvise it in their own jam sessions. These sessions we never penetrated. But in Alma Ata we did hear a snatch of what must go on for many hours in student quarters. A billboard deceptively advertised "An Evening of Light Music" by a troupe from the northern Kazakhstan city of Kustanai. Through a warm autumn rain we strolled to the concert hall. We sat at the back, as young people, many Kazakhs, some Russians, drifted in. Groups of teen-age girls waved, visited, talked with teen-age boys but sat apart. Young couples, hand in hand, settled down together, waiting for the lights to go out. The curtain rose on a small brightly lit stage. There stood four men in shirt sleeves.

A tall red-bearded youth balanced a bull fiddle. A round-faced farm boy with yellow hair wore an accordion around his neck. A dark wiry fellow tended two drums, and a poetic type embraced a guitar. They sprang to life with a cascade of sound and rhythm and color. For perhaps three minutes the young Russians played as if they were possessed by the creative spirit and the love of their instruments. Then it was all over.

A plump young man in a business suit bounded onto the stage and took over the show. In a bourgeois society he might have been a salesman of vacuum cleaners or health food. He was in truth a salesman. He was a Party man hired to transmit the Party line, the approved health food produced in Moscow for good socialists all over the Soviet Union. He was the official master of ceremonies of a Russian road show. None of the material in the show seemed to have been specially adapted to the Kazakhs in the audience.

After a welcome and several jokes, with polite titters from the girls in the front rows, he introduced: a Russian folk dance; a patriotic song and dance by a young man in military uniform; a stout soprano who belted out operatic arias to piano accompaniment; a nervous woman pianist who hurried through two Chopin nocturnes; and finally the feature of the evening. Now the announcer turned artist. He spoke and sang a narrative set to music, entitled *Vietnam, Vietnam*. He was the simple, unsuspecting Vietnamese, his homeland and then his village invaded by the imperialist beast, his home in ruins. And what was this upon the ground? A baby. His baby. Dead? No, no! He falls upon the body sobbing and cursing the imperialist slaughterers, the Americans.

As the show progressed, the audience sagged. Young couples whispered in the dark and nuzzled. A Kazakh girl sitting just in front of us tired of her boyfriend, put her head down on the adjoining chair, and went to sleep. She had come for jazz, not for this.

The four young jazz artists had remained onstage to provide background music for the show. This they did with efficiency and boredom. The tall redbeard scratched his bull fiddle mechanically. At the end, when it came their turn to take a bow, they did it almost with contempt, as if to say to us, "Save your applause for artists who refuse to be tamed." Our feeling for them, perhaps wasted, was simply compassion.

The evening of "light music" had netted us two dividends: a sample of the new Russian jazz that was unforgettable; and another sample of how the Party controls culture. The jazz artists had started by expressing themselves. They ended by playing what the Party prescribed.

The local art gallery provided another cultural surprise. We have written of the obsession with Glorious Victories in Russian opera, ballet, and painting, and of that Eleventh Commandment of Soviet art: Thou shalt not commemorate defeats except, maybe, the centuries of woe under the Tatars. In Alma Ata, we found on a museum wall a reminder of the First World War. In this disaster, Russia lost 1,700,000 men killed. Some local artist had painted a company of Russian infantry, in their long gray greatcoats, marching off to a fire-lit horizon. The simple title was *1914*. It was a reminder of that largely peasant army that died at Tannenberg, and in a thousand other encounters.

In the same gallery we came upon a painting that violated the Twelfth Commandment of Socialist Realism: Thou shalt not paint any Russian who does not look healthy, strong, and happy. Entitled *Home*, the painting showed a coal miner, his face covered with grime, his body near exhaustion, walking home. His house, of unpainted wood, was thick with coal dust from a slag heap in the distance. Since this was the art gallery of the Kazakh Republic, the setting of the painting probably was somewhere in the black country around the mining center of Karaganda. But it was not only the look of the miner or his house that made this a painting to remember. In the background the returning miner saw a vision of the face of Joseph Stalin, looking at him with pitiless eyes. This, the artist seemed to be saying, was the man who ordered you into the mine, who housed you in a shack, who wore you out in stoking the furnaces of an industrialized Russia.

As art, it was just better than amateur. Yet one stood transfixed by it, for the artist had violated still another Soviet rule. He had also painted an un-person, Stalin, whose features, once so glorified, are no longer shown. And he had proceeded to blame this un-person for the wretchedness of life.

Again we felt, as in Tbilisi, that the bureaucratic hand presses less heavily in the border regions than nearer the

Kremlin. In Moscow the subject matter would have condemned these two paintings to a storage basement.

We remember Alma Ata not just for an opera, a concert,
and two paintings, but for a dentist's chair as well. It was
one chair neither of us had planned to sit in during our
Soviet journey.

Unhappily, we are not strangers to dental clinics. We
know just what to expect. The dentist's nurse invites you
into the chair. She clips a freshly sterilized white towel
around your neck. She adjusts the cushioned headrest,
raises it and tilts it backward, and asks, "Is it comfortable?"
She fills a sterilized paper cup with water from a tiny jet
next to the chair. In the white basin below the paper cup,
water swirls and gurgles softly, round and round. The nurse
places newly sterilized picks, mirrors, and other instruments
onto the disinfected movable counter where the dentist
will work. Then, across a floor so well polished that it reflects her white dress and white shoes, she bustles off to
fetch the dentist. A loudspeaker thumps a record of something by the Tijuana Brass.

Except perhaps for the piped music, this is the scene in
dentists' offices not only in America but everywhere in the
West; not only in Canada, England, and all over Western
Europe, but also in Ceylon, Singapore, and Japan, as we
can attest from personal knowledge. In a provincial capital
of the Soviet Union, on the other hand, resemblance ends.
To paraphrase the title of a Swiss journalist's book about
France, in Russia the clocks keep different time.

How different the time, we discovered again in Alma
Ata. The agent of discovery was a tooth. It had loosened
and fallen out, leaving a hole that bled slightly. Home, and
a dentist's office, was a month in the future. It seemed prudent to ask a Soviet dentist to look at the damage and, if
necessary, deal with it.

In the Soviet Union, of course, one does not consult a

private dentist; one goes to a state dental clinic. Treatment is free for foreigners and comrades alike. So, with an intelligent interpreter, we found our way to the local clinic in the capital of the Soviet Republic of Kazakhstan. It was one of several old two-story stucco buildings that formed a medical center.

"Upstairs," said a nurse at the entrance. We climbed wooden stairs and walked down a long corridor, with bare wood floors. The walls were painted shiny black for the first four feet from the floor, light brown paint above. The door of a room on the right was open, and a smiling young nurse beckoned us inside.

Three nurses in hospital gowns clustered around. After all, foreigners don't often ask to be treated in Alma Ata, and Americans virtually never. "Sit down, please," one of them said, guiding the way to a straight high-backed chair. She didn't tilt it, raise it or swivel it, because she couldn't. All three nurses leaned forward to peer at the American dentistry inside an American mouth. This was something they had not been able to do in their training.

The patient, squaring his shoulders against the perpendicular backrest, had only a moment or two to look around him. His was the end chair in a row of three spaced across the twenty-foot room. Behind him three more chairs formed a second row. In the six-chair room, the clinic provided two dental drills, each of them bracketed to a side wall and thus servicing the two chairs nearest the wall. A high cuspidor like a standing ashtray, without running water, stood alongside the left arm of each chair. The only source of running water in the room was a basin at the back. It was reassuring to notice a shiny sterilizer at the side of the room. If the nurses had to bring instruments, they never touched them, but held them with tongs and laid them on sterilized gauze, on a table next to the patient's chair.

Less comforting was a sound from a building across the courtyard. It was the howling of animals that could only have been in pain. The building, we were told, was a laboratory used for experiments. Why the pain was necessary we did not ask. A Western doctor, to whom we later gave this sidelight on provincial Soviet medicine, bristled at the story. There is no need whatever, he said, to inflict pain on animals in experimental work. The Russians, he thought, should have enough anesthetics for this purpose.

We could not tell to what extent the Alma Ata clinic used anesthetics on its human patients. Extractions, it appeared, were done downstairs, in a room that led out to the grass-covered courtyard. Business must have been brisk down there. From the second-floor window we could see a man or woman walk out every two or three minutes, holding a sore cheek and sometimes spitting blood into the grass.

In the treatment room upstairs, the patient from America held the attention, in sequence, of three nurses, an intern, and a dentist. The young intern wore a mask over his nose and mouth; only his almond eyes suggested that he was a Kazakh. The eyes showed intelligence and compassion as he examined the patient and sized up the problem, so that he could report to his superior. Soon the dentist himself came: a slender man of about thirty-five, with a small dark mustache; not a Kazakh, although he might well have been born in cosmopolitan Alma Ata of the nineteen-thirties. He knew his job, as, indeed, all in that clinic seemed to know theirs.

"When will you be back in your country?" he asked through the interpreter.

"In about four weeks."

"There's a slight infection, and I want it to drain. So just keep it clean, rinse after every meal. It will be better to have your own dentist deal with it."

He could not have given any sounder advice. He prescribed a disinfectant rinse, and sent his grateful patient to the nearby pharmacy. Of course there was no charge. For the people in the borderlands, modern medical service is a boon, and one should never underestimate it in appraising Soviet rule.

The next stop was a pharmacy on a busy shopping street —a state pharmacy, of course, with a number instead of a proprietor's name to identify it. Our interpreter asked for the prescribed antiseptic. "Fourteen kopecks," the white-coated man behind the counter answered. While the customer paid the equivalent of fifteen cents at the cashier's desk and got a ticket in return, the pharmacist went off behind a counter twenty feet long, to find the drug.

The shelves held an array of cardboard cube boxes, each with a label. A few bottles contained drugs in powdered form. The druggist handed us an envelope with dried leaves in it. "Put a spoonful of this in a cup, pour boiling water on it, and let it cool," he said. How a traveler was to accomplish this three times a day while living in hotels or riding for days and nights on a Trans-Siberian train—this he did not explain.

In the end we settled for ordinary salt and made a salt-water solution to keep the wound clean. The clinic and the pharmacy confirmed something which we had first guessed in Leningrad—something basic in more senses than one—about the Soviet economy and Soviet life. The Soviet system provides a basic standard of living, one that supplies essentials and little more. The state permits only a few frills one can do without—and those frills are carefully selected.

In the dental clinic, for example, doctors and interns seemed to have a fundamental knowledge of dentistry. They evidently knew and practiced antisepsis, and their clinic had had the basic instruments for drilling, probing, filling. But the state which equipped and ran the clinic clearly did not consider tiled walls and shiny floors essential to bacteria-free dentistry. Nor were high-speed water-cooled drills regarded as necessary, or electric pulp testers, or electric hammers, or recorded music, or other gadgets now familiar in Western clinics. The clinic in Alma Ata gave the citizen the essentials—and cost him nothing. Why should he need anything more?

The pharmacy taught us even more than the clinic about essentials and frills. Clearly one essential is the widest possible range of drugs. As far as we could tell, the Soviet citizen now has access, even in distant Central Asia, to antibiotics, sulfa drugs, and other lifesaving preparations common in the West. Soviet laboratories produce them and pharmacies stock them. But if a drug must be taken in solution or mixed with other drugs, it is up to the patient to dissolve and mix. If boiled water is needed to insure purity, why should the state bother? Let the citizen boil it and find a sterile container for the finished product. The pharmacist sells the prescribed quantity, pours it into an envelope, and lets the citizen do the rest. The price, incidentally, is so low as to be almost a token. Nobody can bring Soviet drug makers into court for gouging. And the state cannot file antitrust proceedings against itself, the biggest monopoly on earth.

The do-it-yourself method applies, in varying degrees, to everything sold to Soviet consumers. Wrapping paper, for example, is a bourgeois luxury seldom used except in shops that cater to foreigners. Even in the GUM department store in Moscow, publicized all over the nation, you use your string bag for purchases; everyone does. Yet the Soviet Union suffers from no shortage of timber for pulp and paper products. On the contrary, the Soviet reserves of timber are nearly inexhaustible. The lack of paper bags and wrapping paper, like everything else in the Soviet economy, is part of the Plan, a conscious decision that people can get along without it, and that resources of timber, labor, and money can be applied more usefully somewhere else.

The state does, however, provide paper and string free

for one small group: those citizens and foreigners who send parcels abroad.

One day we needed to mail bulky books and pamphlets that would have overweighted our airplane baggage. Looking helpless, we asked the friendly fellow who manned the Intourist service counter:

"Where can we get some wrapping paper and string?"

"What do you need it for?"

"We'd like to mail these books to the United States."

"Oh, you won't need paper and string; just take your books to the post office, to the international parcel post counter."

We followed instructions, and they worked. A young woman took the books, opened them, and riffled through the pages. She held them upside down, shaking them. Next she took scissors, cut and wrapped paper, and cut and tied twine, all with the perfection of a professional gift wrapper. Finally she handed back the package, saying, in English, "Write the address, please."

It was a painless way of mailing a package, one that we followed habitually after discovering what the Soviet Post Office would do. Obviously, the government had not arranged it in order to make mailing easier for tourists. It was a device to prevent the concealment of money (although why anyone would send rubles out of the Soviet Union is a mystery) and to make sure that jewelry, national treasures, manuscripts, or secrets were not being exported in a book or the skirt of a toy doll.

At Alma Ata one starry midnight we strolled with the nonchalance of old travelers onto a plane that was to lift us out of Central Asia. The flight ahead of us was 1,500 miles to Irkutsk in Siberia. For part of the way we were to fly roughly parallel to the Soviet-Chinese frontier.

Sitting in a poorly insulated jet plane, a Tupolev 104 that rattled too loudly for sleep; looking out at the clear night sky, wondering which were the low-hanging stars and which the occasional lights below, we had plenty of time to reflect on the Central Asia we had left behind. Far off to our right lay a forty-six mile corridor known as the Dzungarian Gate, a gap in the mountains that separate Russian and Chinese territory. It was through this corridor that the Mongols swept westward to conquer Russia more than seven hundred years ago. Off to our left stretched what used to be the pastures of nomadic Asian tribes. Scattered through these once empty parts of Kazakhstan were raw new centers of mining and industry, evidences of Russia's modern vitality and power.

The Aeroflot hostess, eager to please, brought us a pre-dawn snack of pulpy green apples and soggy buns. They could not compete in interest with the stars outside, or with a pool of blackness below us which probably hid the Altai Mountains. Down there two and a half thousand years ago an early civilization had flourished and died. In the Hermitage Museum at Leningrad we had been shown some of its remains, preserved in ice until they were discovered in modern times: a patterned carpet, the earliest ever found; a leaping deer that was carved in wood; a contemporary-looking rider on his pony.

The Central Asian cities that lay behind us were remnants of another civilization, not yet buried but unmistakably in decline. The pond and the fountains at Bukhara, the fluted blue dome of Tamerlane's tomb, the brilliant tiles on mosques no longer used: what were these but artifacts of a vanishing past? Of the twenty-two million inheritors of those Islamic cultures, some, notably the Uzbeks, still showed energy and talent. But as nearly as we could judge, old Central Asia was being smothered by Russian settlers, Russian soldiers, Russian officials, Russian language, Russian culture, and the Russian political system. A force far stronger than Tamerlane's had moved in on Central Asia and had left it overpowered.

Dawn was just breaking over a landscape of woods and streams when our plane landed at Irkutsk. The sky was gray, the leaves and flowers gone, a hint of snow in the air. We were back in Russia, in the heart of a different kind of Russian empire: Siberia.

VIII

Irkutsk:

THE FACE OF SIBERIA, OLD AND YOUNG

*La donna a sesante anni è come
la Siberia. Ognuno sa dov'è ma
nessuno ci vuole andare.*

—Italian proverb

Before going to Siberia we came to know someone who had been born and raised there. She was a Russian lady who had fled during the Revolution, first to Harbin, then to Shanghai, and finally to Canada. Her birthplace and early home had been Irkutsk, the leading city and the cultural center of eastern Siberia. With some hesitation because of her unhappy past, we asked her to tell us about Siberia. What was it like? For a moment she could not speak. Then, her eyes filling with tears, she said, "It's beautiful, beautiful."

The answer was not just unexpected; it was beyond belief, as if Dante had reported hell as a haven of tranquillity and the devil as a dear man. How could any place with such an evil reputation be "beautiful"? The lady must have forgotten. Or else it was homesickness that gave her memories a rosy glow.

Not until we came to Siberia, not until we strolled among the carved wooden houses of old Irkutsk, stood among the pines and birches of the taiga under falling snow, watched the mountains, rivers, and rangelands slide past our Trans-Siberian train window, did we understand what she had meant. The face of Siberia which we saw is beautiful. It is also tragic.

The tragedy that scars Siberia's face is Russians' inhumanity to Russians. It went on for more than three hundred years and it is not ended yet. Not long after Siberia was added to their empire, the czars began to use it as a place of punishment. As early as 1649, exile to Siberia was incorporated into Russian law. After that the place and its name became accursed. Russian police used it to threaten the guilty and the innocent. Parents used it to frighten their children into obedience, much as English nannies in Victorian times used to invoke the dread name of Napoleon Bonaparte to warn their little charges that "Bony'll get you if you don't behave."

Siberian punishment grew into a system and finally into an institution.[1] As the prison population swelled, St. Petersburg had to create a bureau of exile administration to deal with it. That was in 1823. But eventually the Ministry of Interior took it over and handed responsibility for it to the secret police.

The bureaucracy swelled too, demanding thousands of officials, guards, and jailers, the kinds of dubious and despicable characters that prison systems seem to attract. For the first two hundred years of the system, prisoners walked to Siberia in chains. After being marshaled in St. Petersburg and Moscow, they set out in processions of several hundred, surrounded by armed guards. At night they stopped in stockaded "rest houses," a euphemism for verminous sheds heaped high with exhausted bodies. Those who survived the march were divided among sorting centers in four Siberian cities, of which the easternmost was Irkutsk.

A brick column marked the boundary between Europe and Asia. Known as the Monument of Tears, it was a symbolic Bridge of Sighs and always the scene of loud lamentation, as if beloved Russia ended here. In truth it did.

The system scooped up every kind of human being. Saints, poets, and philosophers marched to Siberia along-

[1] The literature of Siberian punishment is vast, tragic, and sometimes great. In the category of "great" we would mention one American author. He is George Kennan (1845–1924), whose two-volume masterpiece *Siberia and the Exile System* was published in 1891. He was a distant cousin of George Frost Kennan, diplomat and historian.

side murderers, degenerates, and drunkards. In theory, prisoners were divided into three categories for purposes of punishment: criminals, political criminals, and politicals. The criminals had supposedly committed ordinary crimes of violence. The political criminals were allegedly guilty of rioting, killing, or looting for political reasons. The politicals ranged from active revolutionaries to anyone the czars did not want to have around. But the walls between the categories broke down. Priests would find themselves chained to thieves as they went underground to work in gold or silver mines. When the theory worked, politicals were often allowed to live relatively free and decent lives with their families in remote towns and villages of Siberia.

The roster of politicals included most of the "best people" of European Russia, the men and women with education, ideas, skills, and creative energies, as well as social consciences. This was why the czars could not tolerate them. The politicals were the first truly cultivated people to come to Siberia. They made the towns and cities where they lived into outposts of Russian culture. Russian and Polish exiles gave Irkutsk, for example, its nineteenth-century style and melancholy beauty. They gave it a life of its own, with theaters, concerts, libraries, lecture courses, and museums. They wrote and printed dozens of literary weeklies and political tracts, which the police promptly suppressed. Like refugees of all times they gravitated into cliques, they quarreled and argued endlessly. One of them, a writer on politics and economics named Vladimir Ulyanov, got tired of the refugee mentality and exasperated with the waste of time. So he barricaded himself in his Siberian village and spent his exile years writing books and manifestoes on capitalism and Marxian dogma. But in this as in other ways, Lenin was an exception.

Often the politicals had to spend years in prison before being released to the relative freedom of exile. Coming out of mines and dark cells, they stood in the sunshine and clean air and they thought Siberia was heaven. They roamed its fields and forests. After the damp of the cell, Siberia's dry cold hardly bothered them. One of these freed prisoners was able to explore some of the wildest country of the Russian Far East. He was a young Social Democrat named Wladimir S. Woytinsky, who broke with both czarist and communist regimes and eventually came to the United States to write and teach. His memoir, *Stormy Passage*, makes the exile's love of Siberia understandable and moving. Today the Soviet authorities who are trying to people Siberia might learn from Woytinsky. They might people it with released prisoners, some of whom would think it heaven and even choose to stay there.

It is easy to overlook another part of the Siberian experience. This is the story of the settlers. There were people who actually came of their own accord, as well as the officials, prisoners, and exiles, who had no choice. Settlers were slow in coming to the empty East. Russian society was almost entirely rural, and farm people are hard to move. But there was another reason. For the first two hundred years in which Siberia was open to settlement, the bulk of Russia's peasants were serfs, chained to the land. Some were restless and land-hungry, to be sure, but they were helpless. Finally, in 1864, more than twenty million serfs got their long awaited "liberation."

The freedom they had expected, to own land and to work it independently, did not materialize. Instead, they found themselves still chained to landlords by debt and to village communes by law. Even so, the more enterprising, sometimes whole villages, uprooted themselves and moved eastward. If they came without express permission, they were called "irregulars," and these accounted for perhaps eight out of ten migrants. Irregulars got no help on the way out or on arrival. But they staked out claims to good land and set to work. Few educated Russians thought then that the illiterate serf could survive in the wilderness. But often he did survive, as an independent farmer or a tenant or a farm laborer, and Siberia began to be heard of back home as a place to live.

It was not until 1889 that the czar got around to making migration legal and helping it. After that, migrants did receive land, loans, food, and medical service of sorts. The building of the Trans-Siberian Railroad made it all relatively easy. About the start of this century, peasants were loaded into boxcars with their families, their animals, tools, and meager possessions. There were special trains of boxcars, sometimes with a clinic car attached. When regular trains began to bring business and professional people, Siberia had an almost balanced population, however small and scattered and lonely. There was one missing component: a labor force that was not only cheap but large. This the Bolshevists were about to supply.

In czarist times, prison labor had been mobilized for all kinds of heavy work. Peter used it for his capital and his navy; Nicholas II used it to build the railroad across Siberia. On the eve of World War I the Siberian prison population was said to be about thirty thousand. After the czar was overthrown in 1917, Kerensky's government ordered the release of all politicals. Lenin's government reversed the order and created a new arm of the penal system, the "corrective labor camp." How many Russians, Georgians, Ukrainians, and others disappeared into these camps will never be known. During Stalin's rule, according to one careful estimate, the average population of the camps in any one year is believed to have been about eight million. The total number of prisoners who died in the camps may have reached twenty million. Only a handful were criminals, perhaps 5 per cent. Of the remaining 95 per cent, not all were dissenters, by any means. Even good communists disappeared without a trace. The big-name Bolshevists were important enough to be put on trial. But the "little people" were simply picked up, packed into paddy wagons, crammed into cattle cars, and distributed to prison camps across the country.

The system became a business venture. The secret police was not just the jailer and executioner; it was the largest procurer and employer of forced labor in the Soviet Union. A secret police corporation called Dalstroy was put in charge of economic development in northeastern Siberia. Dalstroy's territory was three times the size of Texas, with room to spare for New York State as well. Outside its own immense territory, the police undertook to procure prison labor and to deliver it wherever it was in short supply.

Most economists maintain that this kind of labor is wasteful because it is unskilled and lacks incentive. It can also be argued that an almost unlimited supply of prison labor exactly suited the Soviet needs of the time—as long as one did not count the costs in death and degradation. The workers certainly did not lack incentive. There is plenty of testimony from survivors that prisoners worked hard, often until they dropped dead. They worked to eat. The incentive was life itself, since the meager ration was cut if a prisoner failed to meet the day's "norm." Moreover, Russia did not have many skilled workers or much heavy machinery at that time, to do the basic development that the ambitious Soviet planners wanted done. It was the kind of development that could make good use of millions of unskilled, desperate men.

In fact, these millions of bodies accomplished miracles. Their "monuments," if one can call them that, include the gold mines at Kolyma, the port built at Magadan, and the road that connects the two; the silver, nickel, and lead taken from the Kara mines, the nickel from Norilsk in the Arctic. To this day, the Kremlin has not admitted or repudiated the institution of forced labor. Yet there is evidence that the system as it existed under Stalin has been largely dismantled. The remaining camps are called "corrective labor colonies," and the number of politicals in them has been estimated at about a hundred thousand.

Who will develop Siberia now? Can it be done without forced labor? What will it cost to send out heavy machinery, attract skilled labor, and maintain it so far from the source of supplies? Before these things can happen on a major scale, must Siberia live down its reputation as a place of exile and suffering and cold?

Soviet economists have been debating the question of costs. The official propaganda has set about cleansing Siberia of its evil reputation. And the Party itself has undertaken the most difficult and by far the most interesting part of the job, from our point of view—namely, to train new generations of Russians who will consider it a privilege to work for the greater power and glory of the state, in Siberia or anywhere else.

The Soviet experiment is not without precedent. The Spartan state was able to condition its youth to serve the state, and it kept the discipline intact for two hundred years. With more time, Nazi Germany might have done it in the middle of Europe. With quite different kinds of goals, the State of Israel is fashioning a new kind of dedicated youth. The Soviet experiment has its own character, as we were to discover when we spent a morning with the Young Pioneers in Irkutsk.

Since Soviet schools are no-nonsense, six-day-a-week head-stuffing clinics, they have no time, inclination, or equipment for the extracurricular, athletic, social sides of a child's life. These are the province, instead, of the three Soviet youth organizations. Children from seven to nine are enrolled as Octobrists, named for the revolutionary month. From ten to fifteen they belong to the Young Pioneers. And the final catchall, from fifteen to twenty-eight, is the instrument of Party training known as the Komsomol.

Much as educators in the United States look on the junior high school period as formative, character-building years, Party-minded educators pin their hopes and money on the Young Pioneers. When the authorities want to flatter and upgrade an institution, they call it a Palace. So the clubhouse of the favored youth group is the Pioneer Palace all over the Soviet Union.

The Pioneer Palace of Irkutsk is one of the city's landmarks, a turn-of-the-century mansion. It was built by a merchant prince in the days when private wealth and its display were not only legal but respectable. This merchant prince let himself go. He built a palace of red and yellow bricks patterned in elaborate fretwork, with arched windows and pointed cupolas. In the fashion of the times he ordered a private chapel in decadent Orthodox. Irkutsk still treasures the mansion and expects the foreigner to stand in admiration before it. The whole house, from ballroom to servants' quarters, has been turned into classrooms, studios, and workshops. Perhaps the old merchant pioneer would not have minded seeing the palace he built for his children overrun by today's Young Pioneers.

This is where the children of Irkutsk, the ten- to fourteen-year-olds, spend their free time, which amounts to perhaps three to five hours a week. The house is in use both mornings and afternoons because the schools are overcrowded and many of them have to operate on two-session schedules.

The young directress of the Pioneers greeted us warmly. She was brisk, fortyish, and had a light of dedication in her eyes. She laughed when we asked whether membership in the Young Pioneers was voluntary. "You foreigners, you love to ask that question. Of course it is voluntary, and of course all the children belong. How could they not? It is so wonderful, they could not bear to be left out. If their parents should forbid . . . but why should they?" She led us into a choral class. The children in their pinafores and red scarves (the symbol of the Pioneers) lifted their faces to the music teacher's wand. Such wholesome young faces! They sang out, lustily, a hymn to Lenin. The gist of it, in rough translation, would be, "Lenin is my shepherd, I shall not want." In the shop, boys of about fourteen were assembling models of planes and racing cars under the teacher's supervision. In the old ballroom a class in traditional ballet was under way with an elderly woman playing the Nutcracker music on an upright piano. The little girls were doing their exercises at the bar, and when we came in they gave us a special performance of the classic pre-Bolshoi steps and twirls. A class in drawing and painting was making Socialist-Realist copies of a very green mug and very red apple, in watercolors.

With particular pride, the directress allowed us to audit a leadership class. Near the age at which they graduate from Pioneers into Komsomols, some of the boys and girls are picked for their leadership potential and given special indoctrination and training. Pioneer social clubs and athletic teams are the proving grounds for spotting leadership material. So are the summer camps and work programs that take some twenty million children to farms and forests during the short summers.

One wonders what the Boy and Girl Scouts and these Pioneers would think of one another, and whether they would sense the differences in their training. We saw a basic difference, even in the brief exposure that our visit to the Pioneer Palace allowed us. It was the difference in the approach of authority to the child, and in the child's response to authority. These Russian children—for most Irkutsk children are Russian—"took" it, but they did not give it back as children are usually encouraged to do in the American system, and do whether they are encouraged or not. These Russian children seemed to us docile, well behaved, disciplined, and unaware even of the possibility of initiative.

We walked out into the tree-lined vistas of old Irkutsk in a somber mood.

There are, of course, no private schools in the Soviet Union. The state is the sole educator. In this planned society the education system is the economic servant of the Plan, and the political servant of the Party. The schools and universities must, as we have said, produce an adequate work force. When the Plan calls for the construction of nineteen new dams, as it did in 1969, the schools must turn out the mechanics, engineers, and scientists to build and man them. Furthermore, the workers must be motivated by their schooling, to go where they are needed, whether in Siberia or Kazakhstan or Moscow. Their education involves service to the state anywhere and at any time; this they must accept without question. For the citizen who is properly conditioned, no conflict can exist between his personal wishes and those of the state.

The teaching of work habits and attitudes starts in kindergarten. Children learn to follow instructions, to obey, and to work and play in teams. Vocational training begins early in grade school, where mathematics and elementary science command the highest prestige and rewards. The humanities go comparatively unsung, which makes sense for the national purposes of economic planning. How else could the Soviets have forged their way to the top as a military and industrial power? To accept authority, learn an approved skill, and put it at the service of the state—these are the priority goals for every child. The state tries to enlist parents as allies in conditioning children toward these goals, but without much conviction. Too many parents are themselves in need of conditioning.

Could a heavier load be put on a relatively new education system? It would seem not, but the Soviet system has an even greater responsibility: the political education of children for service to the Party. For this, as we have said, the primary instruments are the three youth organizations. Their mission is nothing less than the creation of a New Soviet Man. The Communist Party has on its drawing board a new order of human being.

The idea has appeal. The human race could do with a new model. It is an old concept. Jesus made heroic efforts in that direction, with results that are still not conclusive. What could have been more revolutionary then, or now, than the ethic of nonviolence, the turning of the other cheek? The Lord Buddha had also tried to suggest a purer version of man by his personal example.

Lenin, it will be remembered, had little faith in the old model of Russian man. He doubted that his countrymen, as he knew them, could create a socialist system and then an ideal communist society. Nikolai Berdyaev, a Russian philosopher who defied both the czars and the Bolshevists, maintained that "Lenin did not believe in man. He recognized in him no sort of inward principle; he did not believe in spirit and freedom of the spirit, but he had boundless faith in the social regimentation of man. He believed that a compulsory social organization could create any sort of man you like: for instance, a completely social man who would no longer need the use of force." To fashion a "completely social" New Soviet Man, the Bolshevists are not gambling on eugenics, as Hitler proposed doing in his search for a pure Nordic hero. They believe they can shape human behavior with their power tools. The tools on which they rely most heavily are the youth organizations.

Watching the Pioneers as they sang their hymn to Lenin was, for us, an unsettling experience. We knew we were in on the making of the New Soviet Man. The Pioneer age-group would seem to be especially malleable for this purpose.

At fifteen, the Komsomol organization takes over. The Party looks mainly to the Komsomol ranks for its leadership and cadres. It carries on a high-powered recruiting campaign, picturing the Komsomol as the ideal of Soviet youth. A Komsomol leader is more than any other Russian the model of a New Soviet Man. The term applies to both sexes, since Russian communism admits of no weaker sex.

If you expect to be jostled by a New Soviet Man on Moscow's Gorky Street or in Kiev's subway, you may be disappointed. He is still rare, still in production. But you can see the production process at work and discover what kind of person he is meant to be. Our portrait of him will be faulty but it will try to do him justice. For who is wise enough to scoff at any attempt to make a better man?

New Soviet Man is first and foremost a believer. Like many familiar words, this one calls for definition. A visitor to the Soviet Union should not be surprised if he is asked, "Are you a believer?" The question startled us for a moment. Did it mean, "Are you disciples of Lenin?" The clue came quickly when the questioner added, "If you are a believer, it goes hard with you here." He meant, it appeared, a believer in the Christian, Jewish, or Moslem God. The good communist claims to be an unbeliever but the claim does not bear inspection. So solidly is belief built into the character of New Soviet Man that he would perish, both physically and spiritually, without it. He accepts the creed of Lenin as absolute truth, the Party as its sole spokesman, teacher, and interpreter. He reveres Lenin himself as the only perfect man, as "the way." He obeys the clergy, in the persons of the Party apparatus. He acts out his role, both public and private, as revealed to him by the Party's propaganda arm, Agitprop, the society for the propagation of the faith. To live by this faith is to reach a new level of human perfection. The very promise has miraculous overtones.

How much of this is new? How does the new Russian differ from his great-grandfather, who was among the most docile if not the most hopeful of believers? Great-grandfather, if he belonged to the masses, revered the czar.

He obeyed the czar's messengers, the Orthodox clergy; he feared the police, the czar's agents. New Soviet Man does not have to leap very far from the old framework of belief into the new. Like his forebears he believes in the greatness of Mother Russia, in her mission to lead the world. But in other important ways his world view has shifted. Although Russia is still surrounded by enemies, and her territory is in danger of being violated, today's villains are not power-hungry invaders like Genghis Khan and Napoleon. They are crusaders of rival religions. But New Soviet Man knows that his own religion has missionaries working almost everywhere, and that it will triumph in the end. For it is the only true faith.

New Soviet Man's faith differs from that of his ancestors in other respects. He is a worker. Work has a virtue of its own; to work for the state is to translate the Leninist creed into action. A special virtue attaches to manual labor. Whether they belong to the Komsomol or not, young people are expected to go out to the farms to dig potatoes and harvest other crops each year. But in this field of action, the Party is building trouble as well as socialism. A Soviet geographer, Dr. V. V. Pokshishevsky, predicts that by the year 2000 "all types of hard manual labor will have disappeared." They will no longer be needed, he says, because the country will be totally electrified, and the implication is that this is a good thing. Will the Party then have to look for a moral equivalent of manual labor? Or will the infusion of socialist faith have been completed?

As the New Soviet Man gives his working life, so he gears his private life to what the state expects of him. According to the conventional wisdom, what is best for the building of socialism is best for him. New Soviet Man knows, for example, that the state expects him to marry and have as many children as he can afford. Does not the state provide marriage palaces, and a wedding ceremony under the portrait of Lenin himself? Does it not honor its most prolific

women with the title of Mother Heroine, and lesser con-
tenders with the Order of Motherhood Glory? Does it not
bestow practical incentives such as allowances and living
space for children? In return, New Soviet Man will raise
his children in the faith, and if they should turn out badly
he will accept full responsibility. His marriage will weather
every storm, for he knows that the state frowns on divorce.

The state also expects every good socialist to keep himself physically fit. How otherwise can he make his full contribution to the building of socialism? This calls for both
time and thought. As a start, New Soviet Man will take
part in the daily programs of calisthenics for which the
state broadcasts radio programs with music each morning.
These programs can be heard over the loudspeakers in
streets and parks, as well as in homes and places of work.
But health means more than daily exercise; it demands a
way of life. The state encourages various kinds of wholesome recreation. New Soviet Man is fond of sports, both
as a spectator and a participant. If he is a city man, he will
spend his afternoon off yelling for the home football team
in the new sports arena. Otherwise he will sit at a television
set at home or in a café. He himself can join in team sports
through his union or club. If he wants to commune with
the great outdoors, he can hike, camp, fish, hunt, ski, or just
take his sleeping bag into the woods. He can go mountain
climbing in the Caucasus, among stunning snow-capped
peaks. Better still, he can spend his holiday at a southern
resort, and even laze in the sun on a beach. All these forms
of recreation the state smiles upon as health-building, and
more.

Workers find a variety of vacation tours open to them,
state-sponsored and usually in groups. Never has internal
tourism flourished as it does today. Busloads of farmers from
collectives in the Ukraine, Moldavia, and even further
afield pour through the Kremlin museums and the Hermitage. Boatloads sail down the Volga, the Dnieper, and the

Don. Group tours flood the Soviet cities and even trickle into the bloc countries across the borders. But to attain the heart's desire of most Russians, to travel in what they call the "imperialist world"—that is still reserved for the Party elite, who are few. Such tours are rare, but we encountered one cruising the Mediterranean. And we heard of another touring, of all countries, Portugal, the last of the colonial overlords (excepting only Russia itself). If a day comes when the state offers world tours to its working masses, on that day we can assume that socialism has been built to last.

Meanwhile, Russians do not lack for things to do and see, provided they can find time and money. Being both melancholy and pleasure-loving, they find solace in drink, and this the state does not deny them. New Soviet Man knows he is free to enjoy wines and beer, but not hard liquor. The state deplores the people's love of spirits. Nonetheless it has not taken vodka and brandy off the market. Nor has it campaigned against smoking, which is a widespread habit. To summarize the guidelines, we would say that New Soviet Man pursues a clean life, and rejects a "sweet" life. He knows that such things as pin-ups of nude women and the striptease "carry an extremely well-concealed ideological burden" which is designed "to draw youth away from the embrace of communism." We quote a Party spokesman for manners and morals.

The New Soviet Man welcomes the embrace of communism, and shoulders ideological burdens that would stagger an ordinary person. His work and play, his code of morality, even his personal health, are loaded with Lenin's messages as the Party interprets them.

Health in the Soviet Union carries a special public message that has no counterpart outside the socialist world. It is a duty to the state. Illness is antisocial. Now we are in a kind of Erewhonian dreamland, in which illness is

crime and crime is illness. Political dissenters are sometimes consigned to mental institutions and "correction"
colonies, as if they were suffering from schizophrenia or
clubfeet. When Russians asked us about the most remarkable of defectors, Stalin's daughter, the questioning invari-
ably ended with their shaking their heads and saying, "She
is sick, sick." Capitalism is sick. In the stock cartoon, the
rich man is unhealthily bloated, the worker starved.

At the other extreme the symbols of socialism glow with
health. How do we know? They surround us. To miss their
message, we would have to shut our eyes and ears, plug
our synapses. One of the favorite symbols, next to Lenin
himself, is a monument called The Worker and the Woman
Collective Farmer. We met it first in Moscow, outside the
National Economics Achievement Exhibition. We stood
dwarfed beneath the figures of a man and a woman striding
into the future. Theirs is the kind of stride that can be made
only with seven-league boots. The man holds aloft a hammer, the woman a sickle. They are cast in stainless steel.
They are fourteen times human size and they weigh
seventy-five tons. How does a piece of stainless steel express health? The torsos are heroic, the limbs massive. So
dynamic is their well-being that you cannot imagine these
two having even a simple sniffle.

We have walked many miles through city streets, stopping to examine wall posters, photographs, and murals,
getting acquainted with socialist over-achievers. They may
be athletes, or astronauts, engineers, scientists, winners of
prizes in production and technology. We wander through
galleries contemplating Socialist Realism in art. There is a
sameness of subjects: men and women on scaffoldings,
building socialism; men and women in fields, harvesting it.
They glow with health; the potatoes and apples and sheaves
of wheat are without blemish. Pests breed only in capitalist
fields. This is not a joke; it is ideology. In the early years of
Czech communism, Czechoslovakia's potato crop was in-

fested with the common potato bug. The regime formally protested to the American embassy, accusing the United States of having sprayed capitalist bugs onto socialist soil.

Of all the goals set for New Socialist Man, health may be the hardest to attain. Soviet medicine shows the effects of confinement in a relatively closed world. Under state discipline, medical science has one foot planted in the twenty-first century, in outer space, to be exact. But the other foot is still mired in the nineteenth century. You can see this either as a gap or a stride. Either way, it enables foreigners with medical interests to find in Russia almost anything they are looking for, anything from the newest in equipment and practice to the most antiquated. For an example of antiquated medicine, you can go to Stalin's deathbed. The account of his last hours, as reported by one who was there, namely his daughter, tells us Stalin's doctors "were applying leeches to his neck and the back of his head, making cardiograms, and taking X-rays of his lungs. . . . An artificial respiration machine had been brought from one of the medical research institutes. Some young doctors had come with it, since no one else had the faintest idea how to work it."

Soon after Stalin's death, the Soviet Union began to offer loans and technical aid to poorer countries of Asia and Africa. In Cambodia we found a Russian team putting the finishing touches on what was to be an ultramodern hospital. And indeed it was. The plans called for the newest of gadgets, including a cobalt treatment laboratory with closed-circuit television, and an air-conditioned surgical wing.

The state's concern about health is exceeded only by that of ordinary Russians. Whether they are reacting to propaganda or hypochondria we do not know. But the Russian prizes his physical well-being as the Greeks prized beauty and the early Jesuits salvation. Sometimes he seems to overdo it. A European friend of ours tells of riding in a

Russian train and falling into conversation with his seat-mate. The Russian turned to him and asked, "What is your blood pressure?" Our friend said he did not know.

"What? You don't know your own blood pressure?" Well, he had probably heard it when he had his last checkup a year ago. But he didn't remember.

"Imagine that. Perhaps you should see a doctor. I must tell you that mine was 190 over ninety this morning. And yesterday it was 200 over 110. I ought to be home in bed."

In the search for well-being, Russians preserve their own counterparts of the European spa. Each year they assemble in the Caucasus Mountains and by the sea to take cures and drink waters. They throng the mountain resorts of Kislovodsk, Yessentuki, Pyatigorsk, and Zheleznovodsk, whose mineral springs are recommended for "circulatory, respiratory, alimentary, and metabolic disorders." They swarm the shores of the Black Sea, at Yalta and Sochi, in search of cures for "diseases of the nervous system, heart, and blood vessels," as well as motor disorders, skin and gynecological ailments. What could be more bourgeois? We are wrong. The state itself maintains the resorts and recommends the waters, which means that they are not only salubrious but socialist as well. Why should not workers take cures, drink waters, mingle with fellow sufferers, exchange symptoms, and compare medical histories?

Disease has other uses. It can be a leveler, as we were to learn one morning in the Russian provinces. We had arrived cold and hungry at a hotel where our room had been reserved and paid for in advance. The manageress stonily refused to have us. Her excuse was that the hotel had been fully booked by official delegations. (In fact, it was half empty, and her refusal to take us in remains a mystery.) At last she relented and released an attic room, without a bath. It was five flights up, and the hotel had no elevator. At this point, one of us remarked, "Well, you'd better reserve a bed in a clinic if I am going to have to

climb five flights of stairs three times a day." The face of
the manageress sagged with concern. "You have a heart
condition?" We had only to nod. Within two minutes she
had found us a suite with a bath on the second floor. The
state assures free medical services to foreign visitors, as
well as to its own people. No good Party Woman, and she
was clearly one, would care to involve herself in landing
a foreigner in a scarce clinic bed.

For us, one of the most ineffable qualities of the ideal
New Soviet Man is his indifference to wealth. According
to the Party blueprint, he is an unacquisitive man.

Is there such a man? In the Judeo-Christian, the Bud-
dhist, and the Hindu cultures, among others, there have
been ascetics. But they have usually been deeply religious
or mad or both. They have stood out on the landscape,
incongruous and lonely. The Marxist-Leninist state has not
just one such man in view, but a whole society of unacquisitive men. They will belong in the landscape, the
socialist environment that Lenin planned. They will be as
natural to it as the acquisitive man is to New York or Paris
or Calcutta.

This experiment in shaping human nature by means of
environment may well be the most daring of all Soviet
enterprises. To the capitalist man, looking in, the Soviet
experiment seems improbable and unlikely to succeed. He
may be wrong. It just may happen—in Russia.

The state holds title to every inch of Soviet territory, all
eight million square miles of it. It owns everything under
the land and water, everything, that is, except the stray
trout or carp that a fisherman may hook. It owns the forests
and the crops, with one small exception. Farmers may grow
flowers, fruits, and vegetables in their state-owned backyards, and either enjoy them or sell them in "free" markets.
There is only one entrepreneur: the state, down to the last
little hole-in-the-wall repairer of jewelry or watches or

shoes, who is a licensed employee, not a businessman. The
state pays each worker what it estimates he is worth. Out
of the total resources of the nation, the state allocates for
labor only what it decides it can spare.

The Soviet system, in other words, is forever stacked
against the accumulation of money and goods by its citizens, deliberately stacked. New Soviet Man, if he leads a
clean life (early to bed and early to rise) can expect to be
healthy and even wise. But he will never be wealthy. This
is not to say that he is condemned forever to the threadbare economy in which he now lives. Indeed, the men who
took Stalin's place in the Kremlin have all promised the
workers a better deal and a more comfortable life. Slowly
and sometimes, it would seem, grudgingly, the state has
been delivering on that promise. A city dweller may look
forward to buying a television set or a small refrigerator,
which will mercifully save him from the tyranny of daily
food shopping. He can even dream of someday buying a
small car, on the installment plan.

A Soviet citizen can bequeath his possessions to his children. And if he manages to save some money as well, he
can will to them perhaps as much as a thousand dollars.
Anything more than this risks an official investigation as
illegal gain. In addition to which the state assures a steady
job, pensions, free medical service, cheap vacations, and
sports. Why should any Russian ask for more?

To anyone raised in a system of private enterprise, the
question can only sound absurd. Why should anyone not
ask for more and get more if he can? The idea of putting a
brake on the pursuit of goods, a ceiling on accumulation
of wealth, is nothing short of heresy. But in a society engaged in the building of Marxist-Leninist socialism, the
question makes sense. Furthermore, it is crucial. To ask
continually for more is to endanger the goals of the society.
And so the system puts a ceiling on private wealth, and it

encases its people in a kind of economic ice pack or permafrost.

This is a world free from private investment, private enterprise, private profits, and private competition. Outsiders may find it hard to imagine such a world.

To experience it is to discover a new freedom: freedom from commercial advertising. There is little in the newspapers, magazines, radio, television, billboards, or in the morning mail to suggest that the state, the sole producer, has anything to sell in the way of goods or services. It follows that the citizen is rarely urged to buy. (The state occasionally announces sales of surplus goods or single items, but the response is cool.) Thus the consumer's life is tranquil, or bleak, depending on how you look at it. Nobody tempts him with rare bargains or cries of "you-get-you-get." Nobody pelts him with claims that "It's new, it's quicker, it's more." Nobody assaults his pocketbook with special offers that expire a week hence or ten-day trials with money back.

Nobody advises him how to impress a neighbor or seduce a mate. This is a world devoid of public incitement to private sex. Aeroflot, the Soviet airline, does not proclaim that its hostesses are "delectable dishes" who will do anything to please you. No Russian cigarette is touted with the sly double entendre, "It's what's up front that counts." Soviet shipping lines are not in the habit of luring passengers with "Getting there is half the fun." If Russia should become a car-oriented society (which Khrushchev said he would prevent) we doubt that a new model will be christened Fury or Cougar or that red banners would urge drivers to "Put a tiger in your tank." So far as we know, no division of Agitprop is figuring out how to play on Soviet man's pride in sexual potency or fear of impotence as a technique of salesmanship.

If without advertising or incitement or guidance Soviet man still burns with the fever to buy, the state has other

ways of cooling him. To buy a single item—a pound of
salt, for example—involves three operations and means
waiting in three queues. The buyer must bring the packag-
ing with him in the form of a string bag or brief case. Whatever he buys he must carry home in the bus or subway.
And when he finally gets it home, he must find a place to
put it. The new apartments, for all their advantages in
privacy, are still crowded places. Their official architects
deliberately failed to provide space for things. Those who
designed them had never heard, or chose not to have heard,
of built-in clothes closets, kitchen cupboards or shelves,
storage attics, and basements.

Naturally, the narrow entrance halls are cluttered with
brooms and baby carriages. This is a subject for complaints
and jokes in *Krokodil,* a weekly magazine of Russian wit
and wisdom. For example, it cartoons the new prefabricated apartment house with a crane just swinging one unit
into place. The unit is complete with outside balcony, and
as the balcony swings upward it is already crammed with
skis, bed-rolls, a go-cart, a bicycle, and other things this
acquisitive tenant spent his rubles for without thinking of
where he would put them. As long as the state produces
cars mainly for official, not for private use, it has the means
to damp down expectation and demand. It has only to
keep the roads in lamentable condition, to limit filling stations, spare parts, and mechanics' services, and to continue
building apartment houses without garages or parking
space.

In the face of so many discouragements, one might expect
the Russian to be a listless consumer. So far as we can tell,
he is not. Indeed, he seems tireless and resourceful in the
use of his two feet and his grapevine. His feet take him on
endless looking-hikes. Never have we seen people plodding
so doggedly through shops. There would seem to be no
time of day when the stores are relatively uncrowded—food
stores, bookstores, commission shops for secondhand cloth-

ing and household goods, children's department stores, general department stores, and free markets. How working people find the time for so much milling around we have not been able to discover. There are, of course, practical incentives. Something new and exciting may have come in from abroad or come out of the state's industrial plan. So it is that people on looking-hikes often end up in endless queues. In foreign countries we make a habit of joining queues just to find out what is at the end of them. In Russia it might be an outdoor fruit stand, where whatever happens to be in season is on sale: crates of tiny blue plums that make jam, small pears, peaches, and even baskets of grapes from Georgia. An old woman weighs out a kilo on request; you wrap them in newspaper and stuff them in the string bag you have brought along.

No queue is longer or more patient than the Saturday morning line at newsstands. It culminates, if you are early, in a copy of *Nedelia*, the weekly edition of *Izvestia*. It is a twenty-four-page magazine of tabloid size, containing feature stories, pictures, fashion news, and food hints. It is easy to understand its popularity if one has been exposed to the bleakness of the daily papers. *Nedelia* is an example of the lengths to which advertising can go in the Soviet press. In one issue it runs two advertisements. One is an appeal to read it and its sister publications. The other is a three-line "personal" at the bottom of page twenty-two which tells about the recording "of a gay concert for schoolchildren," price thirty kopeks, about 33 cents.

Russians rely also on the grapevine to save time and shoe leather. How the word passes around we do not know, but it has the power to unleash a small stampede. On a rainy morning in Alma Ata we took part in one. Something was happening outside the city's main department store. The police were there in force, trying not to break it up but to organize it. They failed. Somewhere in the crowd there lurked a queue. We found it and joined it. It led to a row of outdoor stalls piled high with boxes. Those who reached the stalls emerged in triumph holding the boxes above their heads. On the rim of the crowd people gathered around to examine the prizes. They were children's boots of green or red cotton felt. And they were part of a shipment from Czechoslovakia, which is known to make sturdier and more stylish footwear than anything produced in the Soviet Union. To our critical eyes, they did not seem worth stampeding about or worth the six rubles they cost per pair. Which shows how mistaken an outsider can be. Within an hour at least a hundred pairs had been sold.

What was to be learned from this small fire in the consumer permafrost? Was it because good shoes are in short supply here? Does it show a natural acquisitiveness in the citizens of Alma Ata? Or was it an example of consumer discrimination? Some Russians have in fact begun to discriminate between good and shoddy merchandise. For a time they rejected television sets that were faulty and suggested that the factory name be imprinted on all sets, so that they could choose. This incident was seized upon by American business as a vindication of brand names and advertising. It fortified one side of a continuing argument about human nature and its acquisitive impulses.

In this argument, one school of thought maintains that a baby comes into the world with a kind of Sears Roebuck catalogue of potential needs and wants imprinted on his subconscious. Going far beyond his mother's milk and disposable diapers, it lists in invisible ink every conceivable desire from babyhood to age, down to the senior citizen's condominium apartment he will buy in Florida. In a free enterprise society, it is the role of industry, salesmanship, and advertising to decipher felt and unfelt human needs, to produce the appropriate goods and services, and to alert the citizen to their qualities. Thus private enterprise is said to serve humanity and build a fully employed and ever more prosperous nation.

Where this process goes on, there is a perpetual revolution of rising expectations welling up from the grass roots and demanding something more and something new. As expectations rise, consumers will logically covet not two shades of lipstick, but thirty, not five breakfast cereals but fifty. They will greet with delight new styles that make pointed shoes look right and the old round-toed ones seem odd. Men's ties will be alternately wide and narrow, each banishing the other from the market and the neck. Industry just interprets and provides what Mr. Consumer carries around in his subconscious catalogue of wants.

So goes the argument. Perhaps we have oversimplified it, but we do not exaggerate. It is expressed each day in advertisements such as the recent full page in the two leading papers of Washington, D.C.: "At last! New Milk Cartons you'll be proud to bring to your table . . . all in the new pastel colors that complement your home . . ." How could industry have been so derelict as not to know that pastel cartons had been churning around among the unmet subconscious needs of the American family? At last the wants are met, and thus the society attains its perpetual motion, from demand to investment to employment to production to profits and wealth and advertising, and thence to more demand.

Another school of thought regards this view of human nature as nonsense. Man, it says, has basic wants, and what he considers basic at any time depends on his environment. Once he reaches the point of having these wants satisfied, then his additional desires must be devised by his industrial society. It is not the consumer but industry and advertising that are said to foment a revolution of rising expectations. This revolution puts man on a treadmill, pursuing money. Rarely does he accumulate enough of it to fill all the needs that are being created for him and dangled before his eyes. He cannot be allowed to falter in his race for money and possessions. If he does, the apparatus that invents, makes, and sells things will collapse and bury him in the wreckage. But why should anyone falter so long as his society sets a value on personal wealth and honors him for acquiring it?

Lenin took this view of man's malleable nature and turned it upside down for his own purposes. Believing that environment could shape man, he set out to create an environment and a man that had not been seen in the modern world. Russia was to be made into a great industrial power and Russians were to share the wealth but not to covet it. For Lenin feared that if his people ever got onto a treadmill in pursuit of personal fortunes and things, their energies would be lost to the pursuit of socialism.

In one way, Lenin's blueprint for a noncovetous social man had a better chance of coming alive than Marx's ever had. When Marx looked forward to the rising of the exploited workers, he thought of England and Prussia, where every underpaid factory hand could see other people enjoying the fruits of his labor. Lenin's revolution upset the Marxian timetable. It took over a country which had only begun to industrialize.

Where was the embattled proletariat on which Marx relied? Most Russians—eight out of ten—were country people, peasants mired in poverty and ignorance of the world. They had never smelled factory smoke or the open sewers of factory workers' slums. Only a few had sniffed the aroma of affluence or even of bourgeois well-being. The grievances of the masses of Russians were against landlords, not slumlords. Lenin had the luck to catch his people before modern capitalism caught them, before most of them had even imagined such things as modern European housing, plumbing, mass-produced clothing, gadgets, cosmetics, and patent medicines, not to mention cars. When Stalin mobilized the peasant-workers for his own industrial revolution, he put them onto his own treadmill, geared to the pursuit of social wealth and national glory. There they are today, and there we should be able to find the new unacquisitive man, at least in the making.

He is new and he has lost some of his innocence. The rural-urban balance has shifted. Now a little more than half the people live in towns and cities. Almost everybody can read and write, although the content of literacy varies widely between city and country. Most people can hear and read about what goes on in their own brave new world and even some of the things that happen outside, carefully selected and shaped for them.

How well has the socialist inoculation taken? It is all too easy for the foreign observer to apply his own standards and to come out with quick answers. For example, a stranger who comes to Moscow and Leningrad and sees the hordes of shoppers is likely to say, "Russians are the most acquisitive people on earth." How comforting to find that Russians are really just like everybody else! But he is wrong. He assumes that people here look at things in order to buy them, and have the money to pay for them; that they can buy things quickly and easily. Both assumptions are wrong. Finally, he fails to understand that in their gray lives, shopping is more fun than most other diversions, that it is an escape from cramped living quarters and a release from other frustrations.

What about the infatuation of city people with automobiles? This, too, strikes the foreigner. One of the few luxuries that Russians can permit themselves is to dream about what is clearly unattainable. For a vast majority, cars are in this category. There is, for example, a cartoon in *Krokodil* of a dear old gaffer daydreaming in his rocking chair. And what is the vision that puts an impish smile on his face? It is the Russian notion of the true capitalistic car, a 1922 town car on which the chauffeur sits out front in the rain. This floats in a balloon over the old man's head and he is not —repeat, not—a good socialist for dreaming of such a thing. But, then, what can you expect of the older generation?

We saw another version, a rather touching one, of the car fantasy on a sunny morning in Samarkand. We were sitting on a bench in the Park of Culture and Rest near where an official of the park had left his small Moskvich car. It nestled, new and creamy, under a tree, a lovely status symbol. A Russian family came swinging down the walk. The young mother, who was in the lead, spied the car and stopped. Then she impulsively ran to it and stroked its body. "Hold it," called her husband and pulled a camera out of his pocket. The woman posed, proud and smiling, her hand on the hood of the car, as if to say, "It's mine, so you see . . ." Click went the camera from a variety of angles. Then the two children posed in turn, after which they all laughed and swung on down the path. Somehow the incident took us back to old studio pictures, in which our grandparents had posed against unlikely backgrounds such as the Pyramids or the Matterhorn, dream places they knew they would never see.

While the Russian-made car is a familiar improbability, the foreign model has the exotic feel of a flying saucer. Anyone who has lived in Moscow knows the crowds that collect around diplomatic cars when they are not moving. Outside our hotel, somebody habitually parked a new black Buick LeSabre. It was the center of constant admiration and speculation about its value. "At least twenty thousand dollars" was one guess. "Not a penny under twenty-five thousand" was another. We curbed the impulse to cut in with, "No, it may have cost four thousand dollars, and not more than five." Then a voice, obviously beamed at us, whispered in English, "You people should bring in a hundred of these cars and scatter them around the country. They need to have the conceit taken out of them." It came from a Dutch businessman standing just behind us, and he spoke with venom.

Russians fly into space and they may yet land on the moon. But their rulers have deliberately avoided putting them behind a gasoline engine on the ground. We know of no other society that has so aggressively pushed industry and science, and at the same time so obstinately refused to become car-oriented. Since the economy is totally planned, we must assume that this decision was made in the Kremlin, and deliberately sustained over more than forty years. The reasons must have been cogent.

Could the American example have influenced them? Khrushchev, we know, looked down on Washington from a helicopter in an afternoon rush hour and saw the streams of bumper-to-bumper traffic. At which he is reported to have said, "Not for us," or words to that effect. His words hold today, despite the publicity about the new Fiat works on the Volga, with their planned output of two thousand cars a day. Even if that target is attained and added to the past claim of 170,000 cars a year, the sum total will not bring more than a small percentage of Russians within sight of a family car.

We dwell on this seeming eccentricity of Soviet planning because it has become a kind of bench mark in foreign minds of how the socialist experiment will eventually turn out. One premise is that if Russians go car mad, socialism will suffocate in the fumes of the gasoline engine. Just look at the directions in which the automobile has pushed and twisted American society. Observe, for example, the car as an escape hatch: children escaping from parental authority, youth from sex inhibitions, criminals from the law; the car as a braggart of personal power; the car as a killer of foolish and innocent people; and finally the car as a cunning detonator of the acquisitive passion.

If this kind of picture of the car-oriented society influenced the men in the Kremlin, who can say that their decision does not make sense from the socialist point of view? After all that their experiment has risked and suffered, why should they expose it to the whims of a buzz-box with a bad breath?

It is not easy to find Americans, even experts on the Soviet Union, who take the idea of an unacquisitive man seriously. It is supposed to be contrary to human nature. Whose human nature? Is human nature the same the world over? Or do Americans tend to identify human nature with their own ways and beliefs? As sane an authority as Ruth Benedict, the anthropologist, said that all peoples do; that human nature is not locked in the germ cell but results from conditioning, social habits, culture in the anthropological sense. Not all the social scientists agree with her; many do. And we who are not scientists at all are inclined to agree.

This is not to deny that man has basic instincts, such as in the search for food. But when it comes to food, "human nature" can be anything—from the wild children found living with animals in the forest on nuts and berries, to the Frenchman who assumes that wine with his dinner is simply "human nature." Aristotle insisted that the institution of slavery was inherent in human nature. Some people, he said, are born to be slaves, others to be free. Plato disagreed. And so the argument has gone for centuries until the weight of evidence seems to be slanting it toward the side we take. The record of this century has shown how easily man can be conditioned. After seeing New Soviet Man in the making, we ourselves take him seriously. We would be foolish not to. There is nothing in the Soviet system to preclude a Soviet human nature that puts social values ahead of personal wealth. Just give the Kremlin another fifty years of shutting out the acquisitive idea, the expectation of getting and having things. Who can say that it will not have made a new and unacquisitive man?

When we were asked if we would like to visit an aluminum plant outside Irkutsk, we showed only the mildest interest. The plant was fairly new, having been finished in 1964, and therefore a specimen of Siberia's modern industry. But there was much else to see and do in the Irkutsk area, and tramping through factories was not what we had come for. We did agree, just to be agreeable.

On a conducted tour we learned how aluminum is made, and concluded that when you have seen one ingot you have seen them all. More profitable for us was a by-product of the tour. We got acquainted for the first time with a New Soviet Man, and we learned a little of how he was made.

He was the chief technologist—Americans probably would call him the chief engineer—of a plant employing four thousand workers. For some obscure reason this busy man had been delegated to receive two American tourists and give them three hours of his time. We used some of the time to discover by what processes a man so young—he was only thirty-two—had climbed to so high a rung on the Soviet industrial ladder.

Sitting at the head of a long polished table in the management office, he looked the part of a New Soviet Man: light-haired, clear-eyed, stocky, and fit. His answers to our questions showed him to be intellectually fit as well, one of the brightest Russians we had met. He seemed dedicated in a way that only a true believer could be.

Since Russians do not mind direct questions, we were able to draw him out about his own career. He told us he had been born and schooled in the Ukraine. When the Nazis invaded and devastated his homeland he was only six. Yet if the war had scarred his childhood physically or emotionally, he did not show it.

"Why did you come to Siberia?" was a natural question.

"They asked me to come here, to help in building this plant," he said. "That was only a temporary job, but I liked it. I took night courses at the polytechnic in Irkutsk, and I got my degree. And I decided to stay.

"Last year I got an offer of a good job back in the Ukraine," he went on. "The pay would have been better, but I didn't take it. The Ukraine isn't as good as this. When things get me down around here, I take my sleeping bag into the taiga. That's where I'm happy."

A portrait of Leonid Brezhnev looked down on us from the office wall. This suggested the next question:

"If you were in Mr. Brezhnev's place—if you could order whatever you needed for this factory, and get it without anyone stopping you—what would you do?"

The young man liked the question. He looked pleased for a moment, then serious. Perhaps nobody had ever asked him just that, and he had never dared to imagine himself in Brezhnev's shoes. He answered with a frankness that did him credit:

"First, I would get this factory a supply of properly trained labor. Some of the engineers they send me don't know a thing about production and management. I've had to start a training school for them. I had to get a professor from the polytechnic to teach them at night.

"Second, I would see that this plant gets the materials it needs. I mean materials for the factory buildings, and for the workers' apartments. Nobody seems to understand that a new factory with its own machine shop and housing needs all kinds of machine tools and spare parts."

The chief engineer talked easily and well, through an interpreter, of course. He seemed to understand our questions, but preferred to have them interpreted, thus giving himself more time to reflect. He explained why the plant happened to be where it was, deep in the heart of Asia. Its construction, he said, was part of a program started in Stalin's last days. A mile-wide dam was being built across the Angara River, a few miles downstream from its source in Lake Baikal. Should bauxite and other components of aluminum be hauled to the dam, the source of electric power? Or should the power be carried westward in transmission lines to factories near the mines in the Urals?

The answer, since the aluminum was to be made by electrolysis, was to build the factory near the power plant.

This meant that steel for the building as well as the heavy machinery had to be hauled, in some instances thousands of miles, by the Trans-Siberian Railroad. The bauxite also had to be mined and processed in the Urals and hauled by rail for the final processing and molding into ingots and wire. A new site and a new city had to be hacked out of Siberian forest.

"You ought to like the name of this place, Shelekhovo," our informant said. "We named it for the man who discovered Alaska." The name, not taught in most American schoolbooks, is that of Grigori Ivanovich Shelekhov, an eighteenth-century Siberian fur merchant and explorer. In 1784, on Kodiak Island, he founded Alaska's first permanent settlement.

Again and again the chief engineer indicated that his worst difficulties in the plant were not material but human —problems of his workers and their families, and of the bureaucrats in Moscow. As we started a tour of the factory, we noticed portraits and citations of workers in the front lobby. They were the winners of production awards, and their pictures had been put up, obviously, as incentives to others. (We had seen a similar device used in the language school in Leningrad: pictures of the best students had been mounted in the front hall, as rewards to them and prods to others.) More tangible incentives, of course, were needed in the factory. All workers in this Siberian aluminum plant get 20 per cent more than the national scale for aluminum workers. Those in the Arctic and sub-Arctic industrial centers get a 40 per cent bonus, and sometimes even more. Judging from what we saw of the living conditions of the aluminum workers, even 40 per cent would not be a kopek too much. In early October, by no means the wettest season, apartment buildings stand in a sea of mud. The ugliness is unrelieved by any greenery or any touch of color that might lift the spirits of those who have to live there.

Yet as we hiked through the factory—hiked is the right

word, for the main shed is a third of a mile long—the workers went about their jobs in lively fashion. Women were operating the enormous traveling cranes that hung from the high ceiling. (We were assured that women were not allowed to work in the area of the greatest heat and danger, near the huge vats where the ore is melted and refined.) The men at the vats wore gauze masks but no eye shields, although the furnaces gave off aluminum dust and gas.

Among the young workers in the Shelekhovo plant, men and women, the state had circulated a questionnaire asking: "What made you come to Siberia?" The result, according to the official account—and what outsider can check the truth of such a statement?—was that 84 per cent gave "ethical" reasons. "I wanted to be useful to society," was a typical answer. "I wanted to do as much as possible for my country," was another.

As we walked out of the factory, the young engineer decided it was his turn to question us.

"Tell me," he began, "why do I have so much trouble getting information from the United States?"

He said he had gladly shown his plant to visiting Americans, officials as well as private travelers like ourselves. Why, then, couldn't America reciprocate with information?

"What kind of information do you mean?"

"Mostly chemical," he said. "I do better with electrical information than chemical, but I never get enough."

"Then your embassy in Washington isn't doing its job." And he was reminded of the ease with which an alert embassy can get information from American newspapers and technical publications. He was neither persuaded nor satisfied. He seemed to see no reason why the Aluminum Corporation of America, for example, should keep its newest processes from the eyes of Soviet technologists who probably would copy them.

Not hiding his troubles, the young engineer had lifted

a curtain on the bureaucratic infighting within the Soviet structure. Priorities differ, jealousies appear, vested interests develop in the Marxist-Leninist heaven as well as in the world of capitalism.

The Irkutsk area can show another example of such contention within the political system. This is the controversy over Lake Baikal, without question one of the natural wonders of the world.

The well-trained Intourist guide will tell American visitors: "We have as much water in this lake as in all your Great Lakes put together."

Maybe the official boast is off by a few million gallons, plus or minus, but it doesn't matter. Baikal is an enormous natural reservoir by any calculation. Although it is only about half as big as Lake Michigan, it happens to lie in a canyonlike rift in the earth's surface. The bottom of the canyon is more than a mile down. This makes Baikal the deepest lake of all. Another Soviet statistic has not been challenged: that this one lake contains one tenth of all the fresh water in the world.

Its water is not only fresh but clear like a mountain pond. Within its chilly depths, frozen over for five months of the year, flourish hundreds of natural species not found anywhere else. The Russians count 1,300 species of fish, mollusks, and other animal life, and 600 of plant life, three fourths of all of them unique to Baikal. The rarity of these species and the purity of their watery home has made the lake a political battleground as well as a natural marvel. In the nineteen-fifties the Kremlin, bent on using Siberia's forests for industry, ordered the building of two paper mills near Baikal's southern shores. Scientists and conservationists, working for the government in their respective fields, set up an outcry that went on for ten years.

In the United States such struggles are in the open. In the Soviet Union, clashes of interests among ministries are hidden from public view. Quarrels over ideology are usually fought out at party meetings; the leadership decides what to tell the public, or whether to tell anything at all. Quarrels over economic policies sometimes are allowed to break into print, even into letters to the newspapers, but Soviet leaders usually prefer to have them argued behind closed doors.

The controversy over polluting Lake Baikal broke the Soviet rules. For reasons unexplained, the Soviet leadership permitted one segment of its own structure—namely, the scientists and conservationists—to wage a public campaign against another segment—namely, the industrial developers and engineers. Even the scientists could not agree. One of them, Victor A. Cheprakov, wrote in 1968: "Only socialism, developing its economy according to a plan, will provide favorable conditions for the use and conservation of resources, plants, and animal life on a strictly scientific basis." Yet another, the well-known physicist Andrei D. Sakharov, lamented "the senseless despoliation caused . . . simply by questions of bureaucratic prestige, as in the sad fate of Lake Baikal." Sakharov had apparently given up hope, as if the polluting tide could not be reversed.

Year after year the government refused to stop the development of the paper plants. Finally, early in 1969 it came down on the side of the conservationists. Not only the lake, but its entire drainage basin was declared a protected area. The government-owned pulp mills were put under strict control; the state's industrial developers had to bow to the state's conservationists. Baikal, in other words, became a political as well as a natural oddity, and we were all the more eager to see it.

In summer, and until the end of September, one can ride into Lake Baikal from near the Angara Dam, near Irkutsk, on a hydrofoil craft called The Rocket. The Russians are ahead of the United States in using this kind of transport on lakes and rivers. Soviet rivers are not lined with highways that swarm with cars; the waterways themselves are the highways, as they have been since Viking days. For fast passenger travel, Russians find the hydrofoil a convenience and a tourist lure. They run several of these new craft between Leningrad and the palace of Peter the Great on the Gulf of Finland. The forty-mile trip to Lake Baikal is a forerunner of what will, inevitably, be many more hydrofoil routes of the future.

We were too late in the season for the hydrofoil, and rode to Baikal by car. The road cuts through unbroken forest, through silver birch and larch and pine trees without end. The first measurable snow of the season had whitened the trees on the hills. It softened the harshness of a lumbering village, a place of hundreds of all-alike log houses. The white landscape drove from our minds, for the moment, what we had read about the Siberia of prison camps, that "abyss of miseries." The road came out of the woods in sight of the lake. A pier, a mound of coal, and a black-funneled ship showed us Port Baikal, a famous name in the old days when the Trans-Siberian Railroad was new. Early in this century, all eastbound passengers had to change here to a ferry, an ungainly four-funneled icebreaker, to reach the opposite shore and another train. In winter they crossed by sledges on the ice.

This is the point where the Angara River flows out of Baikal, not into it. The river's source is the lake itself, just as the St. Lawrence flows out of Lake Ontario. The Angara takes Baikal's clear water 1,150 miles north and west to the Yenisei, which in turn flows into the Arctic. If the Angara flowed the other way, into the lake, Baikal would not now be one of the world's cleanest bodies of fresh water. For the human and industrial wastes of the city of Irkutsk, forty miles down the Angara, would have poured into Baikal, and much of the lake's marine life might long ago have been impaired.

Visitors can see specimens of that unique marine life in a handsome stone building at Listvyanka, just beyond the junction of the Angara and the lake. The building houses a limnological museum—literally, a museum devoted to the study of fresh-water lakes, but in this instance only to Baikal. If there is another like it in any country, we have not discovered it. The main exhibit is a glass model of the lake and its underwater canyon. The model makes clear what Soviet scientists have discovered: that there is no underground link with the Arctic, although many of the animals and plants of the lake resemble those of the northern sea.

Among the fish—one can see specimens and models in the museum—is the fat *omul*, a herringlike fish which Russians prize. Another unique creature of the Baikal deep is the *golovyanka*, a tiny fish that bears its young alive instead of laying eggs. It melts into a boneless ooze when it is exposed to warmth and sun. The Baikal inhabitant we most wanted to see, and could not, was the *nerpa*, or Baikal seal. Thousands of these mammals, outwardly no different from Atlantic or Arctic salt-water seals, live in Baikal's fresh water in the northern end, almost 400 miles from Irkutsk. How their ancestors reached Baikal from the Arctic Ocean remains one of the riddles of zoology and limnology. The northern tip of Baikal, where the seals live, is not far from the headwaters of the great River Lena, which winds 2,850 miles to the Arctic Ocean. But this does not solve the riddle; it only tantalizes the searcher.

Continuing pollution from the pulp mills would have endangered the seals, the fish, the plants, the smaller species most of all. The earth's largest reservoir of fresh pure water would have been spoiled, and the uniqueness of the lake, except for the mere volume of its water, would have disappeared. Control of contamination, on the other hand, should keep Baikal a treasure in the twenty-first century. There is only one sizable city on its shores or in its drainage area; this is the manufacturing and railroad repair center of Ulan Ude, on the Selenga River, which flows into the lake. Plans for new industries in the coming decade place most of them on the Angara River, which flows not into Baikal but into the distant Arctic. So the odds are against Baikal sharing the fate of Lake Erie—unless Soviet leadership reverses itself and goes industry mad.

The men in the Kremlin have a chance here to set an example. They can make of Baikal and its watershed whatever they choose. Now that the policy of conserving the lake has been set and announced in Moscow, its enforcement will be worth watching. Can the Russians do by decree what Americans and other Westerners have so far failed to do by debate and consent?

IX

DAYS AND NIGHTS ON THE TRANS-SIBERIAN

The track seemed to represent
an invader that had penetrated
a strange land but never conquered it.

—Richard L. Neuberger, on a
railroad journey in the
American Northwest (1938)

Crossing Siberia by train for the first time is one of the last remaining adventures of the vanishing railroad age. For anyone who finds joy in riding the rails, it is an adventure for at least two reasons. The first is the length of the Trans-Siberian route: 5,786 miles from Moscow to the Sea of Japan. The second reason is that Siberia is one of the world's last frontiers (in the Frederick Jackson Turner sense) and it has been open only intermittently to Western tourists.

The Trans-Siberian Railroad runs along the southern edge of an immensity of forest and range and tundra stretching northward all the way to the Arctic. Even today there is no trans-Siberia highway, and only a few north-south roads fit for motor traffic. One can fly across, of course, seeing a lifeless surface below. The magic carpet that gives a newcomer the least trouble and the most delight is the Trans-Siberian Railroad.

Just as one sniffs the salt air long before sighting an ocean beach, so we sensed adventure even before meeting our train. The Irkutsk station, our starting point, is a monument in the turn-of-the-century tradition of railroading. Its soaring arches, its high-ceilinged waiting room, seem to dignify the traveler and assure him that he and his trip are important. The promptness of the train suggested, also, that we were too important to be kept waiting. It was due at 9:14 in the morning. At 9:10 a headlight blinked far down the track, to the northwest. At 9:14, not one minute more or less, the electric locomotive slid along the platform and brought the train to a stop without a jolt. It was on time although it had already spanned 3,124 miles, which is more than from New York to San Francisco. To paraphrase our favorite gourmet, who says, "It's not just a good soup, it's a great soup," our Trans-Siberian express showed on that morning, and for the next three days, that it was not just a good train but a great train.

After such a long run, who could complain if it lacked the newly washed windows and shining paint work of other famous trains we have known? It had the manners if not the look of a patrician all the same. Below the roof of each car, wide letters spelled the train's name, Rossiya: The Russia. Instead of a printed destination card on the side of each car, there were shiny metal letters saying Moscow— Vladivostok. The names of those two cities, almost 6,000 miles apart, were a form of understated bragging. For they said, in effect: "This car is traveling the longest route of any daily scheduled train in the world."

When you board the Trans-Siberian train halfway along its route, it is something like joining a ship in the middle of a cruise. There is this difference: on the Trans-Siberian you never know in advance which compartment you will ride in, or, if there are two of you, whether you can travel together. All you know is the number of your car; ours was Car Six, which was like knowing that on a cruise you would be on "A" Deck.

Hurrying to Car Six as the train came to a stop, we found a small man in a white jacket standing there. He looked at our tickets, smiled so that the sides of his blue eyes crinkled, helped us aboard, and steered us to Compartment Three down the corridor. He was our "attendant," a combined conductor, porter, and general adviser during the three days of our journey. Each day our admiration for him grew. Now he lugged our two heavy bags into the compartment and lifted them onto a high shelf over the door. To reach the shelf, he pulled a metal ladder out of the wall. It was on hinges and folded back when it was not in use. This is the device by which a passenger reaches his upper berth.

Our compartment had four bunks, two uppers and two lowers, with a short aisle between them leading to a window. The four-berth compartment was not only bigger and higher than the usual two-berth European version; it was peculiarly Russian in another way. Here, in one of the most prudish of all countries, women and men share the same sleeping compartment, with no sense of impropriety. We drew a lower berth and an upper. The other lower already held a young Russian man with wavy hair, sleeping peacefully through the Irkutsk station stop. He wore gray flannel trousers and a knitted open-collared shirt, and his rough wool jacket hung on a hook over his head. The other upper was the bunk of a retired New Zealand farmer, on his way home at the end of a world tour; he spent most of his time aloft, immersed in sea and adventure stories such as *The Wreck of the Mary Deare*.

We cased the Rossiya as one does an ocean liner. Before the train had rolled out of Irkutsk, we had inspected and studied our car. It was one of twelve, including a diner, which made up the train. The sleeping cars were either "hard" or "soft," depending mainly on the construction of the bunk. Ours was "soft," meaning that the bunks were upholstered, with springs inside. They were covered with a blue plastic material. On each was a mattress, a pillow, and a bolster stuffed with cotton, as well as a heavy wool blanket; these were what an automobile dealer at home would call standard equipment. For an extra ruble—about a dollar—the attendant would supply the optional items: two sheets, a pillowcase and a towel, all clean but worn. Bright blue linoleum covered the walls of our compartment, a dark blue carpet the aisle between the bunks. Drapes of blue plush framed the window, and curtains of white muslin covered it.

The four of us shared a small table under the window. At times it held the paperback books, the bottle of vodka, the black bread and plastic cups we had brought along for the three-days' ride. Also on the table, a small brass lamp with an old-fashioned silk shade gave better light than the bulb on the ceiling.

The car's forty-eight passengers competed for two small washrooms with toilet and basin, one at each end of the car. Next to one of the washrooms a niche was assigned to our attendant as his living and eating space. It had room only for a single bunk and a shelf, on which stood a big tape player. This supplied the music that invaded all of the compartments during the day. After rummaging behind the drapes we found a switch that turned down the sound in our compartment until we could barely hear it. There was no way to turn it off completely, but by deadening it we at least struck a blow for human freedom.

You would think that a train compartment without this nuisance would be ideal for reading, musing, or just looking out the window. But it was not. Soon after the train started, we discovered that the joints of the Siberian tracks are opposite each other instead of being staggered. They gave our train a bouncing motion. On a "soft" seat, with springs, we felt after a while that we were exercising on a trampoline. Besides, the window in our compartment (and most others on our train) was crusted with dirt. If we had had to depend on it, we would have seen Siberia through a perpetual smog.

Far better for whiling away the daylight hours was the corridor that ran along the side of the car. There at least one of the big windows was clean enough for a view. If the two folding seats in each corridor were not occupied, we could sit in reasonable comfort and watch Siberia roll by. Otherwise we could stand or walk up and down, as long as too many other riders did not have the same urge. A timetable in a glass frame between the windows gave us an easy way of checking whether the train was on time—easy, that is, if we remembered the time zones. All Soviet timetables, whether rail or air, are on Moscow time, although one crosses eight time zones between Moscow and Vladivostok.

We spent hours at the corridor windows. Riding eastward toward the Pacific, we faced north toward the forest, or taiga, that stretches for hundreds of miles; north toward the mines and hydroelectric stations and isolated towns; north toward the sites of prison camps, some abandoned, a few still in use; north toward the tundra, where the rivers pour into the icy sea. On the platforms of our car we could, for a change, stand at windows looking south, toward Mongolia and, later in the journey, toward Chinese Manchuria, although the actual frontier never came into sight.

The notion that eastern Siberia is mile after mile of monotony is one of those pieces of excess baggage the traveler should leave at home. No doubt if we had had to walk across, like the exiles of pre-railroad days, we would have found one mile like the next, or, as the Russians used to put it, one verst. (The verst is out of date now; Soviet Russians walk or ride in kilometers.) Yet we found no sameness. Each of our three full days was as distinct from the other, in the Siberian context, as the seven days of the Creation.

On the first day we passed through several kinds of country. Snow was driving almost horizontally across a landscape of pine, birch, and larch trees. This was Siberia as we had pictured it: a wilderness of tree trunks against the snow. The seventy-eight-mile stretch up a narrow river valley and through tunnels had been built in 1956 as a double-tracked shortcut to the southern shore of Lake Baikal. It replaced a badly engineered route that had twisted around the end of the lake.

The sight of Baikal brought the first change of scene on the first day's journey. From the corridor we no longer looked out on forests but at gray, whitecapped water. The snow stopped. Near the lake shore, about 140 miles from Irkutsk, the train changed engines. Normally this would not be a moment to remember on a train journey, but here it held some meaning. For at this point, about 3,260 miles from Moscow, we changed from electricity to steam. Already the electrified portion of the line is the world's longest, yet the Kremlin is bent on electrifying it all the way to the Pacific. How soon it will achieve this goal depends on how high a priority it gives to the Trans-Siberian.

We had expected a diesel engine to haul us the rest of the way, since diesels outnumber electric locomotives on Soviet railroads by almost two to one. The old electric slipped off and away, the new engine was hitched on with the usual bumping and clanking, and the train started again. But the motion at starting was the series of jerks that recalled an earlier age of railroading. And when we looked out of the corridor window, low-hanging trails of steam and smoke blew past. To be pulled by steam treated two old-time passengers to an experience they thought they would never have again.

Why steam? More than two thirds of all Russia's 31,000 steam locomotives had been scrapped since 1960. We could only guess that diesels were needed for more urgent tasks than hauling passengers across Siberia. So, for the next two and a half days, we were to hear the oddly comforting sounds of a big steam engine. The penalty was soot that blew into our compartment onto the blankets and pillowcases, even though the window was closed. The reward was recapturing one of the joys of steam-train childhoods. The whistle was the wail we used to hear through the night across the American prairies. And when we caught our first sight of the engine, as it rounded a sharp curve ahead, we could see that ours was a monster of its kind. Two vertical slabs, to deflect smoke, had been built on the sides of the locomotive boiler. Otherwise it looked like a first cousin, if not a twin, of heavy-duty steam locomotives in our own country, something American children no longer see unless they visit a museum.

The walk to the Rossiya's dining car took us over five steeply arched bridges. They join the cars of the train together. You climb two steps uphill, run two steps downhill, as though you were crossing a bridge in a Japanese garden. The diner has a familiar old-fashioned look. No snack bar or vinyl-topped counters, but eighteen tables for four, dressed in white linen cloths. You can indeed buy things from the glass display counter at the end of the car: boxes of candy and biscuits, Bulgarian grape juice, apples when in season, Russian beer, and wines from Hungary, East Germany, Bulgaria, and Romania. Unlike European diners, there are no set mealtimes, no calls for lunch or dinner, no tickets for tables. From eight in the morning until eleven at night, the staff feeds a continuous stream of customers.

At lunchtime the tables were half empty. This puzzled us, but we soon caught on to the eating habits of the Rossiya's passengers. Foreigners like ourselves, with food coupons to spare and money already spent, trekked to the diner three times a day in a futile effort to consume all that the coupons provided. Most Russians stoke up on one hot meal a day. The rest of their eating and drinking—we stress drinking—goes on in their compartments. Russians bring food and drink with them, and also buy them along the way at station stops. That very morning we had watched them at one station hurry off the train and across the platform to a food stall. It was stocked with chickens, sausages, and eggs, all cooked, as well as buns and apples. Behind the stalls stood three ancient women bundled up to their chins, their faces red, their hands blue with the cold. Between trains—there might be six a day—the women took refuge in a shed down the platform. Smoke rose from a pipe in the tin roof of the shed, and we guessed that they spent their spare hours inside, knitting and talking around the stove. Meanwhile, our first lunch in the diner was satisfying: hot cabbage soup, an omelet, black bread, and a glass of tea. It sustained us through a long afternoon of corridor watching.

As daylight faded on the first day of our Siberian crossing, Lake Baikal swung northward and out of sight. The steam locomotive pulled us eastward and then southward across rolling wheat and cattle country. This is the only large-scale farming area in the Trans-Baikal region, and the last one we would see for almost a thousand miles. Long white barns in the distance showed where the animals were sheltered during the fiercely cold winters. The average January temperature in this part of Trans-Baikalia is sixteen below zero, which is as cold as at Barrow, the northernmost settlement in Alaska. In October, the month we passed through, the average is just below freezing. Yet the country east of Baikal looked more like southern Minnesota than Alaska. We saw a bus bringing children home from school. Home appeared to be a collective farm of vast extent, with log houses strung along an unpaved road. Somehow the sight of the school bus was as reassuring as that of another ship at sea; for it meant that there really were children, and families, in this sparsely peopled land.

By five-thirty, we were giving some thought to the bottle of vodka cushioned in our hand luggage. But before we could do anything about it our attendant came down the corridor bringing two glasses of steaming tea with lemon. It was our first sample of this service and of his skill at brewing tea. Twice a day, at eight in the morning and five-thirty in the afternoon, he was to bring us fragrant tea at four kopeks (about five cents) a glass. Just outside his niche, at the end of the car, he kept a brass samovar boiling over a charcoal brazier. His spare charcoal he kept in a pail on the

platform. At stations it was replenished from a cart that supplied the whole train.

The tea ritual that first afternoon caused all the compartment doors to open, and most of our four dozen companions
emerged from their cocoons. The train's cast of characters
was improbable and varied enough to have sprung from the
brain of Alfred Hitchcock. Whoever remembers his film *The
Lady Vanishes* would not have discounted the possibility of
a thriller. Hitchcock could have taken his time, this being
the longest train trip in the world. We were already acquainted with the Russian engineer and the New Zealand
farmer in our compartment. Now we met the neighbors on
one side, a Japanese law professor, his pregnant young wife,
and his son of about seven. On the other side were lodged
three Russian army officers, with the son of one of them.
The two boys, Japanese and Russian, now worked up a ball
game in the corridor. In no time a small Russian girl attached herself to them. She and her mother, a startling
blonde, shared a compartment with an Australian couple in
the middle of the car. Before long, the blonde had attached
herself to the best-looking of the army officers. He was a
handsome fellow, though on the portly side.

Late in the afternoon, with much wailing of the locomotive, we passed more log houses and small warehouses on
the approaches to a city. One puzzle was a dazzling sheet
of light off to the side of the train, under light poles like
those at baseball stadiums at home. The setting sun was
reflecting in a glass cold frame at least a hundred feet long,
under which the government grew vitamin-bearing vegetables during the long, dark winter. The tea party in the
corridor was suddenly suspended as the train steamed into
Ulan Ude, the capital of the Buryat Autonomous Soviet
Socialist Republic.

The Buryats are a partly Mongol, Mongolian-speaking
people. They and their herds were roaming this region just

north of Mongolia when the first Russian Cossacks came in
the mid-seventeenth century. We saw two of their broad,
slant-eyed faces, but only two, in the crowd of Russians on
the station platform. Buryats are still a majority in the
wooded hills and steppes of their so-called republic. But
like the Kazakhs in Alma Ata, they are already outnum-
bered by Russians in their capital city. The chief reason is
that the city is booming industrially. In czarist times, when
its name was Verkhne Udinsk, it was noted only for having
one of the best-kept prisons, and for its mud and backward-
ness. Now it is a factory town of about 175,000, with the
biggest railroad equipment plant in Siberia. It is sure to
grow, partly because of coal and iron ore in its hinterland.

Railroads as well as geography give the place added importance. For if our train had been bound for Ulan Bator,
the capital of the Mongolian People's Republic, and on to
Peking, this is where we would have branched off from the
main Moscow-to-Vladivostok line. (A train was still running
once a week on the Moscow–Mongolia–Peking route in
1970, in spite of the quarrel between the Soviet Union and
China.) Our own train, still rolling eastward, by the next
morning reached Chita, which is a second important junction. Until 1916 the train to Vladivostok had to branch off
Russian territory near here and use the tracks of what was
called the Chinese Eastern Railway, on Chinese soil. This
shortcut was more popular with travelers than our all-
Russian route that rounds the curving northern frontier of
Manchuria instead of crossing it.

For most of our second morning on wheels we followed
the partly wooded, partly cultivated valley of the Shilka
River, a tributary of the Amur. We were to meet the Amur
itself and cross it at Khabarovsk in the Soviet Far East.

At breakfast time, as the track twisted along the Shilka,
the dining car began to fill up with Russians as well as foreigners. We chose for our first breakfast *kasha manle*, which
is hot cream of wheat with fresh butter, followed by fried

eggs and tea. A young Russian couple across the table were already halfway through their main meal of the day: meat stew, potatoes, and cabbage, all glistening with fat. Another Russian across the aisle was starting the day on sausages and buckwheat groats cooked in lard. They would probably come back in the late evening for beer or a glass of tea. The canned music served throughout the day was least bearable at the morning meal. The program seemed then to assume that passengers had sleepwalked into the dining car and needed to be shaken out of their comas. A baritone bellowed military songs with the aid of an army chorus. Lunch and supper music concentrated on Russian opera and sentimental ballads, which one could both bear and enjoy.

All morning the collective farms and occasional clusters of log houses grew poorer. On one hillside near the tracks we passed some gravestones overgrown with weeds. The crosses leaned at crazy angles as if nobody had taken care of them for years. Not far north of here the czars and their successor, Stalin, had run the infamous Kara mines, where thousands of prison workers died. By afternoon the train was headed northeast, beginning to round the Manchurian border. Nowhere along our entire route did we sense such isolation, such closeness to the wilderness. Mountains we saw in the distance, to the northwest, are not yet fully explored. For the villagers here, as for others along the line, the railroad and the river are the only means of communication. We saw no roads; the rivers are their highways—by shallow-draft barges in summer, by sled or jeep along the ice in winter. Nothing, it seemed, had happened here to make life easier since the building of the railway—nothing, that is, except the coming of electricity for lighting and power.

Why would anyone have settled here? The answer is perhaps what lured Americans and Canadians to the frozen Klondike at the end of the nineteenth century. Gold drew free settlers to this part of Siberia even before the railroad made the journey easy. Some stayed, panning the rivers if not working in the mines further north, and doing enough backyard farming to keep their families fed. Once, in the gathering darkness, the train crossed a bridge near a string of lights in the river. The light came from a dredge which was anchored there, our first evidence that gold digging was going on. We were not far from Nerchinsk, just off the railroad, a place with two claims to be remembered in Siberian annals. It was, first, a kind of base camp of the gold-mining companies in the late nineteenth century. It was also the place where Russia and China signed a boundary treaty in 1689, the first treaty with "barbarians" ever made by the ruler of the Celestial Empire.

Towns and station stops were few on this stretch of the line. One advantage of the timetable on the corridor wall was to alert us to the chance of getting a breath of air and a run up and down the infrequent station platforms. For Russians, of course, it was the chance to buy food at the stalls across the platform. This was the busy time for our hard-working attendant. He was always first off the car, heaving baggage to the ground, helping passengers off, hustling new ones aboard and assigning them to the vacated bunks. Through this scramble, his face never lost its sweetness, sadness, or patience. In the remaining time before takeoff, if there was any, we found him polishing the metal Moscow-Vladivostok letters on the outside of the car. Once we humbly suggested that if he would be so kind as to clean the car windows instead of the letters, one might get a clearer view of the glorious Russian countryside. He merely shook his head and polished harder.

If he took first prize for charm, another member of the train crew surpassed everyone in self-importance. She was the Party Woman. In Hitchcockian terms, she was "The Lady Who Seldom Vanishes." Whether every Trans-Siberian train is equipped with an official of the Party, we do not know. But our Rossiya, with its international passenger load, did apparently rate one. Her ostensible job was to supervise all the linens on the train, a superior housekeeping responsibility. In dispensing and collecting bed linen, she had a chance to confer with the attendant on each car. In doling out table linens, she kept in touch with the dining car personnel. Thus she had to roam the train, keeping an eye on the passengers. At every major stop she left the train and disappeared into the station, presumably to file her report.

Hitchcock could not have done a better job of casting. She was big, blond, and bossy. She could also be sickly sweet, as when she detached two Russians from our table in the diner. She all but pulled them from their seats with, "I am sure you don't want these gentlemen to bother you." Her uniform was a starched white blouse and a dark blue skirt, a bit tight over her hips and conservatively below her knees. Her hair was always pressed into a wad on the exact top of her head. She had a splendid complexion. She radiated health, the kind that comes from doing calisthenics every time the official radio tells you to.

During a longish stop, perhaps fourteen minutes, the Lady vanished into the station, doubtless on Party business, and by a stroke of good fortune missed a scene in the dining car. It was a moment in which Hitchcock introduced one of the irrelevant bit parts at which he excels. We had just finished a meal and were about to take a walk on the station platform when a young Russian, a stranger to the train, boarded the dining car. With his tousled hair and his face of fun, he might have been Danny Kaye in a heavy quilted jacket. He found an empty seat and asked the waitress for a beer. She chose to flounce by and ignore him. He tried to waylay the other waitress, who did the same. The fourteen minutes of our stop began to ebb, and the man began to appeal to the waitresses for a beer.

Finally, he rose and put his case to the passengers. It was eloquent. "Why should I be treated in this way? All I ask for is a beer. Why should I be different from all of you? I am not a hooligan, just a thirsty human being. Believe me, I am sober. I have money. I don't ask for anything free. Is this justice?"

The crowd was with him. "Give him his beer," they urged the waitresses, who remained stony-faced. The train began to move and the young man dived for the platform. It was over. When he disappeared, the cause of social justice went with him. The passengers went back to their food and drink. The Party Woman would have expunged him, atomized him. We were glad she had been somewhere else.

On the third morning, the entire landscape changed. The narrow valleys opened into a flat plain, and for the rest of the day we crossed a wide, treeless steppe that might have been the Texas Panhandle. The wheat had been harvested, and there was little for cattle to eat or for tractors to do. The towns along this part of the route showed more sophistication, and probably higher standards of living, than the log villages we had passed the day before.

Our last evening aboard the Rossiya blossomed into a kind of gala, such as cruise ships and ocean liners stage on the final evening. The Rossiya's had the advantage of being spontaneous and basic: no paper caps, no balloons, no artificial noisemakers, only beer, the socialist equivalent. The scene of the gala was the dining car, the only place where "hard" and "soft" passengers could gather in numbers. By nine o'clock the comradely spirit, the joking and moving among tables, had reached a plateau of noise. Even the waitresses joined in. The Party Woman either knew enough to stay away, or had business elsewhere. We suspected the latter.

Among our "hard" acquaintances who showed up were two Australian youths who had been to a university in England and were homeward bound the cheapest way. The long voyage had been rough on their English tweeds, which would be ready for the Salvation Army when they reached home. They had been sharing a compartment with Russians. In the Soviet Union the word "student" opens doors, and of this the two young men were not unaware. They had been around the country, and Russians of their generation had gravitated toward them. Here on the Rossiya they had held a nightly seminar in their compartment. As usual, they found themselves answering questions. Where did they come from? What did their fathers do for a living? Their mothers? Why didn't their mothers work? Did the family have a car? What! Two cars? What did cars cost in Australia? What did their fathers earn? How much living space was the family allowed? And so on, far into the night. Before the seminars ended, the Siberian sun was near the horizon and eighteen Russians had learned about bourgeois life down under. The last question, the Australians told us, nobody could answer. It was, "How can one get to Australia?"

The roadbed that night made sleep impossible. The jump seats in the corridor tempted us more than our jiggling bunks, especially since a full moon was shining on a black and silver landscape. Now the train began crossing what is still called the Jewish Autonomous Region of Birobidjan, a curiosity in the history of Russia and of the Jews alike. In the Soviet Union Jews are regarded as a nationality. In Irkutsk, for example, we asked a teacher whose parents had come from the Ukraine: "Are you a Ukrainian, then?" "No," he said, "I'm a Jew." His identity card labels him as such and he is admitted to universities under a quota, as are students of other non-Russian nationalities. But unlike Ukrainians, Armenians, and the other major minorities, the Jews have no geographical home; they are scattered all over the Soviet Union, mostly in European Russia and the Ukraine.

In 1934 Stalin had two purposes in his policy toward the Jews. One was to rid European Russia of as many as possible by deportation, without creating an international scandal. His own daughter says he was anti-Semitic, probably because of his long feud with Trotsky, a Jew. The other purpose was to plant more people in the thinly settled country along the China frontier. To entice the Jews he created Birobidjan as a Jewish "region," and pretended that he had thereby given them status equal to that of other non-Russians. This equality was a fraud. Birobidjan was neither a separate republic nor a compact home. It was almost as remote as any place could be from the centers of Jewish population and culture. It is a cold and wind-swept region, with a severe six-month winter and a correspondingly short growing season.

Yet as we watched it from our train window in the moonlight, it seemed to us that Stalin could have chosen even worse places than this for the Jews. We had seen worse ones along our route, and in Central Asia. The train stopped only a couple of minutes at the city of Birobidjan, at two o'clock on a clear, cold morning. We had neither time nor permission to get off. We did notice, though, that this was one of the few stations without its bust of Lenin on the platform; that the factory buildings, houses, and apartments looked solidly built; that the town, or what we could see of it, was a modern place, well lighted and well kept. Only 18,000 Jews still live and work there out of about 40,000 assorted people in the city. Those who remain have the advantage of a small metropolis, Khabarovsk, only three hours away. The rest, presumably, were permitted to move back westward after Stalin died.

On our fourth morning, the train rolled slowly across the broad Amur River into the station at Khabarovsk. It came to a stop two minutes early—after a run of 5,298 miles from Moscow. It still had 488 miles to go to reach the end of the line at Vladivostok. But for all foreigners aboard, and for Russians taking the once-a-week ship to Yokohama, Khabarovsk was the place to change trains. Foreigners are not permitted in Vladivostok, the Soviet naval base on the Sea of Japan. Civilian traffic now uses the new port of Nakhodka, about fifty miles to the east of Vladivostok, and passengers must travel there from Khabarovsk on a boat train, like those that connect the cross-Channel ships in France and England. For us, the change was a stroke of luck, for it gave us an eleven-hour day in which to bathe, after three bathless days and nights on the train, and to wander around this industrial center of the Soviet Far East.

At Khabarovsk we saw the last of the neighbors to one side of us, the Russian army officers and their little boy. We wondered about the boy and what memories he would store away of his Trans-Siberian journey. In another fifty years, when he is close to sixty, will transcontinental passenger trains be as nearly obsolete as they are in the United States? Fifty years ago the greatest thing that could happen to an American child was to ride the Overland Limited to California. We grew up in those days before the highways and the airways had become the racetracks of travel. It took the Overland Limited four days and nights from Chicago to cross the Mississippi, the Great Plains, the passes of the Rockies. In winter, snowdrifts sometimes blocked the passes and the Overland would stop dead for twenty-four hours until the plows could reach it and open the way. Then the dining car might run out of fresh milk. But prudent parents would have brought cans of malted milk for such an emergency. They would send the children out for snow to melt, so that the powdered milk could be dissolved. As the train sped along at a dizzying sixty miles an hour, a child could stand on the rear platform of the observation car and watch the tracks rush away. No matter if his eyes filled with cinders. Sometimes there was a moment of suspense when the train made an unscheduled stop in the prairie, to remove a cow from the catcher on the front of the engine. At breakfast the dining car steward might lean over to whisper,

"Would you care for some quail we took aboard this morning in Nebraska?" Or, "I expect to have some fresh mountain trout this evening in Utah."

The Trans-Siberian, like the Overland Limited, had an elegant past. In the days of Czar Nicholas II, privileged passengers slept on soft beds, bathed in marble tubs, and dined on reindeer meat. The Rossiya of today is in tune with the Soviet economy of today. It is basic, serving most needs but few comforts. In one respect, it sets an example the rest of the economy cannot match. It fulfills its plan—or timetable—precisely. Trains do occasionally collide, tracks do buckle, bridges do collapse in the melting of the permafrost, but one hears nothing about this. Such accidents were common in the years after the Revolution, when chaos and civil war gripped Siberia. Today the rolling stock looks sturdy, there are no bandits along the line, and the only antisocialist force still to be reckoned with is Siberian weather.

In one respect, this railroad has not changed since it was built. It is still unique as the lifeline of small, isolated hamlets scattered across continental Russia. Jet planes, to be sure, now link the cities, but without the railroad the thin ribbon of human settlement that parallels the tracks would wither and die. Men may work the land on either side, but they live along the tracks.

The railroad has one companion that is relatively new. This is the parade of electric power pylons on the horizon. They tell better than propaganda that settlements have been electrified, that factories run on power, that even the farmer's hut may now have an electric light bulb. But one looks in vain for other signs of change in the Siberian farm village. It is still a collection of one-room wooden huts, each with its outdoor privy. When the unpaved streets are not frozen, they are rivers of mud. The farm women pump their water from the village well and carry it home in buckets. The Rossiya herself is here on coal and steam. But the pylons march across the sky, promising better things. Khabarovsk, which has two lifelines, the Amur as well as the railroad, is one evidence of the promise.

One does a double take in walking the windy streets of Khabarovsk. This is a Russian city. Everyone looks Russian, talks Russian, acts Russian; there is not an Asian face in sight. The crowds on the streets, on the buses, and in the shops are so overwhelmingly Slavic that one could forget where Khabarovsk is. Only when one remembers that Moscow sits more than five thousand miles to the west, at the far end of a thin thread of track, that China is only thirty-five miles to the south, and that the salt water of the Sea of Japan laps the shore two hundred miles to the east—only then does the drive and scope of Russian expansion take on meaning.

It was the Amur River that put the city here, and it was the river that made us glad we had come to Khabarovsk. Leaning against a northwest wind that cut us to our bones, we pushed down the main street, named of course for Karl Marx. There at the end lay the Amur far below us. It is roughly the same length, 2,700 miles, as those other giants, the Mississippi and the Mekong. At this moment, the end of the dry season, its thundering waters were reduced to about the volume of the Seine in Paris. But the dry riverbed looked to us at least two miles wide, and one could imagine those early summer floods, when the water level can rise as much as thirty feet in no time.

The Amur is one of Russia's great inland waterways, its one sin being that its mouth, four hundred miles northeast of Khabarovsk, is full of sand. This makes it useless for sea-going ships that need more than twelve feet of water, and thus all but useless for foreign trade. And it makes Khabarovsk a domestic supplier of the Russian Far East. For that purpose the city was founded in 1858 at the strategic meeting place of the Amur and Ussuri rivers. It was the year in which the Russians took title to the Amur territory and then ratified the act in a treaty with China, a treaty which the Chinese still lament and repudiate.

For its first thirty-five years Khabarovsk was just a little frontier town. Then came the railroad to link it with the Sea of Japan, and, finally, with Moscow. Today the Soviets, with characteristic enthusiasm, call Khabarovsk a "giant." Considering where and what it is, we cannot argue. In 1968, if Soviet figures are correct, some 423,000 people were living and working there. Among the enterprises that keep them busy are a cable and wire works, an oil refinery at the end of a pipeline from Sakhalin Island, a steel mill, and a sprawl of smaller state factories. The city is still in the making and it keeps a raw, half-finished look. The Amur is its playground as well as its reason for being. The steep shore has been made into a people's park, and a sports stadium named for Lenin stands nearby.

Congealed by the northwest wind (and it was only the month of October) we let it blow us down the main street and away from the river. We mingled with Russians hurrying home at the end of the working day, tough and ruddy-faced men and women. What had brought them to this raw and wind-swept town? Could any of them have been descendants of the original explorers, the Cossacks of 300 years ago? Were they children, perhaps, of exiles or of prisoners? Had their families been deported to the East in Stalin's day? Or were some of them the advance guard of a new and dedicated Siberian Man? If they had come of their own accord, it was hard for either of us to imagine what had drawn them and why they stayed.

X

Nakhodka:

IN THE SOVIET FAR EAST—AND OUT

This abyss of miseries, this
graveyard of the living . . .

—Marquis de Custine (1839)

"All men that are ruined," said Edmund Burke, "are ruined on the side of their natural propensities." He might have said "saved" as well as ruined. But Burke was apparently a pessimist, having failed to persuade his countrymen that they should conciliate their American colonists.

Remembering Burke, and having put most of Siberia behind us, we tried to think of the natural propensities of Russia's Wild East which might explain its past and foretell its future. It is, of course, impossible to do this without also considering the propensities of the men who explored and settled it. Siberia is what it is today partly because they happened to be Russian, not English or Scotch or Dutch or American. It is probably idle to speculate how Siberia might have responded to the English talent for acquisition and order, the Scotch for management, the Dutch for money-making, the American for drive. The subject of our exercise is Russia. Mother Russia's children brought with them qualities of daring and endurance; an almost unlimited capacity for suffering; and, finally, an age-old propensity for submitting to misrule. In Siberia the center of misrule happened to be thousands of miles away, but the Russians submitted to it all the same.

After nibbling at the northern part of Siberia for about six hundred years, the Russians suddenly decided to swallow all of it in one great gulp. It was Ivan IV (the Terrible)

who came to the decision, and his reasons for initiating
the conquest are not entirely clear. Russian fur trappers
and traders had been in the habit of crossing the Ural
Mountains into northwest Siberia, and Ivan had heard complaints that native bands were robbing and killing them.
There were also reports that several shiploads of English-
men had been seen sailing along the shores of the Arctic
and up the river Ob. This particular territory the Russians
had long considered their private hunting preserve. It is
possible that Queen Elizabeth's nosy subjects may inad-
vertently have goaded the Russians to do some preclusive
grabbing, a conditioned reflex that has helped to build
many empires.

Whatever the reason, Ivan sent a band of mercenaries
across the Urals to teach the natives a lesson. At the same
time, a family of merchant princes used the mercenaries to
secure a claim to Siberian territory which the czar had
given them. So well did the mercenaries carry out their
assignments that Ivan (we are told) sent them back to
conquer the rest of the continent in his name.

It sounds like an improbable picaresque tale of the six-
teenth century, which in truth it is. Even less probable than
the conquest were the men who performed it. They were
an unusual breed of Russian peasants, who had fled the rule
of the czars to settle near the Black Sea. There they had
farmed, raided, plundered, and undertaken odd jobs of conquest on a piecework basis. It was these peasants, the Cossacks, who streaked through the wilderness and delivered
Siberia whole to the czars. Being expert boatmen as well
as horsemen, they made use of the great northbound rivers
and their east–west tributaries, sailing and portaging across
the continent until, in 1639, they stood on the shore of the
Sea of Okhotsk, an arm of the Pacific Ocean.

Behind them they had left a chain of stockades and
trading posts, each topped with a cross and a pennant of
the czar. To the European Russia of Ivan, which was

slightly smaller than California is today, they added a realm one and a half times the size of the United States. As piecework, this was not a bad job.

It is easy to understand why the czars wanted all that land. To quote the Russian circus juggler whom we mentioned in our prologue: "All that money!" Siberia abounded with fur-bearing animals and gold. Furs and gold were currency in those days. The czars took care to get the bulk of this wealth by involving themselves and their families in Siberian business ventures. The continent to the east of them was not only rich, it was accessible as soon as the Tatar hordes no longer stood in the way. It was also, for practical purposes, empty. The only people who lived there were primitive hunting and fishing folk armed with bows and arrows. They were few and they were expendable. Finally, like the mountain to the climber, Siberia was there. It is still there, rich, accessible, and only a little less empty today, almost four hundred years after the conquest began.

The Cossacks met no serious rivals until, in the valley of the Amur River, they found themselves up against native peoples who had long paid tribute to the emperor of China. The explorer who made this unpleasant discovery was a particularly ruthless Cossack named Erifeo Khabarov. So efficiently did Khabarov assault and decimate the natives that the survivors appealed to the Chinese emperor for help. In the ensuing battle with the Chinese relief force, Khabarov and his Cossacks added another Glorious Victory to Russia's collection. The emperor's men retreated. So did the czar's men when they finally realized that the Amur region, so close to China, was not a healthy place for Russians. In 1689 the two powers agreed on a boundary that excluded Russians from the region, and signed a treaty, their first, at Nerchinsk. The place survives to this day as a mining town not far from the Trans-Siberian tracks.

To lose the Amur region was one of the few setbacks the Cossacks suffered. How bitter a disappointment it must have been we realized as we rolled for a day in our train along the Shilka River, a tributary of the Amur, and two days later crossed the broad Amur itself into the city of Khabarovsk. What a glorious discovery it must have been for the conquerors: a great west–east river system, long, navigable, and only moderately permafrosted, with blue waters six months in the year and a frozen highway in the other six. This on a continent whose rivers flow perversely northward into Arctic ice. To abandon the Amur region to Chinese, who did not want it themselves but could not suffer Russians on their border, must have humiliated Cossack pride. But a hundred and seventy years later a governor-general of Siberia, Count Nicholas Muravyev, who was impervious to the Chinese as well as to the treaty, retrieved the loss. He founded a city on the Amur and named it for Khabarov. If any of the original native stock survive in the city today, and if they have anything to say, they could scarcely tolerate the statue of Khabarov that broods over one of the main squares.

In addition to draining Siberia of its raw wealth, the czars used it as a springboard for further conquests. Peter and Catherine sent their agents eastward with the idea of making the northern Pacific an inland Russian sea. By 1798 Russians had secured the coast of Alaska and in 1812 they raised the czar's flag over a fort sixty miles north of what is now San Francisco. The Australian geographer J. P. Cole estimates that it would then have taken an imperial messenger six hundred days to span the empire from St. Petersburg to California, traveling at the average rate of those roadless times, which was about twenty miles a day.

On the whole, Siberia would seem to have served the czars' purposes and to have given them little trouble. A source of unlimited wealth, a deep freeze for exiles and convicts, who doubled as forced labor in the mines, an escape hatch for land-poor peasants who might have made trouble at home—what more could rulers ask of a colony?

The idea that anything might be put into Siberia to improve it they either rejected or ignored.

Colonial bureaucracies have attracted all kinds of human beings, and Siberia's was no exception. Muravyev, the governor-general who rewon the region of the Amur, was one of the czars' few outstanding proconsuls, almost in a class with such enlightened empire builders as Stamford Raffles and Louis Lyautey. A more recent governor, we learn, was a kindly and humane man, a former judge. Still another was murdered. All of them, whatever their quality, worked under an impossible system, for the czars steadfastly refused to delegate power or responsibility to the men on the spot. Other imperial systems, those of Belgium, Holland, and England, for example, did give their distant representatives a measure of authority, sometimes with appalling consequences. But the czars never did. They could hardly have devised a better prescription for injustice and stagnation at the end of the long line. Even the best-intentioned administrators were helpless. They had to wait months for decisions from St. Petersburg, and sometimes they waited in vain.

To have delegated authority would have altered the czarist system. It would, moreover, have meant giving Siberian bureaucrats more discretion and independence of judgment than had ever been tolerated close to home. This obviously made no sense in the Russian scheme of things. Nor did the idea of putting back into Siberia a part of the wealth that was taken out—putting it back in the form of internal trunk roads, railroads, bridges, improved prisons, hospitals, schools, and industries. From the point of view of communications, eastern Siberia is not much better off today than when the Cossacks conquered it. Rivers still serve as highways, and the Trans-Siberian Railroad is the sole lifeline joining Far East and West. In this respect, the Russians are still far behind the British, French, and Dutch, who left networks of internal communications in India, North Africa, and Java.

It is curious that in all their centuries of isolation and neglect from St. Petersburg, Siberians themselves never cut loose from the center. Yet they were ideally equipped to do just that. Was ever a colony more blessed with revolutionary leadership? For more than a hundred years, potential founding fathers of a Siberian Republic were tossed out of European Russia and exiled to the wild East. They were by all odds the most courageous and gifted Russians of their respective times, excepting only the handful who managed to escape to the West.

The man who led this procession late in the eighteenth century was Alexander Radishchev. He displeased Empress Catherine with a book attacking serfdom and an ode in praise of the American Revolution. But his book died in a political vacuum, and he himself died soon after seven years in Siberian exile. On the heels of Radishchev came more than a hundred Decembrists, those who were not condemned to death; then early socialists and idealists; novelists as distinguished as Dostoevsky and Korolenko; finally, Marxian socialists including Lenin, Trotsky, and Stalin. There were many others, not all geniuses but cultivated men and women, the cream of nineteenth-century Russia. They had surprising opportunities—to get together, to talk and plot and organize. So far as we can discover, no independence movement was ever born of their presence in Siberia. Many of them led fairly normal lives. They had surprisingly good opportunities to meet and plot if they wanted to. Yet if they plotted Siberian independence, they left no traces of revolutions stillborn.[1]

[1] That Siberian independence was at least thought of, if not plotted, we learn from Prince Peter Kropotkin, sent to Siberia as a soldier in 1862. In his *Memoirs of a Revolutionist* (1899) he reports hearing that young officers

Siberia had not only revolutionary leaders, but a good potential for revolutionary followers. Descendants of the early Cossacks were the only true Russian-Siberians until liberated serfs began to migrate near the end of the nineteenth century. Cossacks, with a fighting and pioneering tradition, would have made a fine revolutionary army. Our guess is that the opportunity never even dawned on the exiles, for one reason: in their minds and hearts, they desired one thing, to go back to European Russia, to go "home." Is there a clearer example of the power of Mother Russia over the Russian soul?

The opportunity disappeared when the Bolshevists came to power. Although Siberia's exile population multiplied a hundredfold during the Stalin years, the luckless ones were kept under guard and made to work. Stalin's industrial revolution took Siberia into the Plan, and not only on paper. A new railway, the "Turksib," linked Tashkent in Central Asia with the Trans-Siberian at Novosibirsk in western Siberia. And the Nazi invasion of Russia transformed Novosibirsk itself from a small provincial city into an emergency center of war industry. From our train window we saw other symbols of the new, no longer forgotten Siberia: the cement, paper, and machine works along the railroad; the electric pylons against the Siberian sky; and not least of symbols, a school bus rattling over a narrow, unpaved road. A new Siberia is on the way, but a very different one from the independent republic the exiles might have made —if they had not been such devoted children of Mother Russia.

Few historians writing about Russia, including some of the most distinguished, have resisted the temptation to compare the Soviet East and the American West. They note

---

around the governor-general, Count Muravyev, "discussed the chances of creating the United States of Siberia, federated across the Pacific from the United States of America."

that the two movements of discovery, conquest, and settlement covered the same four centuries. They see the simi-
larities in geography. The two continents are roughly the
same size and have the same diversity of terrain: Arctic
wastes, forest belts, rangelands, grainlands, mountain
chains, lakes, and river systems. Common motives, we are
told, propelled men across both continents: a greed for
wealth, an urge to explore the unknown and find a passage
to the ocean at the end of the trail.

Having forsworn comparisons at the beginning of this
book, we shall break our resolve only to show how comparisons of this kind can mislead. There is, for example,
the fate of the indigenous peoples. On both continents they
suffered unspeakable cruelties at the hands of the Europeans, whether Cossacks, Spaniards, or Anglo-Saxons. The
white men, moreover, despoiled the continents of much
of their natural wealth, so that beavers disappeared from
the Rockies and sables from whole sections of the Siberian
taiga. The labor forces that helped to push the railroads
across both continents were not exactly free. In Siberia they
were battalions of wretched prisoners under the guns of
guards. In the American West they were men imported
by the thousand from Ireland, Poland, and even China as
indentured labor. We could go on with comparisons like
these.

We could reason, as others do, that Americans and Russians shared the same experiences. They are both continental peoples, both pioneering peoples. Being pioneers,
they are brave, adventurous, resourceful, self-reliant, open-
hearted, and forthright. Enjoying these qualities, they
cannot help but be freedom-loving. Being freedom-loving,
they are of course democratic at heart. And so we come to
the logical but false conclusion that Americans and Russians
are basically the same kind of people.

There are various ways of defining this affinity. It has
been called a "common denominator," a common "outlook

on life." One scholar says, "There can be nothing servile about a man who managed to complete Siberian migration successfully." Another sees significance in the fact that the landing at Roanoke coincided with the Cossack crossing of the Ural Mountains; that Jamestown and Tomsk were founded within three years of each other, and that only six years separated the births of Irkutsk and New Haven.

How can New Haven and Irkutsk fail to feel their kinship? Obviously they should be doing something about it. (Perhaps they are.) Being virtual twins, they might organize pioneer-to-pioneer programs, exchanging books and magazines, conducting two-way visits of housewives and students. Perhaps the Daughters of the American Revolution of New Haven should send a delegation to Irkutsk, and then invite their sister organization, the Daughters of the Russian Revolution, to come to New Haven. What could contribute more effectively to the peace of the world than to recognize that we are all, all of us, basically the same?

We have come a long way down the road to absurdity. To say that Americans and Russians are basically different may be subversive, but it is true. The Russian peasant who migrated eastward shared almost nothing with the American farmer-artisan who settled the West. In their skills, education, political experience, and attitudes toward authority the two could hardly have been more alien. The contrasts between Siberia and the American West of today are a direct outgrowth of these differences.

Historians might apply themselves to measuring the nature of the differences after they have pointed up the superficial likenesses. The Russian peasant never broke away from the authority that had held him in serfdom. Often his new life in Siberia had much in common with the one he left behind. Not all the migrants, by any means, became independent farmers; many landed on Siberian estates as tenants and laborers. The American migrant not only broke with Europe; he even pulled up the young roots that his father or grandfather had put down in the colonies. In Ohio or Iowa or Kansas he founded a new community. Its members made their own laws to suit frontier needs and cope with frontier dangers. In this respect the American frontier was politically more sophisticated than the Siberian has ever been.

Another measure of the difference was technology. The American migrant took with him the most advanced knowledge of his time in woodwork, metalworking, and farming. He was an artisan and he was at least partly literate. After the farmhouse, the next building to go up in the American West was the schoolhouse—unless it was the saloon that doubled during the day as a school. The techniques of farming and building which the Russian peasant took with him to Siberia had changed little for centuries. And the settlers were to wait for education until they were collectivized and Soviet authorities ordered them to build schools. We have no wish to point a moral, but rather to point to differences that help to account for the contrasts of today. The people who created the American West and the Russian East started from different premises. Nikita Khrushchev could talk about "catching up." He failed to see that the two peoples were not on the same historical highway.

Riding a train across Siberia, especially in the clear, dry months of early fall, you cannot help wondering what the Siberian future will bring. What will these forests and plains and river valleys be like twenty, fifty, a hundred years from now? You feel at first that the whole immense region ought to be renamed "Futuria" or its Russian equivalent. By all the conventional American standards, it is a land of tomorrow. It is a physical resource for the unborn generations of man—assuming, of course, that man does not incinerate himself and his planet.

Here is at least one huge portion of the globe where

rivers still sparkle, where the woods still quiver with wild life, where car and factory smog is rare. It is a land where Paul Bunyan would have flourished, and where a booster could feel at home.

One such booster, an American named Perry McDonough Collins, foretold a dazzling future for Siberia more than a hundred years ago. Exploring down the Amur in 1856 all the way to its foggy estuary, he saw the need for a railroad linking the river to Lake Baikal. With such a railroad, he wrote, there would be opened "a system of inland navigation, wonderful in extent, and absolutely past calculation in its commercial results." Siberia then, he predicted, "would be able to contend with England for the commerce of China and India." He offered to help the czar build such a railroad, but got nowhere at all.

Well, the railroad was built. The dream of a connecting link did come true. But today, more than a century after Collins' forecast, Siberia does not "contend" with England or with anyone for the trade of Asia. It is still vastly underused. With two thirds of the nation's hydroelectric potential, it contributes one tenth of the electric power. With half the area of the Soviet Union, it is home to only one tenth of the Soviet people.

Moreover, four out of five of these Siberians are concentrated into its western plain, which adjoins European Russia. They are the factory hands, miners, and farmers who work Siberia's only large industrial complex and its single ambitious agricultural project, known as the Virgin Lands. The industrial complex clusters around Siberia's showpiece of development, Novosibirsk, a city of more than a million people, Siberia's largest. The Novosibirsk region feeds nearby coal and iron into a multiplicity of industrial processing plants. It has its own community of scientists for brain power.

In contrast with this Chicago on the western plain, Siberia's East, where we traveled, is still an encyclopedia of potential wealth with most of its pages blank. But if you pick up the official literature on these empty expanses, you will find the pages printed in rosy ink. In general terms they tell us what the Kremlin has in mind for Siberia. The picture, in inspirational prose and postcard colors, catalogues Siberia's resources. Its forests cover more than half the area of the United States. It has four fifths of the nation's coal reserves. It is rich in natural gas and oil, gold, diamonds, bauxite, and nickel.

But resources do not tell the story. A country can brim over with natural wealth and still be poor. One example we know at first hand is Indonesia, a storehouse of rubber, tin, oil, and rice that could enrich its people and Southeast Asia besides. Nowhere have we seen more indecent poverty than among Java's subsistence farmers or in the urban jungle of Jakarta. The people and government do not know how to organize their own resources, much less make good use of the foreign capital that is pouring in. It does not follow, therefore, that Siberia's resources will necessarily enrich it or the Soviet Union as a whole.

What the Kremlin has in mind for Siberia it tells us only in general terms. Taking the concentration of industry around Novosibirsk as a prototype, it seems intent on repeating this pattern in Eastern and Far Eastern Siberia, wherever enough hydroelectric power can be generated. The newer concentration around Bratsk is one example of the scheme, and there are others in various stages of planning. Bratsk, carved out of the wilderness north of Irkutsk, is now the world's largest power plant. Soon it will be outranked by a larger dam and power station on the Yenisei River at Krasnoyarsk. If dam building on this scale continues, and if the level of the rivers is not lowered too much, Siberia in the year 2000 may yet become, as one Soviet scientist predicts, technologically the most advanced part of the Soviet Union. But Siberia will have to advance in other directions before this can come true. Scientists will have to find ways of overcoming its physical handicaps, the chief of which are its distances and its cold. Only one railroad stitches Siberia together across its five thousand miles. There are several branches to the south, none in the north. Only two long motor roads, costly and difficult to maintain, now give access deep into the northern wastes. The best highways are still the frozen rivers. The sea route along the Arctic coast is open only three months in the year. Most of Siberia's riches, in other words, still remain locked, and nobody has yet made an effort strong enough to open the lock and fling the gates wide.

As for the cold, it has coated two thirds of Siberia's surface with permafrost. And it is the permafrost, in turn, that blocks drainage and causes the annual flooding of fields, the destruction of buildings and bridges, the formation of clouds of mosquitoes, and other miseries during the short, hot Siberian summer. As everything in Siberia costs more because of distance, so the long winter and the cold multiply the cost of construction, food, manufacturing, housing, and clothing for a family.

Before we waste too much sympathy on the Siberians, we should remember that deep snow falls only near the sea or where winds blow moisture from the sea. It was in European Russia, not Siberia, that Baron Munchausen, that prince of fibbers, found his well-known hitching post. As night was falling on an all-white landscape, the baron got out of his sleigh, hitched his horse to a stick that pointed through the snow, wrapped himself in furs, and went to sleep. When he woke he found himself in a village and his horse was dangling from the church steeple. The snow had, of course, melted during the night.

The dry heartland of Siberia, in contrast, congeals quietly in windless and almost snowless winters. We strolled through Irkutsk during the first light snowfall of October, looking for snowplows, sidewalk arcades, and other defenses against the deep snowfalls to come. We found none.

Only eighteen inches of snow fall on Irkutsk in an average year. Beneath their beautifully carved eaves and shutters, the old log houses of Irkutsk have double windows to keep out the cold. Householders lay cotton batting between the panes to close every chink to outside air. They make this precaution a festive sight by scattering confetti on the cotton, and it sparkles like snow.

Official Soviet literature insists that all the fuss about climate is just the invention of unfriendly Westerners. It assures us that "the general impression of Siberia as a land of grim climate and cold comfort, transformed by czarism into a terrible place of prison and exile, possesses the vital power of a myth and finds currency to this day." An Intourist folder wants us to believe that "the tales of Russian frosts are sheer exaggeration." Soviet publicity—let us not say propaganda—informs us, for example, that Norilsk in the far North is "the most beautiful" of Arctic cities. Norilsk, built in the tundra by forced labor, the site of some of Stalin's most cruel prisons, is now the home of more than a hundred thousand long-suffering miners, factory workers, and their families.

Admittedly, Norilsk is an extreme case of hardship. But for the windfall of forced labor, it probably would never have been built. Now that the developers of Siberia can no longer recruit thousands of bodies just by ordering them, who will do the work that must be done, not only in Norilsk but in many less cold and distant places? We have described how the Party through its youth organizations is training up a new generation to serve the state. For the generation now coming out of school Siberia is a testing ground of dedication.

"Go east, young man, and grow up with the country" may sound old-fashioned. But that is what the Party is saying to its youth every day. It is an appeal, it is almost a mobilization, but not quite. The message plays on two dominant themes: romance and patriotism. Life is hard out there, the message says, but it's a good life. Siberia is an exciting place; it's where things are happening. Siberia is rushing into the future and you can hitch a ride. Omsk, Bratsk, Krasnoyarsk, these are where the action is. Young communists like to offer themselves for the hardest tasks (says the Party). They are volunteering by the thousands to build railways, roads, and steel mills. They beg to go "where everyone else my age is." Sometimes they die, to become heroes and have railway stations named for them. This is the "Go East" lure, and the propaganda campaign never stops.

If it is true—and one cannot judge its credibility—then the next century may see Siberia merely underpopulated instead of empty. But there are hints in the propaganda itself that the appeal is not going as well as the authorities would like. Young people come to Siberia perhaps to do summer jobs in their vacations. Too few stay and fewer come back. It would seem that something like dedication still has to be generated.

The government has at least five ways of persuading or compelling workers to go to Siberia. The first is the one that has been used ever since the Revolution: the mobilization of youth, the creation and maintenance of a psychology of struggle. The second, an obvious device, is the use of wage incentives. Wages, as we have said, jump 20 per cent for the southern, less exposed areas, and 40 per cent or more for those in the Arctic or sub-Arctic. The third method is a by-product of the educational system. All university graduates who have had government scholarships must give three years of service to the state in their respective fields. Since Siberia, especially East Siberia, suffers from a shortage of trained technicians, this is where many of the graduates are likely to spend their first years outside the university.

The fourth method is a curious and interesting one, since it adopts the Orwellian technique of "doublespeak." Outsiders call it administrative exile, but Soviet authorities, of course, would not use the term. It is a method of persuading talent to go to remote places without seeming to use coercion. Suppose a harbor master is needed for the timber exporting port of Sovetskaya Gavan ("Soviet Harbor") on the Gulf of Tatary in the far east. It is at the end of the line and has an abominable climate, winter and summer. Good men are not likely to go there of their own free will. A reliable young Ukrainian in the Odessa harbor authority is picked to go. He is told that a fine job is waiting for him, at incentive pay, as well as housing for his family. It is an opportunity for him to get ahead in his profession. Of course he does not have to take the new job, although he cannot expect any further advancement if he stays in Odessa. He goes. He has been sent into administrative exile.

The fifth of the methods of getting young people to Siberia is the use of police power. It may be applied as ordinary exile—that is, in the old-time system which sends a convicted offender to live in some unpleasant place of the government's choice. Such a traditional sentence was the fate of Pavel Litvinov, grandson of the Foreign Minister of the nineteen-thirties. Young Litvinov was sent to Verkhne-Usuglin, a village in the bitterly cold Chita district between Baikal and the Far East. A job as mathematics teacher in the village was open to him. Other Siberian jobs in schools and factories probably are being filled each year in the same way by convicted offenders. How many, the state will never say.

The Kremlin is looking not only for dedicated New Soviet Men but also, of all things, for foreign capital to develop Siberia. The search has taken it to capitalist Japan, just as the search for raw materials has repeatedly led Japanese businessmen to take an interest in the Soviet East.

Several years ago we happened to be in one of Japan's west coast ports that face Siberia. It was Otaru on the island of Hokkaido. There we talked with Siberia-conscious economists about the future of Japanese-Soviet trade. They foresaw the old-style trade: Siberian raw materials for Japanese manufactured goods—namely, logs from the Soviet Far East to keep Japan's plywood mills supplied, in exchange for consumer goods like rubber boots and winter clothing from Japanese factories. But now the Russians are thinking of Japanese capital as well as goods. In 1968, they signed a contract for joint Japanese-Soviet development of timber-growing areas. The two governments have also been studying co-operation in the building of a new oil pipeline across Siberia, in the mining of coal, copper, and diamonds, and in the building of new ports on the coast facing Japan.

Much of this is still a dream rather than an imminent reality, for at least two reasons. First, the Russians cannot find enough non-conscript labor even for their existing enterprises in Siberia; how, then, can they entice, inspire, and mobilize enough for the mining and lumbering projects which they now propose to add? The Japanese, for their part, are tempted by Siberia until they think of other places where they can make more money more quickly. In our talks at Otaru, for example, our Japanese informants conceded that any trade they could hope to achieve with the Soviet Union would amount to far less than their present, actual business with the United States. Japanese-Soviet trade both ways totals little more than $600 million a year. Japanese sales to the United States alone amounted to almost three billion dollars in 1967. It is the known quantity of the American market, rather than the many unknowns of Russia, that will attract Japanese effort.

It is our conviction that the Russians will have to develop Siberia themselves, if they develop it at all. They will get little or no help from outside the Soviet bloc, due partly to their own suspicion of foreign capital, and partly to the built-in handicaps of Siberia itself.

Even if the Kremlin can lure foreign capital to Siberia and as many New Soviet Men as it needs, it will still have to surmount enormous barriers. As Soviet builders have learned how to root new factories and apartments into the frozen ground, so engineers will have to explore ways to move raw materials and goods over the frozen surface of the earth. This is a challenge that has defeated them so far. There is another challenge, one of human engineering. Is it possible within the Soviet system to free Siberian enterprises from the tight control of the center? In the outskirts of Irkutsk we saw how heavy the hand of Moscow could be on a struggling aluminum factory. At a distance of 3,225 miles its young and enterprising management was still tied to the center and dependent on it for every last tool and spare part in its repair shop.

Can the Soviet bureaucracy summon the flexibility that Siberia needs, the willingness to trust the men on the spot with decision-making power? We would be inclined to answer *nyet*. Unless the Russians can change their habit of rigidly centralized authority, their insistence on making all decisions at the center, our guess is that eastern Siberia will remain a colonial economy, a place for extracting raw wealth as the czars extracted furs, and for little else.

The Kremlin has a further motive for populating Siberia that has nothing to do with its development. To have a neighbor of 700 million people bordering your virtually empty land is not healthy. Fewer than five million of Siberia's people live in the eastern areas closest to the overpopulated parts of China.

Are the Russians right in fearing the 700 million? If nature abhors a vacuum, millions of Chinese would long ago have swarmed into the emptiness to the north. The emperor did

exact tribute from the tribes in the Amur valley and the
maritime province until the late eighteen-fifties, but he
never seriously tried to populate these border regions. The
Russians did find Chinese shopkeepers, gamblers, and
coolies in the towns of the frontier region where they took
possession in 1858. But Chinese settlers never came there
in appreciable numbers.

Toward the end of the century, the small Chinese communities caused some trouble for the Russians in the Amur
valley. Emigrants from China, which was just across the river,
seem to have aroused the same fears and hatreds in Siberia
that their southern cousins did and still do in Southeast
Asia. They worked too hard, lived too thriftily, and came
to wield more economic power than the Russian settlers
liked. Many of them had crossed without women into
Russian-controlled country, and stayed to annex wives from
the local population. In 1900, while the Boxers were killing
foreigners around Peking, resentments blew up into tragedy. At the Amur River port of Blagoveshchensk, the Russian commander ordered all Chinese out of the city, and
Russian troops drove five thousand men, women, and children into the Amur to drown. After that, few Chinese chose
to live north of the river.

In general, the record in Asia shows that most great
migrations have moved from the cold north to the warmer
south. Aryans came down into India from the north;
Burma's dominant people trace their ancestry to Tibet, to
the north; Thailand was conquered by Shans, who had
come from what is now Yünnan, in China, in their north.
The Mongols and Manchus drove from the northwest to
conquer China, and the Mongols, of course, erupted westward as well. The so-called Overseas Chinese have been
filtering south and southeast for centuries into the still
warmer climes of Indonesia, the Philippines, and Southeast
Asia. Unless history is a sham, Asians of the past would

seem to have agreed with Thomas Jefferson, who wrote to a friend in 1801:

> I have often wondered that any human being should live in a cold country who can find room in a warm one. I have no doubt but that cold is the source of more sufferance to all animal nature than hunger, thirst, sickness, and all the other pains of life and of death itself put together.

Only occasionally does history show any sizable migration northward—and then as an exception that proves the rule. For example, in the human explosion that propelled the Huns and Turkic-speaking tribes out of Asia's heartland, only one important tribe, or horde, moved northward and down the Siberian rivers toward the Arctic. This tribe became the present-day Yakuts, who survive and seem to thrive in an environment that would have frozen anyone else. One can find a few other northward-moving migrants, such as the ancestors of the present-day Japanese, who crossed from China and pushed the indigenous Ainu northward through their chain of islands. These exceptions do not invalidate our belief that Asians will move to warmer climates when they can, that Chinese farmers still prefer the intensive agriculture of the tropics, and that for these among other reasons Siberia has never attracted them.

It would not attract them today, but they no longer have a choice. Under their present dynasty the Chinese move only where the government wants them and forces them, if necessary, to live. We have seen estimates, unconfirmed of course, that the Peking Government has moved twenty million into Tibet and Sinkiang and another five million into northern Manchuria since 1949. In these regions the primary motive appears to have been political: in Tibet to supplant and outnumber the anti-Chinese and anticommunist Tibetans; in Sinkiang to outnumber the remaining Central Asian Moslems; in Manchuria to stiffen an empty borderland.

Perhaps Peking would like to move millions into Siberia too, but of course it cannot with the Soviet Union in possession. The Russians intend to keep Siberia, every permafrosted square mile of it. To keep it they may have to people it. And to people it they may be tempted to use an expedient such as the Chinese adopted in Sinkiang. The old Russian habit of deporting whole communities of unwanted people to outlying provinces, the Tatars, the Volga Germans, and the Jews, for example, may no longer be practical politics for the Kremlin. But there are other ways of achieving the same results. One is to deploy army units to a strategic border in paramilitary agricultural settlements. We have seen a variant of this in Thailand, where the government could not persuade its own civilian staffs to live and work on the communist-threatened northeast border. So it sent army units to the border on village-aid duty. In somewhat the same manner, young Israelis have been assigned to frontier settlements, to work the land and defend the border too.

A young Russian soldier riding a tractor would at least be something new on the Siberian landscape, something different from the Cossack, the convict laborer, the liberated serf, and the exile. He might even find Siberia beautiful and want to stay.

To leave Siberia and the Soviet Union was a process the Russians made easy and almost casual for us. It was as if the authorities were saying, "Closed society? Police state? Nonsense; see how easy it is to get out." Our Trans-Siberian train with its four-berth compartments had gone on to Vladivostok, the naval base, from which foreigners are barred. Another train took us from Khabarovsk to the coast, one with a conventional European personality. On its sixteen-hour overnight run to the Sea of Japan, we lived in a two-berth compartment like those on any wagon-lit. The train seemed ordinary, but its route was not. Run-

ning for about 500 miles south and southwest from Khabarovsk, the double tracks parallel the Ussuri River. Down
the Ussuri runs the Soviet frontier with China. It was
in this river, on Damansky or Chenpao Island, that Soviet
and Chinese troops fought two battles in 1969. Frontier
"incidents" might well have been going on as we passed.
(Two years later we saw excerpts of a Chinese propaganda
film on a frontier incident of late 1967. The Ussuri was not
yet frozen, and the fight, with fire hoses and boat hooks as
weapons, might have been actually in progress in October,
when we went by.) We saw no sign of tension or trouble
from the train, or in the faces or manner of the Russian
train crew. The tracks are laid on high ground at least ten
miles east of the river frontier. Alongside the river, especially on the Chinese side, the ground is so boggy that any
tracks built on it would sink.

The Ussuri Railway, as it is called, was started in 1891,
several years earlier than the other stretches of the Trans-
Siberian. What hastened its construction was a supposed
threat from the Chinese—a threat not so much against the
Ussuri valley as against Vladivostok, then a small town. Today, three quarters of a century later, the threat to the Russians comes from a far more formidable China. For several
years Vladivostok had already been closed to foreigners
for fear that they might spy on the harbor and the naval
base.

Our timetable made sure that the foreign traveler saw
little of this sensitive border region. Leaving Khabarovsk
late in the afternoon, we rolled southward for less than an
hour through a gray twilight before darkness shut out the
view. What we saw of the forested and hilly Ussuri valley
looked damp and gloomy. The landscape was hardly one
to remember. On the left side of the train rose the wooded
outcroppings of the Shikotan Mountains, as featureless as
the Appalachian ridges of Pennsylvania. On the other side,
lower ridges hid the river and the boundary.

In the morning, as daylight broke, the train had already branched from the main Vladivostok line and was clacking over switches in the outskirts of Nakhodka. Here the woods had disappeared. One saw small farms, and near them a rare sight in Siberia: whitewashed cottages, belonging to Ukrainians whose forefathers were brought to this remote corner in the early eighteen-sixties, soon after it became Russian territory. The train finished its run exactly on schedule. Buses drove us down steep hills to the pier, where an all-white ship of 6,000 tons, the *Khabarovsk*, was waiting to take us to Japan.

At Nakhodka we began to say good-by to the Soviet Union. It was not a final farewell; we still had ahead of us forty-eight hours on Soviet "soil," on a Soviet ship. But it was here, in what airline announcers call the final boarding process, that we parted with a companion of the Trans-Siberian journey. She was a young Soviet official who had come all the way from Moscow on assignment with a group tour. We had found her to be good company on the train. Somehow she had escaped the brassy officiousness of other Party women. Her quiet voice and her well-cut tweeds were sophisticated. We soon discovered the reason. To the inevitable question, "How did you learn to speak such perfect English?" she replied that she had spent three years at a language institute in Leningrad, and had since traveled in English-speaking countries. In addition to the Soviet bloc countries, her travels had taken her to Austria, France, and several times to England. What or who had taken her to all these countries we did not ask, nor did she volunteer the answers. Obviously she had some special access to the rarest of all Soviet privileges: foreign travel. She did, however, mention that her wanderings might include the United States someday. When it was time to leave, we reminded her of the possibility of coming to Washington, our city, and said she could find us in the telephone book. At that moment, as we shook hands, she presented to us a new face. It was closed. "Oh, I shall be much too busy in Washington to get in touch with you," she said. She was a Party Woman, there could be no doubt; the Party could be proud of her.

An official at the pier retrieved the green slips of paper which were our Soviet visas, leaving only two small ink stamps in our passports to show that we had ever been in the Soviet Union. A smooth-cheeked young border guard in uniform inspected our baggage, with special interest in the family snapshots we always carry. He was so young, so pink-faced, that one was tempted to ask him, "When did you last write to your mother?" In his smiling manner, he was the very opposite of the heavy, humorless Soviet guard of most travelers' stories.

We had three hours before sailing time to get acquainted with Nakhodka harbor and with our ship. Standing at the bow, looking out at the blue of the bay, we understood why the place had been named Nakhodka. In Russian the word means a windfall, a find. The Russians who discovered it found something rare and valuable, on a coast that has few good harbors except that of Vladivostok itself. Stalin set up not one but two forced labor camps near the town, mostly for the heavy work of building docks and stevedoring. The harbor is a vast anchorage protected on three sides by hills. As landscape and seascape, we thought it one of the most impressive we had seen in Asia, including Manila Bay. At first sight all the passenger fleets of the world could anchor safely here—except, of course, that Nakhodka is ice-bound for five months of the year. There were other ships in the harbor, some of them white postwar vessels, some ready to steam to Soviet ports in the northland. Some were beaten-up freighters, no doubt bound for Haiphong with civilian goods. War material for Vietnam would, of course, leave from Vladivostok, away from prying foreign eyes.

Our ship was a reminder that Soviet tourism has taken to the sea. Built in East Germany, clearly designed for the tourist trade, it had spacious two-berth cabins where travelers could spend a week rather than two days without suffering the slightest pain. Everything on the ship looked spotless, even to the linen tablecloths and napkins in the dining room. If the *Khabarovsk's* appearance was any guide, the descendants of Peter the Great have learned to maintain ships as well as anyone.

An assistant purser, speaking good English, told us that the previous month this ship had gone on a cruise. "Usually," he said, "we have sunshine every day in September, and no fog. It's the most beautiful month of the year around here." For anyone who had walked along the nearby coast of Japanese Hokkaido in midsummer, veiled in a day-long mist and drizzle, the ship's officer was hard to believe. But he insisted it was the truth.

"We cruised for twenty-two days," he said, "and we didn't have one day of rain."

"Who were your passengers?"

"People from all over the Soviet Union."

A twenty-two-day cruise in Pacific waters, without rain, suggested that the *Khabarovsk* must have gone to sunny ports of call in the south. Not so. Soviet tourism, like everything else, must have social usefulness. So the ship took its Soviet tourists, not to isles of warmth and ease in the south, but north to some of the most forbidding regions of the earth—all under Soviet rule.

"We stopped first in Kamchatka," the officer said. "Would you believe it? Our passengers bathed in warm water in a volcano. Really, it was beautiful"—and he held the "beaut" like an opera singer.

"Then," he went on, "we made two stops in Sakhalin—very interesting, very beautiful—and one in the Kuriles, and back here. You would have liked it, too."

He knew, of course, that foreigners were not yet welcomed on the North Pacific tourist circuit. He intimated that they would be within a very few years. Tourists then could decide whether the pamphlet that called Kamchatka "a primeval land of gaudy Pacific sunsets, the cones of volcanoes, and the roar of geysers" was telling the truth.

Like the officer who talked about tourism, the ship's crew, we felt, were unlike other Russians we had met. They understood the meaning of service. How do we turn off the heat in our cabin? An engineer does it for us in no time, with a grin. May we order caviar for lunch? The plump, dark-eyed waitress assures us, "Of course—and for this evening, too, if you wish." We did not encounter a single *nyet*-woman on board.

Of course Russians who work on ships are trusted as well as privileged. They are among the few who can escape from the closed society of the Soviet Union for short periods, always in the service of the state. No doubt they are watched, as embassy officials are, in foreign countries. But they are at ease in the outer world, and they would not have the slightest trouble in navigating on land as well as on sea if the closed society should open.

At noon, the ship's horn blew deep blasts that echoed from the hills. The ship slid from the pier. All of a sudden we felt the invisible curtains closing behind us, and we knew that we were "out." So did other passengers—Australians, New Zealanders, Japanese, and even Russians. A young Japanese, stationed too long in Moscow, stood up in the middle of the sun deck and sang *O Sole Mio* in perfect Italian as the ship headed out to sea. Everybody cheered, for no particular reason.

What does it mean to come "out" of a closed society? The experience is heady, almost like coming out of Sodium Pentothal. The sense of release had not hit us in quite the same way in leaving a partly closed place such as Poland or a beleaguered country like Vietnam. This time each of us felt gay, and relieved that nothing had gone wrong.

If these were the sensations of coming "out," there must have been a contrasting condition of being "in." Neither of us had been conscious of such a condition inside the Soviet Union. Neither remembered feeling captive, anxious, oppressed, or particularly downhearted, except for a time, as we have said, in Kiev. On the other hand, we did look and listen with more than normal intensity. We did walk with greater care, we did choose our words more deliberately than usual, and we did curb our tendency to lose patience.

Maybe all these disciplines, self-imposed for a few weeks, added up to tension, to an ordeal of being "in." Maybe we did not fully sense the restraints of a closed society until we were out.

XI

EPILOGUE

Oh, if the Queen were a man,
she would like to go and give
those Russians, whose word one
cannot believe, such a beating!
We shall never be friends again
till we have it out. This the
Queen feels sure of.

—Queen Victoria, in a
letter to Lord Beaconsfield
(Benjamin Disraeli), 1878

Why does Victoria's royal anger at "those Russians" fall so quaintly on our ears? It is not just the sound of the Queen-Empress stamping her tiny foot, like Kipling's butterfly, at the strongest land power in the world. The outburst, to our way of thinking, is a measure of the change that has over-taken power politics. In Victoria's time, great powers could go to war and come out alive as nations, even though they might lose their best young men in the battle. The difference now is, of course, in the nature of war.

In our own time it has become trite to say that "nuclear war is unthinkable." This remark seems to us unthinking. Nuclear war, with all its implications, calls for constant and careful thought. How else can one understand what it could mean? How else can one put sense and stamina to the task of making nuclear war impossible? Only to dread such a war, and not to think about averting it, is to squander man's genius for survival.

Nuclear war is not some meteor on collision course with the earth. Nor is it a missile with a warhead that is to be diverted or exploded in midair by another missile. What demands attention is the state of things on the ground. What requires the utmost mental labor is how to keep the missiles from leaving the ground. Of all that is happening on the ground, nothing is more important to know and understand than what is going on inside the Soviet Union.

Near the beginning of these reflections on another world, we suggested some of the questions that would engage us, questions that would probably have to be faced even if they could not be readily answered. It is time to look back and gather together some of the answers we have scattered through this book.

The question that seemed to us central, and the one from which others derive, was whether the Soviet experiment was in general holding to its course, or whether there were signs of a change in direction. It seems to us that the basic structure of the system has come through the more than fifty turbulent years of its life in remarkably good shape from the Soviet point of view. The Communist Party has kept its power intact—even enhanced it—in spite of all its internal rivalries and struggles for leadership. It stands today as the unchallenged ruler of two hundred and forty million Soviet citizens.

The Soviet state has not forfeited any vital part of its monopoly of the ownership, production, and use of the nation's wealth—this despite all the mistakes of its planning and management, all the hardships it has imposed on its people. So strong was its authority that it could afford to make concessions such as permitting the building of private homes and the marketing of private produce.

When it comes to the content of Party teaching, we cannot find any radical departure from the Leninist creed. The same old "truths" pervade the new education system; the same old slogans pervade the very air that Soviet citizens breathe. The Party neglects no opportunity, such as the fiftieth anniversary of the Revolution, and the centennial of Lenin's birth, to rally the people to the cause as Lenin preached it and to reaffirm its own infallibility. As guidelines for the Lenin centennial, it instructed its cadres that "political work should be directed toward indoctrination of the Soviet people in a spirit of fidelity to Lenin's precepts and dedication to communism. . . ." It also reminded the

Soviet citizen "of his duties to our common cause and his civic responsibilities to the socialist motherland. . . ."

It is important to remember who are the people to whom such messages go. Gone are the men and women whom communism could not serve, and who would not serve communism. Russians who survive today are, with few exceptions, those for whom the system was specifically designed. For most of the surviving people, the system has apparently justified itself. By and large, they believe it to be the best system for their own purposes, and often they go so far as to say that it is the best as yet devised by man. On that ground, they will accept the official claim that it will someday prevail over all others in the world.

Ideology has ceased to be a lively issue. Far from being dead, however, as some Western scholars contend, it has entered the national bloodstream. If the people were not constantly reminded of it, they would probably take it for granted. "They know we're socialists," the young woman on the park bench said to us. And she meant it.

In a society shaped by centuries of autocratic rule, the line between acceptance and belief may not be clear. But there is little doubt that Marxism-Leninism enjoys both among ordinary Russians. A Russian might find comparable acceptance and belief in our country, which has an ideology of its own, although the term is in some disrepute. And it would be no less true to say that most Americans carry in their national bloodstream the creed expressed in the Declaration of Independence and inscribed on the walls of the Lincoln and Jefferson memorials. We are not suggesting that all Americans live by their beliefs; only that most of them do come to accept certain values as unarguable.

Lenin's revolution was a coup that lacked mass support. He gambled on gaining mass acceptance, and he won. If he could see the degree of acceptance of his revolutionary creed today, he would surely think more highly of his countrymen. So might Copernicus and Darwin feel vindicated if they could know how their revolutionary theories have permeated scientific truth. But perhaps all three of these great innovators would also be a little bored to find the struggle ended, the disputation silenced, and success achieved in the form of a dreary consensus.

On the Soviet horizon there appears to be no substitute for the Party, the state, or the prevailing system. Russia has never been ruled by a military dictatorship, which is not to say that it never will be. But whenever the influence of the military has loomed large in moments of crisis, the marshals and the generals and the leading officers have been pushed aside, and sometimes liquidated—and they could be again.

There is, of course, another potential source of internal trouble: the dissident intellectual, the writer, editor, publisher, and creative artist who finds the Soviet censorship intolerable. His feelings about living in a closed society were put into words by an Indian dissident, and carved into the wall of the All-India Broadcasting House in New Delhi. The words are those of Mahatma Gandhi:

> I do not want my house to be walled on all sides and my windows to be stuffed. I want the cultures of all lands to be blown about my house as freely as possible. But I refuse to be blown off my feet by any. . . .

As such a man cannot tolerate the Soviet system, so the system cannot tolerate him. It cannot digest him, as some people cannot digest fish or gin. It must regurgitate him. Lenin and Khrushchev talked of the "good" intellectual who served the state, thus showing how little they understood the meaning of the word. The Russian intellectual has always been in trouble. Even in czarist days he made no contribution to the established regime, and he was hardly ever a working revolutionist. His concern was with seeing life as it was, and in Russia life as it was—and is—has always been a reproach to the ruling autocracy.

Among others the Leninist system could not tolerate were the kulaks, or rich farmers. They had to be exterminated. But the intellectual is harder to get rid of because he is vocal and articulate and he has contacts abroad. So instead of exterminating him, the state tries to cow him or bribe him, and when neither of these expedients works, it sends him to prison or exile, or to a mental institution. The state can do this because the intellectual is expendable. In truth, the system gets on far better without him. This is not true of the scientist, the technologist, or even the good factory manager. These men and women are rarely intellectuals in the Russian sense, and so they are rarely in danger.

There are also plenty of tame "intellectuals" who serve the state with varying degrees of sincerity, in the press and publishing, in propaganda, socialist literature, and the arts. The dissident who cannot make his peace with the system is a kind of modern "superfluous man," the Russian whom Turgenev depicted and labeled and made immortal. He is the ineffectual, introspective dreamer. Today, for his courage alone, he makes a splash in the international literary community. Sometimes he commands respect, too, for his authentic genius. But to imagine him as a genuine threat to the Leninist system, or, even more, a liberalizing influence inside the system, seems to us a product of Western romanticism and wishful thinking.

Another example of intellectual daydreaming is the current theory of convergence. This is the assumption that the Soviet and American systems are gradually coming closer together because the Russians are becoming more highly industrialized year by year. And as they become more industrialized, the people will demand and get more consumer goods.

They will get, for example, household gadgets such as

refrigerators and washing machines, blenders and hair dryers. Those who have country cottages will want electric lawn mowers and those who live on rivers will demand outboard motors. The more of these gadgets they manage to get, the more they will want. Someday they will even acquire their hearts' desire, the family car. Little by little the accumulation of material possessions will absorb their interest and divert their energies from the building of socialism. In the end, this will mean the death of the communist system and the triumph of middle-class values. For do not all people, and especially people who are so much like Americans in character and experience, want the kind of affluent society that Americans have made?

By this time it becomes clear that convergence is really a process of Russians becoming more "like us," not Americans becoming more "like them." It is, in short, an expression of American egoism. As the two societies converge, so, presumably, will their national interests and, in consequence, their policies.

The two basic fallacies of the theory are, first, that Americans and Russians are the same kind of people, and second, that a high standard of living is inconsistent with the Marxist-Leninist system. The second fallacy is, of course, a relic of the old myth that Marxian socialism is inherently incapable of satisfying consumer demand. The Soviet economy has already been highly industrialized, and only the priorities set by the Party chiefs have prevented the economy from being oriented toward consumer needs. The Soviet people could have a good many of the gadgets they want, and others they do not need, if their rulers wanted them to. But the men in the Kremlin have two reasons for not wanting them to. One is the priority they give to the building of a vast military arsenal. The other is precisely the fear that an unrestrained accumulation of things would indeed divert the popular mind and energy away from social goals. How sensitive they are to this danger can be seen in their angry rejection of "convergence." Their official publications call the very idea seditious.

What is it that really separates Russians and Americans, who sometimes seem to the casual observer to be so much alike? Their differences are wide and deep. But just because people are different does not mean that they cannot co-operate. Let us look at two opposites, the Soviet and American economic systems. The Soviet system puts severe limits on private property and private trading. This makes it impossible for a Soviet citizen to accumulate wealth. In the United States, the right to accumulate private property and wealth is unlimited, although private enterprise is hedged about by antitrust laws and regulations.

Yet there is nothing in either economic system that prevents it from producing a decent standard of living for all its people. The Marxist-Leninist system could give its citizens an agreeable standard of living; the capitalist system could protect its citizens from air and water pollution and provide all its people with good housing and schools as well. Whatever the abuses or the unmet needs in both societies, they do not derive from the economic systems themselves but rather from the values and priorities that prevail within the systems.

If it is not differences in economic philosophy that prevent their co-operation, is it perhaps their rival political systems? Here the gulf between the two superpowers might seem too wide to bridge. The Communist Party of course permits no opposition, while the United States considers a free choice among opposing political parties and candidates to be among the most precious of its rights. Few in the Western world would give up these rights without a struggle. Yet the United States has open and friendly relations in politics and trade with many countries that have never known democracy, or have lost it. In most of Latin America, in Portugal and Spain, in Tunisia and Greece, in

Pakistan and Thailand, and, of course, in much of newly independent Africa, one party or one group holds all the power. If there is an opposition, it is scattered or in jail.

The real source of the Soviet-American difficulty is not the conflict of their two political systems, as such, but rather the evangelistic strain in Marxism-Leninism and in American democracy as well. In countries which have not accepted either faith, missionaries from both powers are active among the political heathen.

To renounce political evangelism would be an enormous concession on both sides, but even this would only begin to clear the road that leads to mutually useful relations. For there is another barrier between the two countries which is neither economic nor political. This is the fact that the Soviet Union has walled itself up in a closed society. It is the most formidable and the most frightening barrier ever built by man.

Looking back on our journey, we were more troubled by the closed, secretive nature of Soviet society than by anything else we saw or heard. More than anything else, it gave us the sense of moving through another world. It is hard for us to believe that a country so advanced in science and the arts should make shut-ins of its citizens, censor their mail, restrict their travel, and permit them only one point of view, the view of the all-powerful ruling party. This tyranny over the mind has produced a paradox mentioned by more than one Soviet defector: that the world's biggest country, of eight and a half million square miles, is a prison. Maybe the sprawling geography of the country requires prison guards —to keep its people in and strangers out. Maybe the so-called Union of Soviet Socialist Republics would show cracks in its internal structure if its internal discipline were relaxed.

In the past, other countries have paid a crippling price for isolating themselves. One can argue that both czarist

Russia and imperial China collapsed because they sealed themselves off from the winds of technological and intellectual change. Japan of the Tokugawas remained tightly sealed for 216 years; at the end of that time, in the mid-nineteenth century, the nation was dangerously weak and disunited. Only by a supreme effort of intellect, common sense, and will power did Japan's new rulers break the isolation and save their country. There are other instances: Tibet, for example, spun a cocoon around its Lamaistic society, and regarded itself as the center of the world; today Tibetan culture is little more than an artifact.

Of course there is no real analogy between Russia and any other country except perhaps China. Both the Soviet Union and China are so vast, so varied, so populous, so ruthlessly ruled, that physically they can survive their isolation. One price they have already paid for it, and will continue to pay, is an intellectual one. The massive dullness of life in the Soviet Union, and the discontent of many young writers and artists, are direct results of the closed society. Having entered Russia from Finland and left it to go to Japan, our impression is that there is more intellectual ferment in Stockmann's bookshop in Helsinki and Maruzen in Tokyo than in all the dreary, bureaucratized bookshops of the Soviet Union put together. It is even more serious, and more dangerous, for a people to lose touch with reality, so that they are ignorant of the world around them, and of the forces that make for war and peace. These are the thoughts that haunted us as we sailed away, across the Sea of Japan.

At the start of this book we mentioned the anticommunist emotions stirred up by Bolshevism, emotions that have stayed alive in the United States for more than fifty years. We might also have talked of another American mood that grew up during World War II and has never died. This is a longing to live at peace with the Soviet Union, and to find some path to co-operation. The two emotions do not exclude each other. Nobody nowadays wants a war with Russia; everyone wants to believe that peace is possible.

Many who hope for peace are unhappy when it is said, as we in effect say in this book, that co-operation with the Soviet Union is a long way off. To paraphrase Lincoln Steffens, we have been over into another world, and it will be hard to deal with that world for many, many years. No doubt we shall be scolded for saying so. What! Don't you know that this is all One World? Don't you know that nuclear fallout would poison all of us alike? And how can you say that a Russian is different from an American? Hath not a Russian eyes? Hath not a Russian

> . . . hands, organs, dimensions, senses, affections, passions? fed with the same food, hurt with the same weapons, subject to the same diseases, healed by the same means, warmed and cooled by the same winter and summer?

Have we not all one Father? Hath not one God created us?

To these questions there can be only one answer. If the tears shed by a Russian and by an American, in grief or pain, were analyzed in test tubes, we do not doubt that they would reveal the same amount of salt. We might add, with Archibald MacLeish, that Russians and Americans and all mankind are "riders on the earth together." Yet we do maintain, even more strongly since our Soviet journey, that the Russian and the American are indeed different men; that the Russian has for a thousand years been conditioned to absolutism, while the American has for perhaps three hundred been conditioned to self-rule; that the standards, values and goals of the two peoples have little in common; and that they do not yet live in One World.

We say "not yet." It will have to come some day. If the human race does not blow itself up in a fit of madness, the babies born today, lying behind glass screens in their hospital cribs, may live to see the first stirrings of that One World. For those who will not live to see it, the only sensible course, surely, is not to bank on One World, but to work for it.

INDEX

European Community, 130
European Games, 90
Evangelism, political, 288

Famine, 128
Farms, 145–46, 160, 246
Fiat works, 215
Finland, 289
First Circle, The, 59
Fischer, John, 146
Flags, 90–91
Food and drink, 23–29, 107,
    201 (see also Farms); fam-
    ine, 128; on train, 235–36,
    237, 238–39
Frunze, 165
Furtseva, Ekaterina, 67

Gandhi, Mahatma, 284
Garmo Peak, 122
Georgia and Georgians, 29,
    103–20, 171
Germans, 21–22, 91–94, 150;
    Volga, 86, 167
Gibbon, Edward, 125
Glorious Victories, 124–25
Gold, 239–40
Gorchakov, Prince, 140, 141
Gori, 115–20
Gorky, Maxim, 41, 76, 128
Government, 72–75. See also
    Kremlin; specific areas of
    control, leaders
Grandmothers, 71
Great Britain. See Britain and
    the British
Great Game, 141
GUM, 180

Health, 200–5

Hermitage Museum, 114, 182
Herzen, Alexander, 38
History, 120–31
Hitchcock, Alfred, 237
Hitler, Adolf, 150
Holmes, Oliver Wendell, 55
Hoover, Herbert, 128
Housing, 74, 208; Leningrad,
    47–48; Moscow, 60–63, 71–
    72; and Tashkent earth-
    quake, 151–54; Tbilisi,
    108–10
Hungary, 89
Hydrofoils, 222–23

Imanov (Iman-uli), Aman-
    geldi, 169
India, 8–9, 10, 141–42
Indonesia, 262
Informers, 59
Intellectuals, 284–85
Intourist, 17–19, 58–59, 181,
    264; and Babi Yar, 91; and
    collectives, 160; and Geor-
    gia, 112, 116; and Kiev,
    87; and Lake Baikal, 221
Iran, 163
Irkutsk, 193–96, 216–21, 223,
    229, 244, 268; and New
    Haven, 259; and snow,
    263–64
Israel, 271
Ivan IV (the Terrible), 123–
    24, 251–52
Izvestia, 121

Jamestown, Virginia, 259
Japan and the Japanese, 161–
    62, 266–67, 270, 289